W9-BHB-462

PRAISE FOR

Lives in Ruins

"Johnson's wonderful and engaging work peels back the superficial glamour surrounding archaeology and archaeologists. [Her] contribution to this genre is unmatched. Without glitz, the author has created a very enjoyable work that will be appreciated by experts in the field and casual readers alike."   —*Library Journal* (starred review)

"Johnson weaves a serious tale of learning about archaeologists and their craft with humor and insight. The wild cast of characters is the stuff of Hollywood. . . . This book is a delight for all of us amateurs who someday want to become serious archaeologists."   —*American Archaeology*

"Johnson's book is simultaneously a crash course in basic archaeology and a sociological study of the various quirky subcultures of professional archaeologists. Both types of material prove fascinating, and she is a funny and garrulous guide to the terrain. Johnson skillfully captures the vivid and quirky characters drawn to archaeology."
—*Boston Globe*

"Many archeologists credit Indiana Jones with sparking their passion. In this lively love letter [to their profession] Johnson may well inspire a new generation to take up the calling."
—*Publishers Weekly* (starred review)

"An engrossing examination of how archaeologists re-create much of human history, piece by painstaking piece."
—*Kirkus Reviews* (starred review)

"In this gem of hands-on reportage, Marilyn Johnson delves into the lives of the pros behind the finds."   —*Nature*

"A witty, edifying guide to the professionals who, 'armed with not much more than a trowel and a sense of humor,' help fill in the blanks of history. Johnson obviously delights in her subjects—their stubbornness and vision—and trowels out surprises. [She] wears her heart on her shovel and makes us care."   —*Austin American-Statesman*

"In the first chapter of her informative book on archaeology, *Lives in Ruins*, Marilyn Johnson asks, 'What sort of people choose to read bones and dirt for a living?' In succeeding chapters, she answers that question in spades. Johnson writes with clarity (she describes 'a gray tarantula the size of a baby's fist') and humor ('That Neanderthal profile, stocky and hirsute, is quintessential male archaeologist'), and limns wonderful portraits."   —*Providence Journal*

"Through a combination of perception and wit, Johnson discovers how archaeologists are invaluable witnesses 'to the loss of our cultural memories.'"   —*USA Today*

"As archaeologists collect potsherds and spearpoints, Marilyn Johnson became a collector of archaeologists, tracking them to Machu Picchu and to Fishkill, NY, to a Caribbean slave plantation and a Philadelphia beer tasting. In *Lives in Ruins*, she sifts and sorts them, unearthing a treasury of rare characters."   —*Dallas Morning News*

"*Lives in Ruins* holds a surprising amount of weight for such a fun, quick read. . . . It's not the zany characters that make the book so enticing . . . it's their inspiring passion for their work, which Johnson chips away at with each archaeologist she follows, that makes this book profound."
                          —*Publishers Weekly*, Best Books of 2014

"In the process of carving out her own archaeological experience, Johnson digs deep and comes up with a sparkling gem."   —*Book Reporter*

"Johnson is merrily self-deprecating and funny in her anecdotes of the personalities she encounters, but also absolutely serious about the importance of their work. We are all the richer for Johnson's eloquent ode to this dirty job."   —*Shelf Awareness*

"As she did in her bestselling *The Dead Beat,* Johnson writes in a charming and thoughtful manner, weaving in her personal observations, insightful quotes from her subjects, and a wide-eyed fascination with her subjects." —*Seattle Times*

"A lively survey of archaeology and the people who practice it. . . . Johnson writes entertainingly, employing many quirky tidbits gleaned from the likably eccentric intellects she meets."
—*New York Times Book Review*

"As she did in her previous books about librarians and obituary writers, Johnson finds that the line between inspirationally nutty and actually crazy is measured in the joy of the work." —*Entertainment Weekly*

"Johnson throws herself into her subject, taking a field class, following various archeologists into the field (and underwater), and exploring archeology's role in the greater culture. In writing that is funny, entertaining, and enriching, she illustrates why archeologists derive such a thrill from what they do—and why we probably should as well."
—Amazon, best book of the month for November 2014

Lives in Ruins

ALSO BY MARILYN JOHNSON

The Dead Beat:
Lost Souls, Lucky Stiffs, and the Perverse Pleasures of Obituaries

This Book Is Overdue!:
How Librarians and Cybrarians Can Save Us All

LIVES
IN
RUINS

Archaeologists and the Seductive Lure

of Human Rubble

❧

MARILYN
JOHNSON

HARPER ● PERENNIAL

NEW YORK ● LONDON ● TORONTO ● SYDNEY ● NEW DELHI ● AUCKLAND

HARPER ● PERENNIAL

A hardcover edition of this book was published in 2014
by HarperColllins Publishers.

P.S.™ is a trademark of HarperCollins Publishers.

LIVES IN RUINS. Copyright © 2014 by Marilyn Johnson. All rights reserved.
Printed in the United States of America. No part of this book may be used or
reproduced in any manner whatsoever without written permission except in the
case of brief quotations embodied in critical articles and reviews. For information
address HarperCollins Publishers, 195 Broadway, New York, NY 10007.

HarperCollins books may be purchased for educational, business, or sales
promotional use. For information please e-mail the Special Markets Department
at SPsales@harpercollins.com.

FIRST HARPER PERENNIAL EDITION PUBLISHED 2015.

Designed by Fritz Metsch

The Library of Congress has catalogued the hardcover edition as follows:

Johnson, Marilyn, 1954–
Lives in ruins: archaeologists and the seductive lure of
human rubble / Marilyn Johnson.—First edition.
pages cm
Includes bibliographical references.
ISBN 978-0-06-212718-1
1. Archaeologists—Anecdotes. 2. Archaeology—Anecdotes. 1. Title.
CC175.J64 2014
930.1—dc23   2014028450

ISBN 978-0-06-212719-8 (pbk.)

HB 11.13.2020

To Rob

"This has become the archaeologist's grandiose task: to make dried-up wellsprings bubble forth again, to make the forgotten known again, the dead alive, and to cause to flow once more that historic stream in which we are all encompassed. . . ."

C. W. CERAM,
Gods, Graves, and Scholars: The Story of Archaeology

Contents

Contents

DOWN AND DIRTY

Studying the people who study people

❧

No **DINOSAURS** appear in these pages. If you are looking for scientists who study dinosaurs, you want to pick up a book about paleontologists. This book is about archaeologists, people who study people and the things that they leave behind—their bones, their trash, and their ruins.

The archaeologists in this book work with humble stuff, from stone tools and broken pots to dirt. They are expert in the way things fall apart and acute observers of context; the placement and surroundings of an object can make the difference between junk and intellectual gold. To the archaeologist, treasure is something that was buried that has been brought to light, a pebble of information around which the narrative of history now needs to bend. I think of the archaeologist I saw on a loop of video, a young woman up to her hips in a muddy tunnel that would soon be a subway station in New York City, her eyes sparkling under a construction hat: "We found a coin with a date on it!"

There is no better time than now to follow archaeologists; new finds and scientific advances keep revising what we know. The bones of a British king turn up in a parking lot. Bronze Age shoes and Viking mittens pop up in ice melts. Lidar, an aerial mapping tool, reveals a vast and ancient city beneath Angkor Wat. Recurring headlines read: (PICK A PLACE) OCCUPIED (EONS) EARLIER THAN PREVIOUSLY BELIEVED. Technological advances account for some of archaeology's boom, but war, commercial development, violent weather, and warming temperatures—change and destruction—are doing their part to lay bare the layers of the past. The world is mutating faster than archaeologists can keep up.

Yet, as their sites multiply and their profession expands, archaeologists find themselves in the same predicament as other cultural memory workers: with too little support for the hard work of salvaging and making sense of our past. How much progress can they hope to make when their goal is to capture history before it disappears forever? We think we know what archaeologists do, but, like librarians, they toil behind an obscuring stereotype. The Hollywood image of the dashing adventurer bears little resemblance to the real people who, armed with not much more than a trowel and a sense of humor, try to tease one true thing from the rot and rubble of the past.

I assumed that everyone in the sandbox wanted to grow up to become an archaeologist. I spent my childhood digging with garden tools, hypnotically absorbed in the hunt for fossils; part of the appeal in researching this book was the prospect of returning to the ground and learning to sift and scrutinize with fresh eyes. I really wanted to see the earth through archaeologists' eyes. What do they observe in a pile of ruins? How does a shard of pottery or an ancient tooth help them piece together the past? How can they help us recapture and preserve our history?

I chased the real thing for this book, up to the summit of Machu Picchu and down to the chilly waters of Newport, Rhode Island. I became a keen collector of archaeologists and a connoisseur of their skills. I sought experts on different eras who specialize in a variety of artifacts. I hunted for archaeologists in places that don't ordinarily attract archaeological attention: the Caribbean and the weedy edge of Fishkill, New York, where archaeologists piece together history, post-Columbus, from plantations and graves. I found my way to a classical-era excavation in the Mediterranean with a group of "earth-whisperers," and got a taste of Old World archaeology from the Bronze Age to the fall of Rome. I studied ancient humans and followed an archaeologist whose passion is the Ice Age. I followed archaeologists who work with the military, with homicide cops, and with brewers. I met archaeologists from Peru, Japan, Australia, the U.K., Germany, the Netherlands, Israel, and Zimbabwe. I found as many female sources as male ones in this once male-dominated field.

I sweated and excavated alongside my guides; they tossed out most of what I found. In turn, I exercised my own prerogative as a writer and tossed out all the chaff, jargon, measurements, calibrated radiocarbon dates, and theories that seemed too needlessly technical for nonscientists, or that failed to illuminate the essential character of The Archaeologist. What does it take to spend your life scratching into the surface of this planet? Why does it matter—and, by the way, how much beer is involved? Such is the nature of my quest.

One graduate student told me, "When the Apocalypse comes, you want to know an archaeologist, because we know how to make fire, catch food, and create hill forts," and I promptly added her to my address book. *Knows how to make hill forts*—who can say when that will come in handy? "Of course," she continued, referring to the long-term employment prospects for her and her classmates, "we will end up living in cardboard boxes, just as our parents fear." Archaeological fieldwork is messy, usually short-term work for hire assessing land for imminent development, to certify that this skyscraper or that pipeline or strip mall won't destroy an ancient village or a sacred burial ground. Those who persevere in the profession fight like cats to get these jobs and work like dogs to keep them. And for all their expertise, competence, breadth of experience, and even cockiness, they are continually humbled by their subject. For people who know so much, there is so much they can never know. One archaeologist said, with a shrug, "Someone will find most of my first book all wrong"; and another said of his students, "What they'll know in ten years will put us to shame." I was drawn to those with experience, long-term perspective, scars, and stories—the toughest I could find.

FOUR YEARS AGO I stood in the National Museum of Ireland—Archaeology in Dublin, contemplating vast quantities of ancient gold objects churned up by the bogs of Ireland: hammered collars, big gold balls, gold diadems and bracelets and things to stick in your ears (they think). At the time, the Irish economy was tanking. Dublin was running, as far as I could tell, on what spilled out of the pockets of Brits during their bachelor parties. And yet here was all this gold, artifacts floating in display cases like jewelry from Brobdingnag.

Behind the main room of the museum, tucked out of sight and discreetly concealed from casual view, was another sort of archaeological bounty surrendered by the bogs: a cache of human bodies, hundreds and sometimes thousands of years old, strangely preserved by the oxygen-deprived bog waters: Instead of the flesh decaying to leave skeletons, the bones of these bog bodies dissolved, leaving behind flesh, organs, and even hair—natural mummies. A snip of the soundtrack from a looping video was audible. "We can look into the face of an Iron Age man!" the voice exulted. "He still has eyelashes!" Each bog body was displayed in a separate chamber that you walked into as if entering the giant shell of a snail; the bodies rested inside the carpeted walls, where a dignified hush prevailed. I stopped to stare at Clonycavan Man, a little skinny guy with a wispy goatee and a face shriveled to dark leather. His hair was piled atop his head like a prom queen's, pomaded with an ointment made from ingredients produced by a tree that grew only near the Mediterranean, more than a thousand miles away from where he lived and died.

Though Clonycavan had a face, and even facial hair, I was drawn to Old Croghan Man, the big guy. Though at present he lacked head and legs, he would have been over six feet tall when he walked the Earth more than two thousand years ago. His torso, stained dark brown, looked almost maroon in the dim light. His hands were so perfectly cured that scientists had been able to lift fingerprints. Eight of his ten nails had been recovered. He had been beheaded. Big holes had been cut through the fleshy part of his upper arms and threaded with "withy," a cord made of willow, so he could be anchored in the bog by his killers. Also, his nipples had been sliced off. It seems there was a custom in Ireland at this time of showing obeisance to your king by sucking his nipples. No nipples, you could not be a king.

The archaeologists and curators speculated that Old Croghan and Clonycavan had been former kings or chiefs, or potential rulers who threatened those in power, or highborn sacrifices who had been taken to the edge of the kingdom and put to death with such vehemence it seemed ritualistic. (I thought of one of my archaeology sources, laughing as she said, "Don't know what it is? Call it ritualistic.")

Clonycavan and Old Croghan were discovered by chance in 2003, within months and about twenty-five miles of each other, when both were dredged up and damaged by the peat-cutting machinery. The word went out—*We've got tissue!* Who answers such a call? Archaeologists, bioanthropologists, and experts on ancient hairdos came running to perform every manner of analysis on the bodies. Clonycavan and Old Croghan underwent postmortem torture to rival their mortem torture—digital and laser imaging of every sort, infrared, ultraviolet, and regular X-ray analysis, 3-D facial reconstruction, pollen analysis, and gut, stomach, dental, and dermatological workups. Someone figured out what kind of wood was used to make Old Croghan's withy; another identified the species that had contributed the leather of his cuff. Then specialists pickled the bodies, more or less, and sealed them in climate-controlled glass coffins for exhibit. It took dozens of experts to comb through the evidence of the past. Imagine getting to see them all in action. I wanted a team of archaeological experts!

The bog bodies, the ultimate artifacts, were riveting. "Some people will stand rooted for hours," said Heather Gill-Frerking, the rare North American consultant who flies across the Atlantic when the peat machines unearth another body from the European wetlands. While still an undergraduate, she had seen a picture of the head of Tollund Man, whose remains had been found in a bog in Denmark. A 2,000-year-old man (or perhaps a bit older), Tollund Man, like other bog bodies, appeared in a state the reverse of most corpses: although his skeleton was dissolving, his body tissue remained, stained brown but otherwise in remarkable condition. You could see the stubble on his chin and his puckered forehead. His expression was peaceful, in spite of the braided leather rope around his neck. Something in those bogs acts as a preservative. What was it exactly? Nobody knows, Gill-Frerking was told. "Don't say 'Nobody knows' to me," she said, and designed an experiment for her thesis by burying dead piglets and pig trotters (feet) in a bog. She earned three degrees and a postgraduate certificate in forensic anthropology, wrote about mummies and bog bodies, and began an unusual archaeological career based mainly in Europe. She is currently the director of science and education for the traveling show "Mummies of the World" and a long-distance law school student at University College London, specializing in cultural heritage law.

Her Ph.D. thesis about the Iron Age bog bodies of Schleswig, Germany, resulted in the news that the body known as Windeby Girl (immortalized in a poem by Seamus Heaney) had in fact been a boy. Gill-Frerking told me this as if she was gossiping about a mutual friend—"You know Windeby Girl was a boy?" She was also eager to talk about a site in Florida where a pond with a peat bottom preserved numerous bodies—no tissue or organs, but skeletons and, surprisingly, intact brains. "There are only three hundred sixty-nine bog bodies.* That's a very small pool of evidence," she pointed out. Some are in private hands. "You'd be amazed how many people want a mummy." Collectors who traffic in work snatched by thieves from historic sites are the bane of archaeology, and security is a big concern with the traveling mummy show.

I assumed there would be a lot of excavations in bogs, but Gill-Frerking disabused me of this. You'd have to drain the bogs to do a proper excavation—too expensive and too difficult. "These bog bodies are found by accident by the peat machines, which do a lot of damage," she said. "Bogs are wonderful places to bury bodies, or for accidents to happen. A sheep falls in, and a shepherd goes after it and falls in too—it's not officially quicksand, but it acts like it."

Gill-Frerking said that the experiment that got her started in the mummy world, which she published as "This Little Piggy Went to Cumbria; This Little Piggy Went to Wales," involved no intentional killing of piglets, though one sow did die accidentally. She herself can't bear violence or death; she makes her husband catch and release any spiders or flies she finds in their house in New Hampshire. They own a poodle named Ammut, Devourer of Souls, but she would rather talk about Fluffy, the sixteenth-century dog pulled from a German bog that she got to study and prepare for the mummy exhibit. The dog had a skeletal head, but lots of tissue and many organs and lovely brown hair—"the oldest surviving 3-D animal with soft tissue!" she claimed.

THOUGH ONE OF my sources had told me, reassuringly, that, after a while, arrowheads and points just "jump out at you," I had no confidence that any such thing would happen for me. The afternoon I spent hunting for effigy mounds in Wisconsin persuaded me

---

*Other counts differ, but the bodies number in the hundreds. Gill-Frerking's count for the international exhibit was as of 2012.

that I needed a guide. Effigy mounds are a great archaeological feature of the Midwest, piles of dirt shaped by early Indians to suggest animals and spirits. They are, according to the book I carried, world-class archaeological features, on par with monumental works like the Nazca Lines in Peru. Okay, but in the photos, those Nazca Lines—massive drawings of birds and geometric figures scraped into the surface of the desert—looked impressive, while the blackand-white pictures of the Wisconsin mounds, by contrast, did not. Still, I'm a child of the U.S.A., and this is my stuff.

In spite of a map, and a sign, and a viewing platform—a viewing platform meant a view, yes?—I could not see the feature in the landscape. Never mind the animal shape. Where was the mound? I was looking for something 359 feet high; alas, it turned out to be 359 feet *long*. I understood from the guidebook that the mounds had world significance, but I had missed the part where they were described as "characteristically low . . . following the natural contours of the land itself and blending seamlessly into the natural terrain." For some of us, they are more or less invisible. The effigies resemble birds and snakes and panthers the way the Ursae, Major and Minor, resemble bears; in other words, it helps to know in advance what you're looking for. And what about the mounds that are not effigies, not in the shapes of animals? Those look like gentle round hills. Sometimes they contain burials, sometimes not. They are piles of dirt that humans shaped. They are mysteries.

The first archaeological excavation in the United States occurred around the time of the Revolutionary War, when Thomas Jefferson cut a trench through an Indian burial mound in Virginia and made a scientific report of the human bones and other artifacts he found there. I can only presume his mound had been easier to see.

Later I heard an archaeologist named Diana Greenlee enthuse about the Poverty Point mounds in Louisiana. She claimed that these mounds and ridges in Louisiana comprise a site significant enough to rank with our other UNESCO World Heritage sites, right up there with the Grand Canyon, Independence Hall, and the Statue of Liberty. The Grand Canyon and . . . Poverty Point? Greenlee explained that thousands of years ago, people from certain lower Mississippi Valley cultures took time from their hunting and gathering to transport vast amounts of earth by hand, basket by basket, from distant spots, and made their own hills, concentric ridges, and a massive plaza. We don't know why. Poverty Point is particularly significant because (a) hunters and gatherers rarely built mounds, (b) they built this mound with great speed, and (c) the scale of this site is so enormous that, according to Greenlee, its 400 acres of mounds and other dirt constructions dwarf Stonehenge. The only created landscapes comparable in size to Poverty Point are Black Rock City at the Burning Man festival and an office complex in Florida, she declared, and by then, I felt humbled. And sure enough, when the next list of UNESCO World Heritage sites was announced this summer, Poverty Point topped the list.

Who knows this stuff? I want to shake the world and have all these experts fall out. Who can tell the difference between a human-made mound and an ordinary hill or hillock, a difference so subtle that someone with a map and a big sign can't detect it? What sort of people choose to read bones and dirt for a living? If the Late Woodland Indians who built the panther mound that I couldn't see and the more ancient Native Americans who built the massive and sadly named Poverty Point are intriguing, then the people who discover them and study them intrigue me even more. And how much do we miss without them?

L. Adrien Hannus told me one day about the hole he has been digging for a decade at a prehistoric Native American village in South Dakota. He has found pottery fragments there, and sharpened stones, and ash from ancient campfires, but the best part, the really great part, this long-haired archaeologist said, was finding a mess of fire-cracked rock and chopped-up bone, evidence of bone grease production. This is why I was sitting in a diner in Rapid

City, South Dakota, eating greasy eggs and learning all about bone grease.

There is no denying the appeal of archaeologists, but they do seem to relish the squeamish side of their work. Hannus, who ordered his bacon burnt (if he doesn't ask to have it "burnt, charred, incinerated, they bring it to me half raw"), was an expert in bone grease, the Crisco of the Neolithic, a stable fat hidden deep inside the big bones of animals that was an important part of ancient people's diets.

Unlike marrow, bone grease requires a ton of work to extract. Hannus laid it all out for me: you gather quite a few large bones, crack them, and then scrape off much of the periosteum, the membrane around the surface of the bone. You cannot simply scoop out the grease; you must boil the bones. Unfortunately, the pots that the Native Americans of the Plains made weren't sturdy enough to hold boiling water. These people fired their pottery in campfires that reached only 1,000 or 1,200 degrees, and ceramics need to be fired at a couple thousand degrees if they're to hold boiling water. Instead, these people dug a pit in the earth, lined it with treated hides, and filled it with water and cracked bones. Then they heated up a bunch of big rocks until they were superhot, somehow fished the hot rocks out of the campfire, then dropped them in the hole full of water. If all went well, the hot rocks sizzled and popped, the water boiled, and the precious bone grease bubbled to the surface, where it could be skimmed.

For all the effort, Hannus said, only a small amount of fat is extracted. The process leaves lots of debris for archaeologists to study, from fire-cracked rock to characteristic hack marks on the bones. And all that debris, representing so much effort, shows just how important bone grease was to these people. Unlike Hannus's crisp bacon fat, or the fat that marbles animal flesh, bone grease can last for years. Native Americans used to stockpile the stuff. It kept them from starving when the hunt or the harvest was bad. It lit their lamps and waterproofed their animal hides. They mixed bone grease with dried meat and berries to make pemmican, the energy bars of a thousand years ago, and with a pouch of pemmican, the Native Americans were good to travel far and wide. (If you can't pack portable food, you spend most of your time hunting and foraging). Pottery fragments from Cahokia, seven hundred miles away, have turned up in Mitchell, South Dakota; bone grease made such widespread travel and trade possible.

Hannus has harvested bone grease himself, in the manner of the Native Americans of the Plains, using bison bones and prehistoric tools. Then he made his own pemmican with dried meat, dried cranberries, and bone grease. How did it taste? He finished his bacon and grinned. "Disgusting," he said.

Archaeologists are not in it for the food. A field archaeologist described lunch on a dig: "We take bologna sandwiches and mustard and peanut butter and jelly and cheese, maybe a pickle, wad it up into a ball, slam it down, and get back to work as quickly as we can."

They are not in it for their health, either. "Let's see," another archaeologist said, ticking off his job-related setbacks. "I had a form of dysentery and turned into a scarecrow. I had malaria four times. But I've never been shot at. Hang on, let me think. . . . No."

From a distance, this kind of work might seem to fit the Indiana Jones fantasy, full of treasure and danger. Up close, the glamour can be hard to detect. Archaeologists are explorers and adventurers—Hollywood got that part right—but not exactly in the way you'd think.

The site can look like an empty lot. The artifacts can be microscopic, the feature too subtle to see. The drama takes place in a muddy hole, with our heroes surrounding it, respectfully, on their knees.

BOOT
CAMP

FIELD SCHOOL

Context is everything

❧

FIELD SCHOOL is a rite of passage. If you are studying archaeology, or even thinking about it, you need to apprentice yourself to an excavation specifically set up to help train field-workers. This usually takes place in a desert or jungle, a hot and often buggy place at the hottest and buggiest time of year. A century ago, field school meant signing on to a dig under the supervision of an archaeologist, who would teach you the fine art of excavating while hired locals did the hard labor. Now the locals work as translators, drivers, guides, or cooks, and the students do the heavy lifting, moving rocks and hauling dirt and slag—for instance, in a foul pit in Jordan that, back in the tenth century B.C., was a copper smelt. "I can't prove it," the lead archaeologist at that site told *National Geographic*, "but I think that the only people who are going to be working in this rather miserable environment are either slaves . . . or undergrads." Students not only work without the prod of a whip, they pay for the privilege. Field schools got that *school* in their name by charging tuition, quite a lot of it, usually thousands of dollars. Where would archaeology be without these armies of toiling grads and undergrads? Are they the base of a pyramid scheme that keeps excavations going with their labor and fees?

Field school is the short cut to a dig. You apply and get your typhoid and hepatitis vaccines, and stock up on antibiotics and Imodium and maybe malaria pills, and someone who has already beaten a path to "the field" tells you where to go and how to get there. You work hard under primitive conditions. You sit around at night with kids who play drinking games and tumble in and out of each other's bunks. You sweat.

From a tribute written in 1930 by a student who did time at the Chaco Canyon, New Mexico, field school:*

> I love your ruins, every one,
> That keep me out in the baking sun,
> And, too, my happy domicile
> Where the breezes play and the dunes do pile—
> I'll miss you, yes, and the words you learn us,
> You sweltering, accursed canvas furnace . . .
> Nice water you have, but only for drink. . . .

Wait. Nice water, *but only for drink*? Did that mean no showers? When I read this ditty, I had not yet been to field school, and was already sweating, scribbling notes at the museum exhibit "Chaco Uncovered: The Field Schools 1929 to the Present." Obviously, the experience of field school involved suffering of one sort and another: grubby quarters—perhaps a "sweltering, accursed canvas furnace"—canned food, insects, sunburn, dirt, and skeletal remains. Fine, bring it on. I could handle heat and discomfort. I could live without wifi or cell phone, or even deodorant; but no showers? Chaco Canyon was 6,200 feet above sea level, in the high desert, an improbable place to build a massively complex city, though Pueblo Indians did just that about two thousand years ago. This meant the site was more than a mile closer to the sun than the regular

*From an exhibit at the Maxwell Museum of Anthropology, Albuquerque, New Mexico.

desert. I imagined a high desert crew, unwashed over a span of days and weeks, digging shoulder to shoulder, armpit to armpit. Is that why bandannas always appear on the packing list for field school, to wear bandit-style, over the nose?

I spent weeks searching websites like shovelbums.org and ar chaeological.org, poring over listings for field school opportunities. I considered a field school in some Roman ruins on an island off Spain, a short walk from the beach, and one in Peru, though students there bunked in a community center "with the only flush toilet in the village!" That exclamation mark worried me. What were the odds that while I was there this toilet would break from the stress of being the only toilet, and no one in the village would know how to fix it? I never imagined I was claustrophobic until I read about another field school in Peru: "Please keep in mind that excavations are made inside the tombs which have a very narrow entrance and limited space inside." One school on a lovely Greek island in the Aegean offered students a whole cemetery, the largest ancient children's cemetery in the world. The burials were in *amphorae*, pots, so "As well as bones, you will get a chance to handle a large range of Classical Greek pottery." The cost of this grave-digging and pot-stroking (not including the therapy to recover from it) topped $7,000.

Something less intense, perhaps?

I kept returning to a listing for St. Eustatius, an island I'd never heard of in the Caribbean, a part of the world that hurricanes regularly try to erase. What kind of archaeology was going on there? St. Eustatius, I read, had "the densest concentration of colonial period artifacts and sites for any location of comparable size anywhere in the world." Shipwrecks, churches, taverns, old sugar plantations, and slave quarters—I might do fieldwork in any of these. The sponsor was not a university but an independent archaeology center, the St. Eustatius Center for Archaeological Research. SECAR seemed particularly suitable for volunteers like me, people who didn't want or need college credit for their work, so it was a relative bargain, $500 a week to dig and bunk at the center. Also, unlike many field schools, SECAR ran from January to September, closing only for hurricane season and the holidays. You could pick your weeks. Perfect. I lived in the cold northeastern United States, so the thought of going to the Caribbean in January to dig in the warm earth delighted me.

"Don't wait," Grant Gilmore, the director of SECAR, advised via satellite phone from the field. "You never know what's going to happen. And if you come next week, you can meet some archaeologists from the Netherlands." So, on the last day of July, I threw a bandanna, bug spray, sunscreen, and a dozen energy bars in a backpack and flew to the furnace of the Caribbean—over the big islands, Cuba, Jamaica, Hispaniola, and Puerto Rico—and landed in St. Maarten. There I hopped a tiny plane southwest to St. Eustatius.

A few hundred years ago, the Caribbean was the London or New York of the world, the hub, the place where the connecting lines on the global map intersected and grew dense. The lines were densest on St. Eustatius, called Statia by its residents: eight square miles of volcanic rubble and tropical vegetation. Under Dutch rule in colonial times, it had a free port, where a teeming multiethnic trading center sprang up with merchants from everywhere, including one of the largest populations of Jews and free blacks in the New World. Its port Oranjestad was the busiest in the Atlantic. From the 1750s to the 1780s, Statia's influence had been global and the island was so wealthy it was nicknamed The Golden Rock. It sent arms to the American revolutionaries, and when the American man-of-war the *Andrew Doria* sailed into port, the guns in the Dutch fort above Oranjestad gave it a welcoming salute. The British were furious. They took the Dutch upstart by force in 1781, auctioned the contents of the island's warehouses, and burned them down. St. Eustatius recovered and even thrived, but then the French swooped in and imposed taxes in 1795. That was the end of the modern world's first experiment in free trade—and the end of Statia as the center of the Atlantic.

I'd be searching for the remains and material culture from those early and dramatic days. I liked the idea of starting my archaeological education in a place I had never heard of, in a forgotten crossroads of the world.

THE ARCHAEOLOGY CENTER turned out to be a funky mint-green house on a steep hill with a bleached cow skull presiding over the backyard.* SECAR: my grandmother's attic, if my grandmother collected broken pottery and lepers' bones. The door from the backyard opened onto a tiny kitchen at the end of a cavernous central room. Most of that room was stuffed with dusty display cases, trays of seventeenth- and eighteenth-century tobacco pipes (stems long gone), rusty cannon balls, plastic storage bins full of artifacts, and other detritus accumulated since the place opened in 2005. Off the main room were the dorms, men's and women's, with room for four volunteers each. I rigged my lower bunk with a spare mosquito net that a friendly Canadian named Kelly loaned me and fell asleep to the cacophony of the tropics: lizards scurrying over stucco, cows mooing and complaining, a mosquito whining through the net. A storm was moving toward the island, but not fast enough to move this air. There was no fan. The heat settled over me like a down blanket—but at least there was a shower.

Our leader, Richard Grant Gilmore III, arrived at eight the next morning from his home across the island, and cheerfully began loading the Land Cruiser with high- and low-tech equipment: cameras and fancy surveying tools, shovels, buckets, trowels, plastic bags, nails, big mesh screens, metric rulers, and a few mangoes from a nearby tree. Gilmore was a coastal Florida native, part Filipino and Jamaican ("My mother is brown"). He was brawny and not yet

---

*SECAR moved in early 2013 to less gritty quarters in Oranjestad.

forty; his close-cropped hair showed bits of silver. He herded the day's volunteers and students into the back of the truck and we sat on benches installed along the windows: Matt, a big guy who came a couple months ago and never got around to leaving, Kelly, in her forties, on an adventure vacation (both in cutoffs and old T-shirts), and me, the oldest, in my nylon shirt with sunblock protection and my pants treated to thwart insects. We would be looking for fragments of pottery and glass, bits of trash from long-dead people, but it felt like an adventure, a reach into the unknown.

And then we were off, no seat belts, bouncing through the steep and colorful streets of Oranjestad, the only town on the island, perched on a bluff above the ocean. The landscape was dominated by the peak of an inactive and overgrown volcano that rose behind us; but giant white oil tanks built on a nearby hillside, roving bands of cows and goats, and half-finished houses gave it a patchwork texture. Though the island is tiny and hilly, the oil company had brought some jobs here; we passed a bright-yellow Hummer on the narrow street. I had been looking for a place with an exotic background to learn the basics of fieldwork, but you can't separate the work from the place where it happens. Place is not the background of archaeology—it's the point. As any archaeologist will tell you, context is everything. Digging in Statia meant getting to know Statia, now and before.

The island's history stands somewhat apart from the history of the rest of the Caribbean. People enslaved on plantations on Jamaica and Barbados and Puerto Rico lived a nightmare under the control of their masters; but, as Gilmore told us, the excavations of St. Eustatius's slave quarters are telling a different story. The island wasn't large enough or wet enough to support big farms; its sugar plantations were small operations, more like country estates for the squires who lived in Oranjestad. Statia had used its free port to become one of the world capitals of trade, playing host to a thriving black market. The other islands secretly shipped tons of sugar here, where it was repackaged to be sent untaxed into the world, or refined or turned into rum in factories like the one in ruins near where we would dig. So many ships came in and out that in the mid-1750s, the merchants of Statia couldn't build warehouses fast enough for all those goods. Gilmore and his diggers had found everything from Chinese porcelain to German seltzer bottles. "They were so friggin' rich, they even imported mineral water," he marveled.

Slaves on other Caribbean islands lived under the watchful eye of their masters; here in Statia, by contrast, the cabins of the enslaved had been found way off near the sugaring operations. They had also been put to work in the rapidly expanding black market. In addition to Afro-Caribbean pottery, Gilmore and others had found porcelain pieces, ivory combs, and hand-blown glass in the slaves' quarters. This wasn't the usual bounty at slave sites.

Gilmore said the relative autonomy of Statia's enslaved could be detected in the written record, too—not the history books, but the primary documents, which he had read in the Royal Dutch Archives in The Hague. "Why else would they have to make laws against slaves galloping on horseback through town firing muskets, or against slave children setting off firecrackers under carriages?" he asked. The place was too small to harbor runaways, but people enslaved on Statia had the means to earn money to buy their freedom. Those who did so tended to stay on the island, as merchants and landowners, and even as slaveowners themselves. At least one of those free black slaveowners was a woman.

IN ADDITION TO learning something of the history of the island, we were also getting to see what life was like for an archaeologist who supervised multiple sites and coordinated the work of a shifting population of experts and volunteers. Down the hill toward the harbor, in the heart of charming Oranjestad, Gilmore stopped first at the St. Eustatius Historical Foundation Museum, housed in a pretty seventeenth-century building. Behind it, a replica of a colonial blacksmith's shop was being rebuilt under the direction of Grant's wife, Joanna Gilmore, a slender, blond archaeologist from the U.K. Grant gave her Matt as an assistant for the day, a gift of muscle and enthusiasm. Matt grinned, picked up a sledgehammer, and immediately began wielding it, chain-gang style, to break down the old, fake-looking kiln.

Gilmore and Kelly and I sped off in the truck along the coast another mile or so, past a graveyard of ornate monuments decorated with photos of the departed and masses of flowers, populated by black-and-white goats and donkeys roaming freely. We stopped by a low-slung modular building where the Dutch archaeological team was housed. The hills behind their dorm were dotted with those big, round, white storage units holding a total of 13 million barrels of oil. The Texas oil conglomerate NuStar Energy wanted to double its capacity by building more tanks, so the Dutch archaeologists and SECAR had been doing contract work for weeks, digging and sampling two wide trenches through the vivid green hills to see if such an expansion would disturb any potential archaeological sites. So far, and much to their surprise, the archaeologists had found nothing.

Gilmore leaned out the Land Cruiser's window to chat with Corinne Hofman, professor of archaeology at Leiden University and one of the Dutch team's leaders. After a dozen rapid-fire exchanges in two languages, she volunteered her son, Yann, a biology student, and his roommate, Thomas, a law student, two tanned university dudes in surfing shorts and mirrored sunglasses, to be our dig partners for the day.

We roared through the gates and deep into the rolling expanse of the former sugar plantation, crisscrossed with rutted roads, cows and goats scattering ahead of us. Here and there the remains of a stone wall marked a potential archaeological site, though more modern garbage also appeared: a hill of rubble sparkling with broken glass, piles of tires, and rusted earth-moving equipment. Gilmore barreled through the potholes and stopped under a tangle of vines and "sting stop" plants. He pointed out the ruins of the slave quarters he and his team had surveyed the week before. We picked our way through the foliage on slightly higher ground to the ruins of an eighteenth-century sugar processing facility. We'd be digging outside its crumbled walls.

"We cleared the site three weeks ago and all this has grown since," Gilmore said. "We found tons of bees' nests, so if you get stung, break off a piece of the 'sting stop' and rub the sap on your skin." Then he warned us about the manchineel trees over by the foundation of the main plantation house; if it rained and we took shelter under a manchineel, we would emerge with second-degree burns and blisters. Even the smallest dissolved drop of its sap was corrosive, and if we consumed the fruit, it would eat holes in our stomach and we would die an excruciating death, or wish we had. Gilmore gave a short bark of a laugh—*Ha! Those crazy tropics!*—then we gathered by the crumbling sugar factory wall, for a lesson in excavation.

Gilmore showed us how to dig a "test unit," or "test pit"—a hole in the shape of a square that we would use to sample a site, to get an idea of what had happened there. Then he directed us to set up two of these test pits in open ground. There is an art to finding the right place to dig: If I had been one of these eighteenth century plantation workers, where would I sleep, cook, drop my trash, bury my dead? Most archaeologists would measure out the square for their test pits, one meter long on each side, then stretch string between the corners to give it boundaries, but Gilmore has tripped over too many strings, so we made do with only the nails marking the corners; tied with a piece of red plastic, they gave the corners a jaunty look. We split into pairs, women and dudes, and measured the ground. We used shovels to bite neat edges around the sides, being careful to keep the perimeter square and straight. Then we pulled up the foliage on top of our test pits and started lifting off the uppermost layer of sediment.

I used a shovel to scoop out some soil and brought it to the screen, a rectangle of mesh in a wooden frame, a simple and ingenious thing with two wooden legs on one side; Kelly held up the other side, balancing the screen, wheelbarrow-style, at her hips, while I dumped dirt. Then she gave the screen several aggressive shakes, rocking it back and forth on its hinged legs. Each shake sent loose soil sifting through the screen to the ground, and soon a "spoil" pile accumulated at her feet. After a few shakes, what was left on the screen was the flotsam too big to sift. Rocks? Treasure? Or lumps of dirt? We eagerly brought our heads in and picked through the debris. Our task was to pluck out anything made or possibly used by humans—pottery, nails, bits of glass and bone, shells, the fun stuff. We squashed the lumps of dirt and rubbed the rocks. Nothing. Then Kelly gave an expert flip of the screen, and the unwanted bits of rock and soil flew off to the side. Gilmore left us with the mission to dig down through the topsoil to the gray layer several inches below the surface, and fill a plastic bag with meaningful shards—the story of the people who worked this sugar plantation hundreds of years ago and who spoke to us now through their trash.

The work was repetitive and might have been boring had we not had the suspense of the hunt for artifacts. And there we were in that sublime setting, on a faraway island, a tropical storm brewing in the Atlantic, surrounded by toxic trees.

While we battled poisonous undergrowth and sifted dirt in the hot sun, Gilmore was crisscrossing the island, doing everything from manual labor—he scavenged a load of heavy stones from an old site and heaved them over the fence of the museum for use in the blacksmith shop—to negotiating for a private pilot to fly a consulting geologist and his bulky ground-penetrating radar equipment off the island. Now our leader had returned. He squatted where I had filled a bag with possible pottery chips and fragments of brick, poured them into his hand, and without breaking stride, tossed them over his shoulder, into the creeping vines. "Next!" My first morning as a shovelbum, and already I was a failure.

The Dutch guys had better luck, or sharper eyes. The test pit they dug a few feet away had yielded more promising artifacts—a couple of rust-crusted nails and what might be a piece of Afro-Caribbean pottery, crude and red. "You find one of these with markings on it, I'll buy you a case of anything, beer, rum, Ting [Jamaican grapefruit soda]," Gilmore announced. "There are maybe a hundred good, marked pieces of Afro-Caribbean pottery in the world, and SECAR has a quarter of them."

BACK AT THE center, we wrote up our field notes, recording the day's yield of nails and pieces of pottery. Gilmore told us a cautionary tale about a student who was entering site records on a laptop in the field; instead of creating a new file to record the finds from each test pit, she would type in a fresh set of data over the old set and hit "save." What should have been the records of sixty pits ended up being the record of only one. This was the risk of using volunteers and students on excavations: mistakes would be made. Fortunately, Gilmore was, in the words of a colleague, "that rare thing, a type A personality with the ability to let things roll off his back." Every day, from early morning to late afternoon, he coped, drove, fetched, strategized, taught, trained, mocked, challenged, and forgave us our lapses. Then he swam off the sliver of a black-sand beach in Oranjestad harbor with Joanna and their four-year-old daughter and two-year-old son and headed home to eat with his family. At night, while the volunteers relaxed and headed for Cool Corners, the bar down the hill that served not-too-bad Chinese food, Gilmore would hole up in his home office, researching until late in the evening, tracking nearby tropical storms and the appearance of looted artifacts on eBay, and piecing together Statia's colonial past through its history and archaeology, the subject of his writing. He wrote about Honen Dalim—the second-oldest standing synagogue in the Americas, built in 1739, which he had helped to excavate and preserve on Statia. Reading that report, I could sense the urgency that drives his profession, the bulldozers looming on the edge of so many excavations. As Gilmore concluded, "The complete destruction of this amazing structure was narrowly avoided."

More often, the archaeological literature of the Caribbean was about what was missing. Gilmore had been a contributor to *Preserving Heritage in the Caribbean*, a collection of dispatches from the islands that charted the challenges of practicing archaeology in a place where development to stimulate tourism frequently destroyed places that might have attracted tourists. Hurricanes weren't the only force trying to erase cultural heritage here. In St. Thomas, one owner agreed, after long negotiations, to preserve a former slave village on his land; then he sold the land to a developer who, without warning or notice, destroyed the site. In Barbados, archaeological sites were nominally under the protection of the Preservation of Antiquities Act; but the act was enforced by the Antiquities Advisory Committee, which had no members and had never convened. Noting such illogic, the editor wrote that Samuel Beckett himself should "give the legislators of Barbados a special award."

Gilmore's stories, filtered through his research reports, were full of heartbreak. One man building a house on the island discovered human remains in his yard, so Gilmore and his team went to work. After a few days, the man grew impatient with the pace of archaeological recovery and took a backhoe to the yard. Gilmore wrote that "due to the lack of legislation to protect archaeological remains at the time, little could be done to prevent the wanton destruction of the burial site," possibly "the first known slave burial ground excavated" on the island, and one of the few in the Caribbean. Gilmore concluded his paper with the mantra of archaeologists everywhere: "Much important history has been lost forever." This is the most common thread in the archaeological literature, not just in the Caribbean but everywhere, from the bulldozing of a pre-Inca pyramid in Peru by developers to the dynamiting of Afghanistan's massive Buddhas of Bamiyan by the Taliban.

GILMORE'S SPECIALTY, HISTORICAL archaeology, is the study of the recent past, particularly the last few hundred years; it uses the documentary record alongside the artifacts. He likes to poke fun at the archaeologists who study earlier periods, which is to say, most archaeologists. *His* sites were full of artifacts like ivory combs, medicine bottles, meerschaum pipes, and the industrial parts that helped turn sugar into rum; what did *they* get to study, stone tools? When a new student, fresh from a pre-Columbian dig in the Dominican Republic, arrived, Gilmore teased, "Find any postholes?"— these were the dark, moist dirt where wooden posts for dwellings might have once been sunk. Yes, the student said earnestly, he found three postholes in a circle. We acted impressed, though I, too, found ivory combs, glass bottles, and other eighteenth-century artifacts vastly more interesting than dark, moist earth; imagine digging for weeks to find three postholes! As for Gilmore, I had the feeling that his japes and barbs were the language he spoke to keep his spirits up. It could be lonely on this island.

Gilmore seemed energized by the Dutch crew—Corinne Hofman and her husband Menno Hoogland and their students— who were in Statia for a few weeks to survey the land where the new oil tanks would go. The relatively small numbers of Caribbean archaeologists could breed rivalries, but these people collaborated, on digs and on monitoring the larger political climate. Statia had been part of the Netherlands Antilles, which was dissolved in 2010; now it was a Dutch municipality, subject to Dutch laws and treaties. Part of Gilmore's job, as he saw it, was to team up with Hoogland to lobby the Netherlands to preserve archaeological resources here—time-consuming political work that would pave the way for all their archaeological work. Gilmore, Hofman, and Hoogland also functioned as old-fashioned rural neighbors, pitching in to help when needed. "There's so much development, we do a lot of 'rescue' archaeology," Hofman said. "We go everywhere. Last month we all went to [the island of] Saba when a developer ran into skeletons that needed excavating."

That neighborly coexistence flourished in late afternoons, when, overheated from a day in the field, we hung out together at SE-CAR's headquarters and did the other work of archaeology, washing and recording our finds. Hofman, an expert on pre-Columbian populations of the Caribbean, held court at the picnic table in the backyard. Two of her Ph.D. students and I cleaned artifacts with old toothbrushes, scrubbing dirt and grime from fractured pottery and goats' teeth. Chickens pecked under the clothesline and lizards (brown, striped, and green with blue heads) scurried over the broken porch and around the bucket where an old anchor, another artifact, soaked. Hofman, in her early fifties, was tan and languid in shorts and a low-cut T, ball cap pulled over dark hair, gold earrings flashing—a dead ringer for Ali MacGraw. Her students call her the *god* (her husband was the *demigod*, their son, the *semigod*). One told me, "Picture her with everyone gathered around, awaiting her instructions. The question is, who gets to wave the fan?"

I asked Hofman if she ever had to work with organic remains, and she said no, but her husband, Menno, was digging some graves from the 1820s in the Netherlands recently and "he had to deal with facial hair and *eyeballs*." Eyeballs! She grimaced and I shuddered, but the two lovely Ph.D. candidates on the picnic bench didn't flinch; one was an expert on teeth and the other on the cranial modification of infant skulls. Cranial modification apparently occurred all over the ancient world, with parents clamping and flattening and binding their babies' skulls to grow into—"Not points!" I interrupted—but, yes, some of them did what was necessary to make pointy-headed children. Others preferred their children's skulls to bulge at the top, like Megamind. I could see how this could make an irresistible thesis topic.

Suddenly, Hofman slapped her hand on the picnic table and

announced, "I have a wonderful idea. We will go on an Indiana Jones expedition—how about that? Grant? Can we all go out Friday looking for prehistoric sites?" At this, Gilmore emerged from the cluttered gloom of SECAR, where he and a group of students and volunteers had been entering data for the 3-D computer map of the island. He agreed. We would consult the maps left by their colleague, an archaeologist on St. Maarten, who had walked across the island in 1989 with a troop of students, noting surface finds and likely locations for digs. There was a spot halfway up the old volcano called the Quill that we could check out, and another in the jungle near the top of the Quill where one of Gilmore's students found a tool fashioned from a shell.

EXPLORERS' DAY DAWNED with the call of a mad, strangled-sounding rooster. When Gilmore came at eight to pick us up, we spilled out from the bright-blue doors of the back gate into a misty rain and an already-packed truck. Field School Goes on a Field Trip! "Come on, everybody," Gilmore said brightly. "This Land Cruiser holds thirteen Marines!" So ten of us, including a couple new volunteers and the Dutch Ph.D. students, squeezed into a cheerful jumble and bounced up the road to the Quill, backpacks full of insect spray and water bottles. Once again, I was swathed in lightweight nylon, long sleeves and pants, boots, thick socks, and a floppy hat with a cord under my chin, prepared for the tropics to attack at any minute. The Dutch were in sleeveless tops and shorts, cool and bubbly with anticipation; the others showed only slightly less enthusiasm and skin. Gilmore parked up the Quill where the road was rutted out, and one of the guys used the GPS to find the area the students from the eighties had marked.

We walked up a lush, green lane. Hofman leaned down and picked up a piece of coral and turned it over. "Look at this," she said. "Do you see this flat side? This was absolutely altered by hand." The students marveled at Hofman's laser-beam ability to find the ancient tool in the landscape; I was impressed by her certainty. How do you discriminate between an edge shaped by humans and a break made by natural forces? That takes experience, and an eye for subtle differences and the patterns a human makes. Matt ran back to the Land Cruiser and returned with a sharpened machete, and began hacking away at the vines behind where the coral tool had been spotted. Hofman grinned. "It's nice to point and say, 'Do this' and he just does it, yes?" The hacking disturbed nests of what the Dutch call "jacky" wasps, which hovered in the lane, looking vicious. "You don't want them after you," one of the Ph.D. students said, so we poked around on the ground gingerly, but, finding nothing else, abandoned the spot. We wandered farther down the path and emerged in a cow field, on a promontory high above the gorgeous Atlantic side of the island. The beauty of the surroundings was simply the most obvious reason to be a Caribbean archaeologist.

We regrouped and hiked back to the road, leaving the coral tool guarded by hovering wasps, and headed up to a trailhead, mostly overgrown, to climb the Quill. Gilmore took the lead and we filed behind him, up an ascent that had me gasping; everyone else was flashing brown muscles and chattering as they climbed. When we reached the area where his student had reported finding a tool, Gilmore told us to look for fruit trees. No matter when they lived, in colonial, pre-Columbian, or ancient times, people gravitated to fruit trees. We fanned out, balancing and picking our way like goats around giant termite nests and spiderwebs. We located a mango tree by the rotting smell of its windfalls and concentrated our search there.

We all felt the anticipation—ancient people walked here!— and the suspense was delicious, but my eagerness had a particular edge. After the second day digging at the plantation, Gilmore told me I could fill in our two test pits. I filled the holes carefully with dirt, but the nail markers at the corner looked messy, so I gathered them up, too, as if tidying up after children. Later I heard two of the Dutch guys surveying the area shout to Gilmore that they couldn't find the markings for two test pits. "Was I not supposed to remove the nails?" I said. "Did I tell you to remove the nails?" Gilmore replied calmly. I tried to fix the depth of my error. "Not as bad as erasing sixty sites?" I said. "No, no," Gilmore allowed. "You erased only two." So on Explorers' Day, least trained and most repentant, I looked harder than anyone. And I found something under the mango tree, two things, in fact: broken shells. Unbroken, they would be nothing special, but broken might mean someone had crafted them into tools. Gilmore came over and examined one of the shells, an act of attention that was gratifying. He pointed it out to one of the Ph.D. students, who didn't bother to stop. "It's most likely hermit crabs," he said. So much for my redemption.

Suddenly a commotion broke out above us on the hill. "Bees!" someone shouted, and another slapped at her ear. One of the Dutch archaeologists yelled, "Get out!" and suddenly all ten of us were in a downhill rush, crashing through the undergrowth. Thomas the law student was slapping at his head, so Gilmore stopped and pulled a bee out of his long hair. The Dutch crew stumbled past, yelling. I stuck close to Gilmore, who hesitated again partway down and pointed. "Lilies," he said, reaching down for the leaves of two plants. "They don't grow wild here, but slaves planted them at grave sites," and of all the markers we had seen today, this would seem the most promising—but he would have to note it on a map for later investigation. "Hurry, they're still on us!" came the cry from the volunteers farther up, so we stumbled down the last stretch of the slope. When we broke through to the road, Thomas had his head bowed and Hofman was pulling another bee out of his hair with a tissue. One Dutch student was nursing a sting at her waist, one shrugged off a sting on his arm.

Bees, you say? A band of fit and hearty archaeologists brought low by little flying insects? I know it seems silly, but consider the words of the archaeologist who listed all of the terrible snakes and spiders and scorpions he encountered in the course of excavating in Central America, then waved his hand dismissively—snakes are stupid, spiders are kind of cute, and our fears about these creatures are irrational. Then what would be a rational fear? "What is deadly in the jungle is the mosquitoes," he declared. What is most likely to kill us? "The bugs."

And these bugs were not little honeybees. "Africanized bees," Gilmore explained. "They appeared on the island about five years ago. They have sentry bees who patrol their territory. They'll bounce against your head, bump into your forehead, and then, if you don't get away, they'll come after you." Ah, bugs that stalk people.

But the archaeologists didn't seem horrified, or upset. Everyone's cheeks were flushed. They seemed recharged, in a heightened state of—could this be pleasure? Why yes, they were having *fun*. Even Thomas, who had had two mad bees trying to drill through his skull, was shaking off the stings and grinning. This was much more fun than law school! This was the adventure we longed for, the Indiana Jones adventure, starring us and a swarm of—let's go ahead and say it—*killer* bees.

GRANT GILMORE WAS sitting in his comfortable home on the north side of the island, on Zeelander Bay, beaming at his wife as she told me how she fell in love with archaeology as a teenager. Joanna, a decade younger than Grant, was soft-voiced, gentle, but steely at the core; she had analyzed bone damage in the skeletons of leprosy victims. She first came to Statia to work with Gilmore when she was a master's student and he a doctoral candidate at University College London; she returned as his girlfriend, then moved in as his wife. "Grant gave me a human skull for my birthday one year," she told me, shyly. "Really? Which year?" I asked. And they discussed it, back and forth in the night breeze blowing off the bay, their children asleep in the back of the house.

"Twenty-one?" she guessed—". . . no, later. Not Christmas, surely." He said, "No, your mother would have freaked. Valentine's Day?" It was a puzzle—people who were trained to take any puzzle out there and pin it to a map and date it couldn't quite locate this oddly endearing event in their own past.

The rain from the tropical storm that had been threatening since I arrived finally came, a hot August downpour. It kept our little band of volunteers indoors for pottery lessons and a show-and-tell about eighteenth-century pipes, mirrors, and ink bottles, some of them marked POLICE EVIDENCE because they had been confiscated from a doctor trying to smuggle them out of the country.

Why do we study pottery? Because it endures; because, for thousands of years, most cultures have made it in one form or another; because it appears in breathtaking variety and tells us stories about the people who made and used it. I rubbed the pieces of creamware and pearlware from Europe and Asia and felt the rough salt glaze on a local piece of stoneware. Gilmore quickly figured out that Courtney, the newest volunteer, had taken pottery classes, and used her experience to explain the differences in how each was made. Then he told us about the beautiful hexagonal blue beads of Statia, the famous blue beads worth $150 or $200 apiece to collectors. I briefly entertained a detour into the archaeology of beads, following bead archaeologists, subscribing to the *Journal of the Society of Bead Researchers*, flying to the International Bead Conference in Borneo—it was not too late to go to Borneo. Whenever there was a storm, beads and other goods that had sunk when the British burned Statia's warehouses would wash ashore. "I bet you there are thirty or forty people combing the beach after this storm, looking for blue beads," Gilmore said.

The next day, a steamy one, we returned to the plantation, this time to learn how to operate the "total station," a surveying tool that measured distances and helped archaeologists map their sites. Gilmore carried the high-tech tool and an equally important low-tech one: a nineteenth-century edition of Diderot's *Pictorial Encyclopedia of Trades and Industry*, with its detailed drawings of how various industries, including sugar mills, worked. You can't identify artifacts if you don't know what they are—it's one of the challenges of historical archaeology, industrial archaeology, military archaeology, any type of archaeology: you have to know what you're looking for. Which meant, since we were digging in a sugar plantation, we had to know the components of a sugar mill, so we could recognize the pieces that went into refining sugar and turning it into rum. If we looked sharp, maybe we could find a conical sugar pot used to drain molasses from raw sugar.

After the lessons, Gilmore worked the sifting screen with a volunteer while I peppered him with questions and took notes.

"Oops, spider," I heard Gilmore say, but I was scribbling and didn't see him pick it off the screen and toss it over his shoulder. A few minutes later, it reappeared—a gray tarantula the size of a baby's fist—on the front of his shirt. I felt fur sprouting around my heart. I had never seen Gilmore motionless before, but there he stood, frozen except for his eyes, which looked at me expectantly. It was one thing to obliterate two test pits, another to stand by and let my first archaeology teacher be attacked by a tarantula. I couldn't let him down twice. Also, I needed him; he was my source, my guide to poison trees, my ride to the airport. I used my pencil to get under the spider, and tried to lift it off his shirt, but the determined thing kept creeping up toward Gilmore's neck. When I finally got under the meat of its thorax and flipped it over Gilmore's shoulder, he said not "Thank you," but, "I think you hurt its leg."

"You're worried about its leg?" I was flabbergasted.

"Come on, it's harmless," he said. Then he resumed picking through the dirt on the screen. We saw the blue glint at the same time and he lifted it up. "A blue bead?" I asked, breathless, as he held it close to his face. "Nah," he said, "it's the egg case of a cockroach," and flung it away.

NEAR THE END of my time in field school, I peeled off from Gilmore and the SECAR volunteers and followed the Dutch archaeologists on a beach walk. The beach where we sometimes swam was small, perched between the old pilings of a pier and a stone outcropping. Statia has its charms, but when it came to Caribbean beaches, the island lost out. If you wanted to walk the shoreline north from town, you had to go past one of the diving centers, cut through a parking lot at the back of a hotel bar, ease past its trash cans and a portable toilet, and pick your way over the rocks. I followed Corinne Hofman and two of her students, Anne and Hayley, around the tourist spot and across a spit of sand toward the abandoned leprosarium. The waves lapped in over the rocks.

We could see where the water cut into the land; a cliff face about six feet high dropped off from the grassy outcropping to what was left of the beach. Anne pointed to a whitish surface poking out of the rough gray cliff. "That's part of a skull," she said. This shocked me. "Human?" "Yeah," she said, and she and Hayley moved in to get a closer look. Hofman was examining a nearby pile of rocks and shells. "This is a midden," she said, "a garbage dump, about a thousand years old." All these rich sources of archaeological knowledge, sitting out in the open, exposed to the elements; some would be washed away in the next storm. "Who owns this land?" I asked her. "It's government land," Hofman said. "I don't know whether they would think it's worth excavating."

I picked my way over the rocks and almost stepped on a shard of painted pottery, lying on a rock in the harbor in low tide, winking up at me. What do you know? I picked it up and turned it over in my fingers: a delicate piece of—was it stoneware?—about three inches long, painted with a band of blue under the lip, and a blue and reddish-brown scene, too worn to say for sure what was pictured. Was this a remnant from the warehouses that had been burnt by the British? I pocketed it and brought it back to Gilmore.

"That is a nice piece," he said, turning it over and calling to Matt to come look. His verdict: Westerwald, most likely seventeenth-century. I felt a glow. He didn't scold me for picking it up, though archaeologists like their artifacts in place, the better to understand where they came from and how they fit in the historic landscape; this piece would have disappeared under the waves had I left it in context. Instead, Gilmore added it to the endless cubic feet of artifacts filed in the SECAR building, old shards plucked out of the earth or sea, carefully labeled, and tucked away—an archaeological record in which I now had a stake.

THE SURVIVALIST'S GUIDE
TO ARCHAEOLOGY
Our ancestors were geniuses

J OHN SHEA carried a sheathed Swiss Army knife on the back of his belt, and his teaching assistant lugged a big old Neolithic ax over his shoulder as they strode across the windswept campus of the State University of New York at Stony Brook. The campus, the terminal edge of a glacier from tens of thousands of years ago, is littered with rocky boulders, its winter bleakness relieved only by the young specimens of *Homo sapiens* milling about. In his lectures for the Archaeology of Human Origins class, Shea drew a picture for me and the other students of what various early humans would look like coming over the horizon. Our ancient ancestors, *Homo erectus*, were tall and thin, hunters able to run prey to the ground; they would have swarmed over their quarry like a pack of "wolves with knives." Neandertals, on the other hand—and Shea trained me to spell those early humans Neander*tal*—were lumberers. They had a barrel-chested build, like football linebackers, or the Boston Bruins—"or me," Shea said. That Neandertal profile, stocky and hirsute, is quintessential male archaeologist. It commanded the landscape: docile Stony Brook students, working their smartphones or talking in small groups, yielded and gave way when they saw two armed men looming like Neandertals. "I have been stopped by campus police," admitted Shea.

In his office, all manner of weapons, blades, triangular points, and axes were arrayed on his desk, windowsill, and bookshelves, mementoes from his digs or the products of his skill as a flintknapper who fashions his own stone tools. Shea is a paleoanthropologist and lithics specialist who studies ancient humans and their tools. A boyish forty-nine when we met in late 2011, Shea had spent his childhood in the woods in Massachusetts, behind his working-class family's home, and in northern Maine near his Acadian grandmother's. "They all knew I was going to be an archaeologist when I was, like, seven or eight," he said. "I was digging holes in the backyard, making primitive tools. The Last Child in the Woods, that's me. I was snowbound one winter in the late sixties, and the Time/Life book about prehistory came just before the snowfall did, and here it is—pictures about how these early humans are making the tools and different kinds of points—and I thought, 'Gee, that would be fun.'" Good raw material for flintknapping, quartzite or basalt, was hard to come by in Shea's neighborhood, but glass was plentiful at the town dump, where he worked in college. "Dump keeper, the perfect job for an archaeologist," he said. Once he discovered that the bottoms of cheap wine bottles yielded the best material, he began knapping wine bottles. "You can make big arrowheads out of those," he said.

"For me, archaeology is basically a part of natural history, and stone tools are a connection between humans and how they dealt with their environment. So, they're tools; they're a means to an end. I look at an artifact like this—" He held up a hefty old ax blade, a big bearded man lifting a weapon in a darkening office, and I held my breath. "My colleagues will say it's a type three Maya classic ax." That was fine as a label, and an expert could explain how the type three differed from the type two or one, but Shea's experience as a flintknapper made him look at it as something more, a unique artifact with a particular history. "I can see the scars. I can see this fracture pattern. [Its makers] probably broke it when they were resharpening it. It's like, I look at a stone tool just like you would look at a text in your book."

When Shea talked about the early humans who have been in the news recently—the *Homo erectus* skulls discovered in faraway Georgia, or the tiny *Homo floresiensis* (nicknamed "the hobbit") unearthed in Indonesia, or the little finger bone used to identify a branch of *Homo sapiens* called Denisovans—he was not talking about remote ancestors whose lives interested him only as archaeological subjects. He identified with them. He, too, built fires, made string, tracked animals (though he doesn't hunt; "I think hunting for sport is cruel"), spent hours chipping stone and making points. How could you understand early humans if you didn't try to experience how they lived?

Stone tools pried open Shea's career. His practical experience with them earned him a spot on an excavation in Belize, where a graduate student digging nearby offered to introduce him to the famous South African archaeologist Glynn Isaac, who had just been hired at Harvard. "They'll let anybody in," the student told him. Harvard's graduate school had already rejected Shea, but Isaac met him and asked about his tools. Shea reached into his loaded backpack and began pulling out points and blades, and Isaac arranged a full scholarship to Harvard for him. Shea has since been on excavations across the world as the stone tool expert—"I'm the Forrest Gump of archaeology," he says. He has worked in Europe and in Jordan and Israel (where he picked up a nasty fungus on his lips and gum; "The kibbutz doc said, 'Yah, you got mushrooms in your mouth.'"). He recently wrote an encyclopedic guide to the stone tools of the Near East. He has worked in Eritrea and Tanzania, in Kenya with his Stony Brook colleague Richard Leakey, the son of legendary archaeologists Louis Leakey and Mary Leakey, and in Ethiopia, where local kids run around carrying Kalashnikovs.

It was in Ethiopia that Shea made his latest contribution to the archaeological record. Back in the sixties, Richard Leakey had found pieces of ancient *Homo sapiens* skulls, which he estimated were 130,000 years old, at Omo Kibish in southern Ethiopia. "It's a very remote area," Shea said, "very difficult to work, and tribes are constantly cattle-raiding each other, so it's dangerous, but several of the anthropologists here decided, 'We have new methods for dating rocks. Let's go see!'" They wanted to find the burial site and try to date the undisturbed rocks around it, but Leakey's earlier expedition had predated GPS. "We piled in the Land Rovers with the geologist and we found the sites by matching up still frames from Super 8 millimeter movies made at the time." It was almost forty years later, but—"We found the same bush, same trees, and same gravel exposures, and pieces of the same bone with the fracture that fit right back together. It doesn't get much better than that." Dating the rocks above the skulls, the team estimated the Omo Kibish bones to be not 130,000 but 195,000 years old, which made them the oldest *Homo sapiens* fossils yet found—"A Stony Brook discovery," Shea said with pride.

Omo Kibish also gave Shea fresh evidence to support his belief in the intelligence of our prehistoric ancestors. He is one of a growing cadre of scientists who see the genius in "primitive" peoples. The idea that at some point early humans began to think and act like modern humans had always bothered him. He told *Science* magazine that that was "a nineteenth-century model, the idea that evolution is directional and ends with us. . . . It's an embarrassment, and we don't need it anymore."[*] According to Shea, the stone points that he found while hunting *Homo sapiens* fossils in Ethiopia were so well made that the people who fashioned them could not have been primitive. "These were people just like me," he declared, people as smart and adaptive as contemporary humans, and as different from

* As reporter Michael Balter quotes Shea in a profile in *Science* February 8, 2013.

each other as we are from other humans; they simply had different environments and challenges than we do.

Shea is like a one-man antidefamation league for our genus and species. Neandertal was the only primate whose name has become an insult, he pointed out, but *Homo neanderthalensis* survived as a species for hundreds of thousands of years. Shouldn't that command some respect? Naturally, Shea was a fan of the old GEICO commercials with their intelligent and maligned cavemen. "There's an element of truth in those," he said. He enjoyed the commercials so much that he wrote a fan letter to the advertising agency that created them, to say, " 'Thank you. You just made it so much easier to teach paleoarchaeology.' " Though no one at the company ever responded, GEICO later gave him permission to reproduce a photo of its misunderstood caveman in one of his scientific papers.

John Shea's passion could be narrowed down to an epoch, specifically the Middle Paleolithic, from 200,000 years ago to 40,000 years ago (2,000 centuries to 400 centuries ago). "I'd like to live in the Ice Age. I'd like to be one of those first people coming out of Siberia down here into the Lower 48, one of the first Americans, just to see the brand-new world," he said. "One of the advantages of living in the Ice Age would be that there are not very many people around. You're constantly moving, and you have to live by your wits. You can't just have fifteen different kinds of tools, you can't carry them. And no villages—no village idiots. Imagine a world free of idiots!" Idiots, he liked to point out, "don't survive in environments with lions."

The least probable habitat for someone like Shea was where he was most often found, at Stony Brook, amid the suburban sprawl of Long Island. He remembers flying over this place as a student. "When I was coming back from Egypt, my first trip overseas, the plane pulled out of JFK and then rolled to head up to Boston. I looked out the window and all I could see was Nassau County— you know, house house house house house, car car car car car, swimming pool swimming pool swimming pool swimming pool swimming pool. I said to one of my professors, 'Look at that. I could never live there.' Then I got this job, and I called him up. 'Good for you, John. Where is it?' he asked. I said, 'You're not going to believe it.' He says, 'Long Island?' I said, 'Yep.'"

Shea lives with his wife, Patricia Crawford, also an archaeologist, two minutes from campus by mountain bike, close enough, he said, "to hear the human sacrifices in the dorms." He and Crawford cope with the claustrophobia of the suburbs by routinely biking thirty-five miles or more, and Shea usually heads to Africa for the summer dig season. They recently bought a little place in Santa Fe, and travel there four or five times a year. The high desert is where Shea feels most at home. "You just walk out the door and you're in the mountains. We have mountain lions running around the neighborhood."

What could be better, except possibly waking up 200,000 years ago in Africa? If you were one of those creatures, *Homo heidelbergensis* or *Homo erectus*, "You know what your biggest problem would be?" Shea asked. "Getting to the ground alive. Because you probably had to sleep in a tree. Why did you have to sleep in a tree? Cuz there are at least five different kinds of carnivores living in your neighborhood and they all hunt at night. They can see at night, they can smell for kilometers, and guess what, you're on their menu." A grin lit up his wolfish face at the challenge of outwitting his stalkers. He'd be fine. I'd be meat. And you?

But never mind the carnivores. Could he help explain the archaeology of ancient humans? I had been lost in a thicket of *Homo* this and *Homo* that—the subfield called paleoanthropology—and who better a guide than someone who helped find some of the oldest evidence of *Homo sapiens*? I asked Shea if I could sit in on one of his classes, and he promptly made space for me in the Archaeology of Human Origins. I didn't tell him I had never quite managed scientific detachment. In high school biology class, when I went to dissect my anaesthesized frog, it pulled up the pins in its legs and jumped free.

Twice a week, over a winter and spring, I took John Shea's class, a virtual tour of significant archaeology sites around the world. Shea wanted to teach his students to think like archaeologists, so we looked at what the professionals uncovered, and tried to make sense of the fragments—tools, art, buildings, and burials. I was rewarded with hours of enlightenment, delivered in Shea's irreverent, almost gonzo patter. Did you know our proto-human ancestors had brain cases big enough to hold two beers, whereas ours are big enough to contain the contents of a six-pack? I began to grasp how tiny and fragmented and bewildering these bits of archaeological knowledge were in the vast expanse of time.

I started to absorb the language of archaeology, and began to call the humans that once roamed Europe, barrel-chest out-thrust, stone tools at the ready, Neander*tals*. My husband thought I sounded pretentious. "Don't you think somebody who teaches paleoanthropology would know the right pronunciation?" I said. I pointed out that a recent documentary on PBS, or National Geographic—one of the channels without space aliens—featured an announcer, obviously a civilian, who called them Neander*thals*, and a parade of archaeologists who carefully said Neander*tals*. I threw in with the archaeologists and leaned hard on the last syllable like a badge of defiance.[*]

Along with a sprinkling of anthropology graduate students who also audited Shea's course, I joined fifty or sixty undergraduates in a classroom from the previous century with a chalkboard and projection screen and teacher's desk up front. Through the long windows we could hear construction vehicles beeping as the university raced to build more and sleeker classrooms. The grad students were

[*] As for the spelling, the official museum in the Neander Valley in Germany still uses Neanderthal (pronounced Neandertal), and the journal *Evolutionary Anthropology* still spells it the old way, but I spell it the way my teacher does.

grunges, without vanity except for their glorious high-top sneakers, purple, orange, even turquoise. They planned to drive to an archaeology conference in Memphis in mid-semester, with roadside stops in Tennessee to harvest flint for their flintknapping. They were excited to check out a bar in Memphis that had a live goat tethered to its balcony. For them, the goat was not just a gimmick with the whiff of a fraternity prank; they had lots of experience with goats. They had studied goats in the history of domestication, eaten goat in the Middle East, observed herds of goats around the world, identified goat bones and teeth in their digs. Goats would play a small but key role in our class, as Shea announced, to the grad students' delight, that the Anthropology Society would once again host the Annual Spring Goat Roast. He would show us how to make our own stone tools, which we would then use to butcher a goat. It would be, he assured us, "the social event of the spring." The goat would already be dead, a whole carcass from a nearby meat purveyor, but I couldn't help remembering that frog that came back to life when I gave it a timid poke of the blade.

JOHN SHEA HAD an unorthodox idea for organizing his class in the Archaeology of Human Origins. After twenty years of teaching the conventional narrative, beginning with the earliest variations of humans and moving through time toward the present, he had decided to reverse direction. The narrative form has been around for five thousand years, and "it's a behavioral universal among the people of *Homo sapiens*," Shea said, but he considered it a flawed structure for a science class. "Narratives close off the complexity of reality," he declared. "You're rooting your story of human origins amongst the data about which you know the least. If you make a mistake identifying the ancestor, or identifying the cause that pushed them out of the trees, or identifying whether it was tool use or bipedalism or some other factor that led them to be successful, that mistake early on in the narrative means that every single thing you inject into that narrative is wrong." He framed the same thought for those of us who would have been eaten by lions in earlier times: "This class is like going back in a time machine. Hot-tub time machine, only without the hot tub, and without the embarrassing memories of the 1970s."

To start, he chose a dozen or so archaeological sites out of the thousands or even tens of thousands that date back to about 6,000–8,000 years ago, then ranged through the Middle East, Europe, China, Indonesia, and North and South Africa, before ending up at the few available ancient sites in East Africa where apes and apelike humans lived. (The Americas are of less interest to paleoanthropologists; they're too young—there's little verified evidence of humans on these continents until about 13,000 or 14,000 years ago,* and as Shea said, "I don't even start paying attention until twelve thousand years ago.") Before we went on our imaginary journey, though, we had to absorb several scientific principles, especially one that archaeologists borrowed from geology, *uniformitarianism*: In explaining the past, we use only those processes we can observe in the present. "This takes fairly pernicious ideas off the table, like ancient alien stuff," Shea explained. "Has anyone noticed aliens coming down today and giving us advice on buildings? 'O space lords! Thank you'? No!"

Shea also wanted us to separate our observations from our interpretation, as good scientists do. He set a water glass on the desk and asked us to describe it. Half full? Half empty? Either involved a judgment and colored our description. A good scientist would describe it simply as a half glass of water. Alert for inadvertent bias in

---

*Older sites like the Monte Verde site in Chile (which dates back about 14,800 years) and the Buttermilk Creek Complex in Texas (which dates to approximately 15,500 years ago) have been controversial, but are increasingly accepted by the archaeological community. Older human sites in the Americas are still disputed.

description, we also had to remember that some artifacts of culture simply don't show up in the archaeological record. "If an ancient hominin [human] butchers a goat, and makes several canoes, and a guitar, ultimately there will be no remains of the wooden efforts. After a few ice ages, it's a goat butchery site." Why are paleoarchaeologists obsessed with flint? Because that is what survives.

Another important lesson: Shea wanted to disabuse us of the notion that everything in the world could be divided in two. The convention that there were two sides to every story eliminated the third and fourth and fifth sides. Even dividing the past two and a half million years into the "Neolithic" (the new stone age) and the "Paleolithic" (the old stone age) was reductionist. "Write this down," he said. "Dichotomies are for idiots." Throughout the winter and spring, he threw it out there at odd moments, "Who are dichotomies for?" and back come their young, strong voices, like Neandertals preparing to ambush a mammoth: "IDIOTS!"

WE STARTED THE class in the Middle East, in the dense Neolithic village of Jericho, also known as Tell es-Sultan. (A *tell* is a mound that grows gradually as successive generations live and build on it.) After many centuries, the people of Jericho found themselves living atop a mound seventy feet high. I am not exactly sure why someone would want to knock down an old mud-brick house and build on top of the debris instead of moving down the road, but the result is a boon for scientists who come along centuries later. Archaeologists love *tells* because they're like layer cakes, with the trash of the pre-pottery people at the base, and deposits from more recent people, including their pottery and gnawed animal bones, near the top.

As I sat in an uncomfortable molded seat, watching the professor draw little figures and diagrams with chalk, I meditated on how much of archaeology involved graves and garbage. Even from the distance of eighty centuries, I could smell the rot. Archaeologists opening the jaws of those early, hardworking farmers found "lots of periodontal diseases," Shea told us. "These guys were shorter, squatter, and sicklier than us. They probably have only half their teeth, if that." Teeth are gold mines for archaeologists, "like fossils in your mouth," one archaeologist told me; and burials—well, we would be crawling into a few on this journey. The people of Jericho kept their dead close, under their living areas, and buried their children as well. Hunter-gatherers of even a few thousand years ago threw the bodies of their dead infants in the trash.

Painted, decorated human skulls were found at Jericho, along with stone bowls, obsidian, and cowrie shells originating from distant places; and there really was a wall around it, and a tower, too. But Shea, naturally, bored in on the *lithics*, the stone weapons. A few different kinds of points were found in Jericho: tiny stone arrowheads, long ones with many notches that did terrible damage to their prey, but also "ginormous arrowheads, super-sized, and almost guaranteed to break when they slam into something," Shea said. "Maybe these were designed to cripple the target—but you don't want to wound an animal that then runs away. When would crippling be preferable to killing?" I looked around at the blank faces on my classmates. We were people who bought our hamburger already ground, if not cooked, and were clearly at a disadvantage in this game. "Any military veterans here?" he asked. "How about shooting to wound or maim, as in combat? Shoot to kill, you take out one person. Shoot to wound, you take three people out of the fight. These weren't weapons for hunting, they were weapons for war."

Shea dialed back the time machine 25,000 years to the Upper Paleolithic, when people started spending huge amounts of time crafting tools and making art, and told us about the exotic site of Dolní Věstonice in what is now the Czech Republic. Mammoth bones littered the site and framed the round dwellings built on stone foundations. The people of Dolní Věstonice loved their mammoth bones, which they burned for fuel (imagine the stink!).

They also carved stout little figures out of ivory and other materials, giving them small heads, big breasts and hips, a slit for the vulva, and stylized feet. This was not unusual; such "Venus figures" have been found from one end of Europe to the other. What was unusual about Dolní Věstonice was its pottery, which was made, not into vessels for food or drink, but into statues of animals. These earliest potters also made round balls of clay spiked with copper oxides and salts. Heating the animal figures made them durable; heating the balls made them explode in colored flames, like ancient firecrackers.

The burials were the oddest part of this odd site. Most striking was what Shea told us about three young bodies, arranged so deliberately that I couldn't help but think that those who buried them were trying to tell us a story. Shea described the scene: on the left, a male skeleton in his early twenties, his skull covered in powdered red ochre, rests one of his hands on the pelvis of the middle figure, apparently female. The figure in the center has a crippled back and is slightly curved toward another male on the right; their arms are interlocked, and both of their heads, too, are covered in red ochre. A soap opera, a love triangle, an ancient version of Romeo and Juliet? Mostly, it was a mystery, in meaning and in the details. Take the ochre. We can guess why ochre made great chalk for pictures or body paint, but why would people be buried with it? Yet both *Homo sapiens* humans and Neandertals buried their dead with such mineral pigments. Who knows why? Who knows why Venus figures appear across Europe? Who knows why big piles of hand-axes are found littered throughout Africa, Europe, and Asia? That's a phrase that should crop up in every archaeological paper: *Who knows why?*

Archaeologists live with mystery. Teasing open a site and studying it from all angles not only doesn't answer all our questions, it mainly leads to more questions. So we study archaeology to gather authentic fragments of our human past, but the further back we go, the more we see what an incomplete picture we have of human history.

There was another odd burial at Dolní Věstonice, this one of an older woman. She was found in a fetal position under the shoulder blades of a mammoth, near a fox skeleton, and scientists said her facial bones indicated paralysis on the left side of her face. Also found nearby at Dolní Věstonice: a carved ivory head and an ivory plaque with an incised face, and get this—both had faces that droop on the left. The carved head was the size of a thumb, and "that ivory would have taken dozens of hours to carve," Shea said with respect. That woman was somebody.

The people of Dolní Věstonice might seem cryptic and strange, but reaching back twice as far, to the Middle Paleolithic's Neandertals and then even further by hundreds of thousands of years, first to *Homo heidelbergensis* and then to *Homo erectus*, was like watching a badly damaged, flickering black-and-white time travelogue. Neandertals ranged across Europe and the eastern Mediterranean (the Levant) into Russia, and lived in caves. Did they live in other dwellings, too? We know only about the ones preserved in caves. For a time, *Homo neanderthalensis* and *Homo sapiens* both inhabited the Levant; then, for a significant period between 80,000 and 50,000 years ago, *Homo sapiens* disappeared from the archaeological record in this area. Again, who knows why?

Did Neandertals and *Homo sapiens* reproduce with each other? This is the hot question ever since a laboratory sequenced the Neandertal genome in 2010 and scientists announced that a small percentage of Eurasian DNA could be traced to Neandertals. The results percolated down to the popular press—"It's Fred, Wilma—And You!" and "Who're You Calling a Neanderthal?" As with most paleoanthropological news, though, the conclusion was soon challenged. Do humans carry traces of Neandertal genes because they interbred or because they shared a common ancestor? Evolutionary genetics "is a young science," Shea noted. "They only got Neandertal DNA in 1996. The jury's still out." To an archaeologist, that's like yesterday. The laboratory at the Max Planck Institute for Evolutionary Anthropology, which sequenced the genome,* has a stellar reputation, Shea acknowledged, but his experience with laboratories overall is not reassuring: "All you have to do is look sideways at a sample to contaminate it." From an archaeological perspective, "There is no clear and convincing proof that either hominin set eyes on the other." You never find these people's tools or bones in the same place at the same time. He refers to Neandertals as "our cousins" and conceded, "At most, the Neandertals are ancestral only to some of us." He attributed part of the fascination with the species to the fact that their remains are easy to find and there are lots of specimens, and also to European scientists' traditional preference for excavating in their own backyard, within easy reach of wine, cheese, and pâté.

WHAT REALLY INTERESTED Shea were the tools, and there were places, like the caves he helped excavate in Israel, where there was evidence that *Homo sapiens* had used the same kinds of knives and tools as Neandertals. "The complex projectile weapons seem to be uniquely *Homo sapiens*, though," he said. "Neandertals don't seem to have used them."

Through Shea's vivid descriptions, I finally learned to distinguish a few of the tangled branches of the human tree. *Homo sapiens* who lived in caves put trash in front and slept in the back; not so in the caves occupied by *Homo heidelbergensis*. Those humans, probably the last common ancestor of *Homo sapiens* and *neanderthalensis*, lived like frat boys 700,000 to 300,000 years ago, "flinging shit everywhere"—and the idea of slovenly boy and girl ancestors fascinated me. "Big heavy stone tools . . . probably solved things with brute force. Commandos without too much thought," Shea riffed. "If you were going to cast *Jersey Shore*, you'd go with *heidelbergensis*."

---

*This laboratory also analyzed the DNA from the little finger that was used to identify another branch of the *Homo* genus, Denisova.

The even more ancient *Homo erectus*, the tall thin guys who ran down their prey like wolves, began in Africa between a million and two million years ago. Most *Homo erectus* fossils, creepily, are missing part of the skull. Were they eaten? I think of the comic Louis C.K., another guy with a somewhat Neandertal build, who reminds us that we don't have to worry about being hunted and eaten on our way to work every day. "We got out of the food chain!" he crows. "That is a massive upgrade."

And then there was *Homo floresiensis*. The three-foot-tall hobbits are a twenty-first-century discovery from Indonesia and lived on the island of Flores, apparently until about 18,000 years ago. "You want to make a name for yourself? Learn the language of Indonesia, get a permit, and start digging holes there," Shea advised.

As for variations of our even-more-ancient ancestors, the proto-humans *Paranthropus* and *Australopithecus*, genera that appeared two to four million years ago in Africa, they had outsized teeth, the better to eat masses of vegetation. "The first thing you'd hear as you approached them is farting," Shea said. There, now—we won't ever confuse them with *Homo erectus*, let alone *Homo sapiens*.

It was Shea's idea that I should sit and take the exam for the Archaeology of Human Origins with the undergraduates. In spite of my crush on *Homo heidelbergensis* and newfound comfort with various extinct species of humans, I was horrified. I thought that was half the point, *the* point, of auditing—that I wouldn't have to write a paper or take a test. "No, it'll be good for you, it will focus your mind," Shea said. "Just see how you do." It must have occurred to him as I eased out of the classroom that my pallor and anxiety might have something to do with my age. "How long has it been since you took a science test?" he asked. Let's see, tenth-grade biology—forty-two years? He was impressed.

All the students who signed up for the class but didn't bother to attend the lectures showed up for the exam. The teaching assistant had to go hunt for extra desks. Shea prefaced the test with a short lecture that distracted me briefly. He talked about Shanidar Cave in Iraq, excavated in the fifties and sixties by the married archaeologists Ralph and Rose Solecki, who found Neandertals buried there with evidence of flowers. The startling find, which has never been replicated, quickly worked its way into the popular culture and became the primary inspiration for Jean Auel's fur-bodice-ripping bestsellers that began with *The Clan of the Cave Bear*. But Shea wondered, had those Neandertals been deliberately buried with flowers, or had the flowers been introduced by a native burrowing rodent? I am a skeptic; I voted for the rodent.

Then Shea passed out the exam: mostly multiple choice, about global temperature shifts and the timing of geological epochs and stone weapons and grave goods, and a short essay based on *The Humans Who Went Extinct*, the book by Clive Finlayson: Why, according to its author, had Neandertals died out? And what was the most important factor in the evolutionary success of *Homo sapiens*? I fussed over my answers, circled back, erased, watched as drops of sweat dripped onto my words: Neandertal lived in small groups and had a narrow niche and few strategies when the climate warmed up and their prey changed. *Homo sapiens* people communicated and traded widely, and were flexible and adaptive. If their cereal crop failed and there were no more reindeer, they'd pack up and head to cousin Joe's.

After the class, with dangerous levels of adrenaline coursing through my veins, I had a delayed realization on the drive home and banged the steering wheel in frustration. Damn it! *Chance!* I forgot chance! Chance and luck—huge factors in evolutionary survival.

In New York City the next day, heading down the subway stairs, I began to feel a tightness in my chest. I slowed down and let the others of my species flow around me, variable and complex. If I collapsed in a subway car, they would find my notebook, full of the advice and maxims of Shea, who once called himself "Beardo the

Weirdo": "never camp by the edge of a waterhole"; "don't screw with hippos"; "baboons are like German shepherds on crack"; and "any of you had seal? very good"—and what would the forensics team make of these? Such a shame to die before the goat roast. Maybe skeletal remains and the explicit consideration of extinction were getting to me. When the tightness persisted and began to feel painful, I took myself to the emergency room. Pinned to an IV line, an EKG machine rolling up to capture my flutters and skips, I considered the nurse's routine question: Had I been under stress?

I looked into her kind, concerned eyes. I had just taken a science test for the first time in decades, I told her. Could that send me into cardiac arrest?

I was not in cardiac arrest, but, just to be safe, I spent the weekend in the hospital, where I read the assignments in *The Human Career*, our thousand-plus-page textbook, and submitted to more tests, including one where, surrounded by emergency personnel, I walked faster and faster on a treadmill. My heart did not fail.

Shea e-mailed the results of my archaeology test, which I also did not fail. "32/33," he wrote. "Not bad." Not bad? Are you kidding? All but one answer right? I felt the weight lift from my chest. Not mentioning chance as a factor in extinction hadn't hurt me, but I did miss a question about the Natufians, a *Homo sapiens* culture* from 10,000 years ago. The lovely Natufians flourished for several thousand years in what is now the Middle East. They domesticated dogs and used mortars and pestles and spent hours making

---

*Once you master the variations of human, you can go for extra credit and study the archaeological version of "cultures," in which people are named based on the style of artifacts they left. Another reason the Neandertals might be popular is they all have the same culture: Mousterian. (The names are based on where the artifacts are first identified.) *Homo sapiens* have zillions of cultures, for example, Acheulian, Chalcolithic, Natufian, Clovis, Folsom, Oldowan, Jomon. . . .

polished bone beads. I pictured them: good cooks, laid-back folk, artsy-craftsy. If I had to go back in time, I'd be a Natufian, me and my dog, Homer. We'd eat gazelle. Even now I can hear Shea's voice: "Gazelle—the Big Mac of the Natufians."

"THE NAKED CHILD ran out of the hide-covered lean-to toward the rocky beach at the bend in the small river." My heart beat faster hearing the first sentence of *The Clan of the Cave Bear*, the audiobook that kept me company on the long drives to and from Stony Brook. Jean Auel's novel, set about 25,000 years ago, tells the story of a lost *Homo sapiens* girl adopted and raised by Neandertals. A monster bestseller in 1980, it was followed by five sequels, the last just published in 2011. The series, called Earth's Children,* combines adventure and romance with a manual on survival in the Ice Age. Auel's biggest achievement was to replace the image of a brutish caveman with a beautiful, intelligent, resourceful cave woman. In Ayla, Auel created the most famous figure of the Upper Paleolithic, after, that is, the Venus of Willendorf. Auel was enabled in this by archaeologists, who furnished the groundwork for the ingenious, detailed, and complex societies that she worked out in her books.

Originally, Auel said she imagined "a story about a young woman who was living with people who were significantly different, but they let her stay because she was taking care of an old man with a crippled arm." She wanted to set the story in the distant past, but knew nothing about it. "What kind of character is a caveman?" she wondered. In her research, she came across the books of Ralph Solecki, who, with his wife, had unearthed the Neandertal man killed in a rockslide at Shanidar and supposedly buried with flowers. "In life he was blind in one eye and lame and one of his arms had been amputated at the elbow. Here's my old man with a crippled arm! He really existed!" Auel devised a set of questions—"How did

*Jean Auel has trademarked the phrase "Earth's Children."

a Neandertal caveman, who was half blind, one-armed, and lame, survive to be an old man? What did he have to offer [to the other Neandertals]? Who amputated his arm, who stopped the bleeding, controlled the shock?"—then worked out the answers in the course of her first novel. Her Neandertal, she concluded, was a respected shaman, looked after by his sister, a skilled medicine woman. They stumbled upon the orphaned Ayla, obviously one of "the others," but took pity and adopted her into the clan. When the shaman's sister died, Ayla laid a wreath of medicinal flowers on her body in tribute. In her acknowledgments, Auel wrote how moved she had been by Ralph Solecki's work and apologized "for one instance of literary license I took with his facts for the sake of my fiction. In real life, it was a Neanderthal who put flowers in the grave."*

Clearly, Auel had read archaeologists besides Solecki, some of whom argued that the great caves where prehistoric art has been found were seasonal gathering places for far-flung tribes, and others who have described Neandertals' bone damage from close-range hunting that looked much like the bone damage of rodeo cowboys. She studied cognitive-science papers to devise a language for the Neandertals, assuming that their vocalizations would sound more guttural than those of *Homo sapiens*, and she gave them gruntlike names, like Uba, Goov, Creb, Broud. Artifacts found in European and Middle Eastern sites appear in her books, like the ubiquitous Venus figures, which she took as indicators of an earth-mother-centered religion shared by even far-flung bands of *Homo sapiens*. She sought out archaeologists with a particular expertise in artifacts like baskets and textiles that disintegrate relatively quickly, leaving little trace of ancient women's work. Auel knew that these two different peoples, Neandertal and *Homo sapiens*, overlapped for perhaps 10,000 years in Europe

---

* Auel pronounces it Neandertal and spells it Neanderthal, so I defer to her spelling in the written quote.

(50,000 years or longer in the Middle East), and might have had contact, though there is no archaeological evidence of it. So she devised a storyline that kept them at a hostile distance yet gave them plenty of dramatic opportunities to interact.

In Auel's hands, Ayla becomes a kind of ambassador between the slow, tough, paternalistic Neandertals, and the flexible, innovative, woman-centered *Homo sapiens*. After the death of her protectors, Ayla is cast out by the clan and lives alone in a remote valley until the traveler named Jondalar reintroduces her to the world of *Homo sapiens*. Jondalar's people, who despise and fear Neandertals as "flatheads" and "animals," have difficulty believing Ayla's stories that their grunts and gestures constitute language and that their society is as complex and elaborate as their own. Ayla alone understands that both genera are people, children of the Earth. She is the first populist.

Auel telescopes thousands of years of human evolution through her heroine. (*Ayla, Auel*—coincidence?) Ayla masters arithmetic and multiple languages and invents animal domestication, horseback riding, spear-throwing, sewing with bone needles, and starting fires with flint. (Auel gives another character credit for inventing pottery and soap.) Ayla is also a formidable hunter and an awesome cook. She is a healer and can set bones, administer herbal anesthesia, concoct hallucinogenic cocktails, prevent pregnancy, and cure hangovers. She even discovers Lascaux cave, and finds the artist to paint it. And there's more! She whistles birds down from the air and tames not just horses and a wolf, but also a cave lion, all of which obey her perfectly. And though her Neandertal rescuers view her as ugly, she is beautiful, naturally, with cascading yellow hair* and a body that won't quit. ("Oh! mother! oh Doni!" her lover Jondalar often exclaims, invoking the female deity.) Like Ayla, Jondalar is

---

*Daryl Hannah starred in the disastrous film based on the first book. Auel was so dismayed she bought back the rights, and no one has made a film about Ayla since.

tall, blond, and well-built, with blue eyes the color of a glacier.* A little Aryan, maybe?

The series runs for more than four thousand pages of pelt-ripping—182 hours on audio—but I couldn't stop. I found Dolní Věstonice woven into a story about a despotic leader who poisons a trio of young people, and an elder with a partially paralyzed face who helps bring down the despot. I read soliloquies about how great it is to have fat in the diet—always welcome news. (If the ancients visited our world, they would be astonished by smartphones and drone warfare—and our fat-free diets.) I stayed with Auel long enough to see Ayla the mighty hunter face down a vicious wolverine, armed only with the spear-thrower she had helped invent, while her baby clung to her back. Jean Auel brought us into this dangerous world, but we're with Ayla, whose competence and courage and intelligence tame most of the challenges in her path. The occasional startling image, like the description of Ayla's Neandertal guardian, reminds us what a difference 25,000 years make: "Her hair was snow white; her face, dried parchment stretched over bones with hollow cheeks and sunken eyes. She looked a thousand years old. She was just past twenty-six." Boom!

---

*There is a profusion of explicit rolling-around-on-furs in the books, though no one, Neandertal or *Homo sapiens*, can figure out how pregnancy begins. "Will you share my furs tonight?" is how the respectful *Homo sapiens* men initiate sex, which is fundamentally about the Mother's Gift of Pleasure—particularly female pleasures—to her people. Sexual relationships are open. Men and women mate and "share a hearth," but they are free to screw around, especially at festivals and summer meetings. Men introduce their mates' children as "the children of my hearth." If a child happens to look like them, they say this is "the child of my spirit," but the child's creation is magic concocted by the great earth mother, not any doing of theirs. Neandertal men, by contrast, are . . . well, a little Neandertal. They make a gesture to "relieve their needs" and a woman is expected to drop to her knees and present herself, baboon style. It is unthinkable for a Neandertal woman to refuse a man's request. Finally, one person makes the connection between sex and procreation. Ayla!

Auel's books, author interviews, and lectures all pay tribute to her authoritative sources. Paleoanthropologist Ian Tattersall sat on-stage with Auel at the Museum of Natural History in New York soon after the publication of her series' sixth and final book. "For thirty years [Jean Auel has] entranced an audience of millions of people," Tattersall said, introducing her. "Anybody who's trying to re-create these vanished worlds with any claim of credibility has to have done their homework. That's where paleoanthropology is very fortunate. . . . Jean has done her homework, and very diligently indeed." Chris Stringer, a renowned anthropologist and *Homo neanderthalensis* expert, appeared with Auel at the Natural History Museum in London. He wasn't as effusive as Tattersall, but he did look astonished when Auel said she had tanned a deer's hide with its own brains. "The author did her homework, you have to give her that," one archaeologist told me, echoing Tattersall. If you want to know about ancient herbology, butchering a mammoth, making sanitary napkins out of mouflon (wild sheep) wool, or badgers' anal glands, Auel could tell you. And she has "given back a lot," as Tattersall noted; among other things, she and her husband hosted a symposium in 1993 near Portland, Oregon, where, according to *Archaeology*, "an international gathering of scholars gave talks on Paleolithic symbolism and enjoyed Dom Pérignon and Château d'Yquem from the Auels' cellar."

But resentment among archaeologists of Auel's success and the privilege that came with it was inevitable. It wasn't just about her money. "What drove people crazy," one archaeologist told me, "was that she'd go to the South of France and be welcomed at all these sites. She got to handle what some of us would have killed to handle." He sat in the audience at one of her talks—"seven male archaeologists and fifteen hundred women." It was a tough evening for the guys, I gathered. On the one hand, here was an author who had single-handedly obliterated the image of the primitive, brutish caveman, and conjured instead a brilliant, adaptive action heroine. Like Shea and other scholars of ancient humans, Auel believed in the sophisticated ancestor. And look at all those lay people she had gathered under the tent to marvel at archaeology's promise! On the other hand . . .

Given a platform to address the Society for American Archaeology's annual conference in 1990, Jean Auel assured the assembled professionals that "no one has more respect and admiration for scientists and researchers than I do. . . . In fact, I'm sort of an 'archaeology groupie.'" But she went on to say that it was essentially the archaeologists' fault that people knew little, if anything, about their fascinating research. "I sometimes think scientists are required to take a class entitled 'Obfuscating English,'" she complained. Maybe they should stop sounding so scientific and quit using jargon like Clovis, microblade, Pleistocene, and Paleolithic.* "Write at least some of your reports in clear, understandable language," she went on. "Romance the public. Let them know that what you are doing is not only important, but fun, exciting, fascinating. Get them involved. Show them how sharp a stone tool is—nothing turned my thinking around so dramatically as the first time I made a blade out of obsidian and cut a piece of leather with it.

"Romance the public," she repeated. "They'll love you for it."

Wait—weren't these the people who had done all the excavating, the hard science, and the sophisticated thinking that formed the foundation of her work? Weren't these the people who put that work in her hands and interrupted their own work to answer her questions? Add this to the list of challenges archaeologists have to face: that the careful practice of their not-very-profitable profession might be interpreted by its most conspicuous beneficiary as a failure, not a choice.

---

* The managers of the Archaeological Society of New Jersey's discussion board advise members to avoid jargon, though they mean words like "cryoturbation" and "selectionism," not Pleistocene.

JOHN SHEA'S REPUTATION as a wild man of archaeology has been fed by stories like the one that opened the profile of him in *Science*. "One day in the late 1980s, an alarmed secretary at Harvard University called campus police. An apparently crazed young man had cornered a deer in the courtyard of the university's Peabody Museum and was hurling spears at it," the piece began. The deer was dead, of course; the scene was a lithics experiment in progress; the young man was neither crazed nor crazy.

I saw John Shea in verbal combat more than once. One of his tools is sarcasm; in class, he questioned the intelligence of the average archaeologist and university administrator and frequently "dropped the F-bomb"—and when the grad students looked shocked, he laughed them off. At the annual meeting of the Paleoanthropology Society, a brutal two-day dawn-to-dusk series of technical presentations like "Howieson's Poort: New Data from Sibudu Cave," Shea relished the heated debates in the short question-and-answer sessions and didn't hesitate to puncture presumptions. Woe to the colleague who labeled an ax unfinished (like a would-be scientist who labeled a glass half full): How did he know it was "unfinished"? One dapper archaeologist suggested that the tools found at a site in South Africa were so unusual they deserved a new name, and this drew Shea's objection. "Does the world really need this?" he said bluntly.

The way tools are classified and named in archaeology is bewildering. In a paper for *Evolutionary Anthropology* subtitled "Some Advice from Uncle Screwtape," Shea took on the conventions of stone-tool classifications. Like C. S. Lewis in the original *Screwtape Letters*, Shea adopted the persona of a demon advising a young person, in this case, about how to make the study of the most durable artifacts irrelevant to human evolution. "Dear Nephew," wrote Shea, in character, "I am delighted to learn that you have decided to take up the study of stone tools. A wise choice. The talking monkeys have been dragging these shiny objects back to their caves for millions of years. You will never be at a loss for things to write." Then he advised: "If you and your colleagues disagree about how to classify particular artifacts, create rival typologies. . . . When you write about stone-tool function, don't waste time doing experiments. . . . Use your intuition and embed your hypotheses about stone tool function in the tool names themselves (for example, scraper, handaxe, chopper)."

How reasonable: conducting experiments with stone tools was a great way to figure out what they were designed to do, and of course one shouldn't label a tool a "scraper" if you didn't know what it did. As for the classifications, Shea told me, "Everyone says it's chaos, even the people who have worked at it a long time." Why did archaeologists want to give a type of stone tool a new name? Because then, whenever that name was mentioned, the person who thought up the name had to be cited.

After the meeting, Shea shrugged off his verbal sparring as no big deal, though he admitted he did enjoy the bloody intellectual battles at the small paleoanthropology meetings. People were too polite for his taste at the larger archaeology conferences. After watching him in action, I expected him to be sharp-tongued off duty, as well. I visited his wooded backyard one evening and sat in a webbed lawn chair while he and his wife told archaeology stories from the Middle East, where they had both dug. Shea was mild and relaxed under the trees. I told him that I had read Ralph Solecki's *Shanidar: The First Flower People*, Solecki's book for general readers about Neandertals burying their dead with flowers. I imagined we would snicker together: What kind of scientist subtitles his book *The First Flower People*?* But it was a mellower Shea who responded that I should give the old archaeologist a break. "Don't forget, the book is fifty years

*It was published in London, more sensibly, as *Shanidar: The Humanity of Neanderthal Man* (Allen Lane, 1972).

old," he said. In multiple ways, I saw the blunt teacher and provocateur of paleoanthropology be kind and solicitous.*

In his backyard, he held out a peanut to a chipmunk edging closer while his wife watched him fondly. "The birds love him, too," Pat Crawford said.

They met when Shea was a college senior, sitting in on a graduate seminar at MIT. She was older than he and "all she knew of rock 'n roll was the Beatles!" he said in a can-you-believe-it voice. He had taught her about Pink Floyd and Black Flag. She took him to the opera and the theater. "*A Doll's House*—I wanted to scream, 'Get me out of here!'" Shea recalled, "but we were both happy with Shakespeare." On their first date, they went to the library. They go to their local public library two or three times a week and read, not surprisingly, voraciously; they were each in the middle of literary novels. Crawford, an adjunct in the archaeology department at Stony Brook, works in a laboratory now. She told me she "pinched pennies like mad," which was how they could afford the place in Santa Fe. I took in their modest home in Long Island, its original kitchen and bath, the pet rabbit's cage in the dining room—none of it any more decorated than they were. Their lives were completely purposeful.

When Shea and Crawford dug together in Roman ruins in Jordan, "We used to sit in the old Bronze Age Temple mound up above our excavation. The sun would go down. We'd have a drink, and we'd watch the kids playing musical tents, sneaking in and out. It was Jane Goodall and the chimps. The alpha male is going to the beta female . . ." He laughed. "I love my job." He talked about the dig in Ethiopia where everything went wrong. "We had cattle raids, we had brush fires, we put the car into the river. You name the di-

---

*He was especially kind in dealing with my ignorance. From the transcript of our first interview: "Shea: You've heard of Omo Kibish? Me: That's the oldest something, right?"

saster, we had it." His students' response? "Let's do it again next year!" The students who became passionate about archaeology were especially rewarding, but all seemed to amuse him and Crawford. "You want to have comic relief, bring a bunch of twenty-year-olds on an expedition."

THE MORNING OF the goat roast was brilliant, an April sky bright blue with streaky white clouds and just enough of a chill for a sweatshirt. I drove around Long Island looking for the wilderness site and finally found it, at the intersection of yesterday and nowhere. The location felt like a Scout camp with a circular road for school buses, and a field alongside it with wooden stocks. Yes, stocks, those public tools of shaming from colonial times. The site was a destination for school groups studying American history. Shea had found that rare spot with few rules or regulations or insurance anxieties where students could play with fire and sharp knives and projectile weapons without anybody freaking out about liability. He bustled around in a bright-red shirt, supervising the digging of a coffin-sized pit behind the red outbuildings where the students would pile sticks and build a fire. Fire! When Shea talked about fire in class, he grunt-laughed like Beavis (or was it Butt-head?). "Fire! Hunh hunh. Fire is cool! Hunh hunh hunh."

I had told everybody I was going to a goat roast; bragging was more like it—I had milked this goat roast. But it turned out the supplier was fresh out of goat. So we stood around the fire pit, drank coffee from a Dunkin' Donuts Box O' Joe, watched Shea unpack his flintknapping kit, and waited for the car of grad students who would deliver . . . a lamb. I dropped my head to scrawl my disappointment in a notebook. *I butchered a goat* seemed so cool, semibarbarous, but *I butchered a lamb*? No. Even the way it sounded—the brutish hard *g* and hard *t* of "goat"—was preferable to the soft baby mewls in "lamb." Shea avoided calling it a *lamb*, I noticed. "They've got the dead animal and are en route," he reported.

At last the rusty transport vehicle arrived and the grad students dragged out a plastic sack with a pitiful, dead lamb inside. It didn't look like nearly enough to feed the thirty or so people gathered—grads, undergrads, and even two of Shea's fellow professors, but Shea was unconcerned. Perhaps he suspected that, after the butchering lesson, some would lose their appetites. The bloody sack waited while a group of us assembled in the shade in front of the sandbox and Shea shook out bloodstained mats and laid out hammerstones, a bag of low-grade obsidian, and a first-aid kit. He draped a piece of leather over one of his thighs for a safe work area. "You *will* get cut doing this," he said gravely.

The obsidian came from a dealer in Texas who "supplies thousands of us," according to Shea. The dealer got the volcanic rock from Washington state, "and it's sharp enough to shave with." With that, Shea passed me a hunk of obsidian and a striker, and I looked at these objects. But what was I looking for? I breathed in and, trying to imitate him, brought the striker down forcefully on the obsidian. Instantly, a chip of the glassy rock flew into Shea's cheek. Bloody hell—I could have put out his eye. "No, that's okay," he said, wiping his face. He put on safety glasses for the rest of the lesson.

Then he took my lump of obsidian, my *core*, in flintknap-speak, and, rotating it, looked for a good angle for me. Somehow, with intensive coaching, I managed to flake off a few thin, triangular points. With the first point, I abraded the side of one piece to dull it so I could hold the thing without slicing my hand, and shaped it—and there was my knife. Then I made two more, crude but sharp. "You are now a cavewoman," Shea told me.

The Band-Aids came out several times as nicks appeared in the students' fingers. When a dozen or so of us had made our tools, Shea wrestled the lamb out of the plastic and, with help, hung it upside down from a corner of the sandbox's wood frame and placed a big sheet of plastic on the ground. The lamb's head had already been removed. As Shea explained, "The head is complex. Good meat, lots of structure, but it takes time to extract, and working around the teeth is dangerous." Ice Age people had to practice speed butchery while looking over their shoulders for lions; they would have carried the head home rather than try to field-dress it. Holding one of his stone blades lightly, Shea knelt down and sliced and peeled back the lamb's skin, then ripped it back so that it hung below the neck cavity like a fluttering cape. The sacrificial carcass, rib bones visible and little lamb feet dangling in front of the cape, managed to look both vulnerable and intimidating.

Shea washed his hands after handling the skin, the dirtiest part of the animal, then lifted the foreleg, "the easiest to take off—the bone floats right there. And I haven't made a single cut mark on the bone yet," he said pointedly. Cut marks were one way archaeologists registered ancient human activity, and the literature is full of dissertations and papers comparing natural breaks on bone with deliberate cut marks made by one sort of tool or another. Shea continued his careful butchery, using an ax to cut the ribs off—"Don't grab near the severed bones" (too sharp)—then he took off the long back steaks. "There's great sinew here, excellent for bowstrings or sewing up wounds, and it's pretty. Anyone want to render it out?" He cut along the throat, then wiped the blade on his jeans to get off the gummy fat. The smell of raw lamb, almost the same as the smell of cooked lamb, permeated the air.

Shea divided us into butchering teams to separate the ribs and cut up the steaks on a clean tarp. "Scrape it," he suggested. "Some of the best meat is on the bone and on the underside of the vertebrae. Don't worry about the flies," he said. "They're there to tell you the food is still edible." I tried to get into the spirit of the enterprise, and not think about fly-borne illnesses, or the goop on fly legs.

I sliced dutifully with my stone knife, which worked better than some of the cutlery in my kitchen, but because the knife was small, I got lamb blood all over me. Then I washed my hands in the clean restroom and watched little bits of lamb go down the drain. I wandered to the pit where the students were laying the ribs and sliced meat on grills and setting them in the fire. They were talking about the crazy stuff they had eaten in their travels—Bavarian wild boar, mare's milk, eyeballs.

"Were you here last year when we played football with the head?" one asked. (I bet it was a goat head.) I ate some grilled lamb steak on a round pat of homemade pita, delicious and disgusting at the same time, and stood with Shea, who grinned as he gnawed on a leg bone with still-bloody hands. "Not bad," he said, and I recalled that "not bad" was what he told me when I got all but one of the quiz questions right. "Not bad" was good.

Then he rounded up a group for a lesson in atlatl throwing and ran down to the field with a handful of spears. Not an unusual weekend for the archaeologists and the archaeology grad students: have a barbecue; throw projectile weapons.

Shea's wilderness and flintknapping experience had shaped his work, and he wanted his students, too, to benefit from such practical knowledge. Encouraging us to get familiar with fire, stone tools, and butchery and engage in experimental archaeology was really just uniformitarianism in action. "I want you to expand the range of experience about which you can make observations about the past," he said. Shea occasionally offered a class called Primitive Technologies, where, a mile from the Long Island thoroughfare of big-box stores and fast-food joints, he taught suburban students to flintknap, throw spears, and make fire. He doesn't want the current crop of *Homo sapiens* to forget what we can do.

Shea's motto, he told me, was "Never effing quit. My students were out there making fire in the snow one year, 'Eww, it's cold. It's wet. Can we go inside?' 'No, if you make fire now, you'll be able to make fire anytime. This is the perfect opportunity. You should thank the Great Spirit for this opportunity. So shut the ef up and make that goddamn fire.' And it got to be where a couple of them couldn't do it, so students who could have gone in stayed out to make sure every single member of that class finished. Co-operation among big groups of strangers is another derived human characteristic—you can't get chimps to stay on the same topic for more than a few minutes—and these students were systematically finding different ways of making fire to bring everybody in. I was so proud of them. I told them, 'Now you are human beings.'"

EXTREME BEVERAGES

Taking beer seriously

ॐ

T HE PLAN for my first conference, the annual Archaeological
Institute of America meeting, was simple: to have a drink
with the keynote speaker, Patrick McGovern, "the Indiana Jones
of Ancient Ales, Wines, and Extreme Beverages." *Extreme beverages*
was McGovern's term for mixed wine, beer, and/or mead. Our ancestors' desire for inebriation is a topic that I could relate to, and as I
pored over the conference program on the train to Philadelphia, the
site of this year's gathering, I worried that it might be the only topic
I could understand. "Rock-Cut Sanctuaries in the Eastern Rhodope
Mountains: The Gloukhite Kamani Cult Complex"? "Cretan Connections in Middle Bronze Age Ayia Irini, Kea"?

I made my way to the lobby of the Marriott Hotel, and studied
the people thronging the halls. Who are you? I wondered. Thirty-
two hundred archaeologists—voluble, bearded men in jeans and
khakis with sun-damaged faces, and women in exotic earrings and
kitten heels and just about any piece of clothing that you would
never find in the field. They sorted themselves out, heading de-
cisively in the direction of the Rhodope Mountains (Bulgaria, it
turned out) or the Middle Bronze Age. They had heard the call of
the desert or the jungle or the catacombs; or they had thrown their
darts at a map. They were part of an action profession.

Archaeological curiosity can take you almost anywhere, but I wanted to ease in on more familiar turf and contemplate inebriation. The organizers of the AIA conference, in their wisdom, must have known that the lecture on the topic of our ancestors' pursuit of intoxication would be a crowd-pleaser, appealing to professionals and enthusiasts alike. They had secured the auditorium and the beautiful Chinese Rotunda of the University of Pennsylvania Museum of Archaeology and Anthropology two miles from the conference hotel, and invited the public. Then they ran packed buses from the hotel to the museum to deliver all the archaeologists who craved edification on this subject.

The mixed crowd of amateurs and professionals, eight hundred or more, was buzzing. We settled into the seats of the musty old auditorium to consider the science of drunkenness and its persistence through history. Patrick McGovern was a slightly distracted man in his sixties, with a shock of white hair, a full white beard, and a mustache more black than white. He had directed a University of Pennsylvania excavation in Jordan for years and served as a pottery expert on several sites. Somewhere along the way, he told us, he decided to take a close look at what some of those old pots contained. He turned to the university storeroom, two floors above his laboratory, where bronze amphorae from Midas's tomb at Gordion in Turkey that had been excavated by Penn archaeologists back in the fifties were still "sitting in their original paper bags," their interiors sticky with unanalyzed residue. "It was one of the easiest excavations I was ever on," McGovern admitted. He collected scrapings, and, applying his background in chemistry, subjected the gunk to a series of tests ("I won't bore you with all the details," he said kindly). In some amphorae, he discovered the residue of a feast of barbecue lamb and lentil stew. In others, he found "a mixture of grape wine, honey, and barley beer. I'd never heard of mixing these things together." In fact, he said, "It kind of made me wince, thinking of drinking all these things in one go, beer and wine together." Then he thought, Maybe Midas and his people were on to something?

Stories about McGovern routinely filter into the popular press. *Smithsonian* magazine summed up his discoveries: "He has identified the world's oldest known barley beer . . . the oldest grape wine . . . and the earliest known booze of any kind, a Neolithic grog from China's Yellow River Valley brewed some 9,000 years ago. . . ." With his deep knowledge of the history and primacy of alcohol in human cultures and his enthusiasm for the technical properties of those crusty patches of alcoholic residue, McGovern is apparently welcome at bars and other watering holes around the world. He often finds himself a guest or guest speaker at various long tables where libations are both subject and refreshment. At one such gathering on the topic of microbrews, McGovern spoke about his harvest of residue from the dirty bronze vessels in Penn's storerooms, and threw out a challenge to the brewers in the crowd: come to my lab at nine the next morning if you want to try to reverse-engineer Midas's drink. He told the crowd at Penn that twenty microbrewers took him up on the challenge; the last man standing was Sam Calagione of Dogfish Head Craft Brewery, who had been experimenting on his own with a medieval plum drink. The two men joined forces to cook up Midas Touch, a mix of honey, white Muscat grape, and saffron. The award-winning brew led to other concoctions, all reverse-engineered from archaeological remains. For the brewer, it was intriguing business; for McGovern, it was experimental archaeology in action, "taking the clues from the past and seeing if we could come up with a modern day scenario of how these beverages were actually made."

Speaking to the rapt audience at the AIA conference about the "extreme beverages" at the heart of his research, McGovern expressed just the right amount of concern about problems of addiction and overindulgence, which not only defused a loaded topic, but also reminded us of the transgressive nature of studying intoxication. Because he was operating this evening at the intersection of scholarship and entertainment, his talk also included a screening of several YouTube videos of elephants and monkeys getting drunk. All creatures enjoy alcohol! It's not just us! Malaysian tree shrews love it, too! And the crowd lapped it up. "When you drink a fermented beverage, as you will later, some of you, it triggers a pleasure cascade," he pointed out. Then he offered, solicitously, that he didn't want to keep us from the reception, and soon we were swarming up the stairs to the gorgeous, huge galleries with vaulted ceilings, dotted with treasures and stocked with bracing drinks.

McGovern's talk was free, but the reception cost $29. That sounded a little steep to me, particularly if you wasted your single drink ticket on a bottle of Yuengling or Bud. But here they were serving the very special microbrews that McGovern has helped Dogfish Head create since that first collaboration on Midas Touch: Chateau Jiahu, a rice/honey concoction based on nine-thousand-year-old residue McGovern found in China; the chocolatey Theobroma, based on a Honduran drink; Ta Henket, an Egyptian beer; and even the rare and hard-to-find Chicha,* inspired by a South American maize drink and fermented with the help of Calagione's and McGovern's personal saliva. (No thanks.) None are cheap; occasionally I can get a four-pack of Midas Touch at a specialty market for $20. The price was partly due to the saffron, the most valuable spice in the world, that turned it golden.

I FOUND MCGOVERN in the rotunda after his talk, sitting at a folding table, making change for a fan who had just bought a copy of his

*Since this lecture, Dogfish Head has debuted the following archaeology-inspired brews: Birra Etrusca Bronze from ingredients including pomegranates and Ethiopian myrrh, based on 2,800-year-old residue found in Etruscan tombs; and Sah'tea, a rye-based drink from ninth-century Finland; Nordicthern Europe, with bog myrtle and bog cranberries, a mid–fourth century B.C. concoction; and Kvasir, from a 3,500-year-old Danish drinking vessel.

book *Uncorking the Past: The Quest for Wine, Beer, and Other Alcoholic Beverages.* Here was the triumphant keynote speaker who had just lectured, and who was also, by virtue of his position as scientific director of the museum's biomolecular laboratory, our host. It seemed undignified for him to be selling his own books. I offered to get him a beer and take over the handling of his money box, freeing him to sign autographs and talk to his fans. He looked nonplussed, but the beer offer was too tempting. After talking for an hour about our ancient thirst, he was thirsty.

The bartender was delighted to pop the top on a Midas Touch for its cocreator. McGovern and I clinked bottles and savored our first sips. To describe it as a "honey beer," or an ale/wine combo, doesn't do the beverage justice. It is divine. I didn't want to swallow, just hold each sip in my mouth. McGovern called it a "Phrygian grog," and I liked that. Yes, a wonderful Phrygian grog! It took me a while to figure out the reason the stuff tasted so delicious—perhaps because it had about three times as many calories as an ordinary beer. If beer is liquid bread, Midas Touch is liquid pound cake, drenched in honey. It did not inhibit me from making correct change for McGovern's admirers, and I made it my job to push copies of *Uncorking the Past*, which I had already read and found stimulating, effervescent, even intoxicating, its chemical geekery leavened with enthusiasm. After expounding on the details of some fermented banana remains in Africa, the author exulted, for example, over an "archaeological bombshell" that had rocked his world: "At one fell swoop, the date for the earliest banana in Africa was moved back three thousand years."

For the rest of the evening, I got to observe the beer archaeologist under assault from his fans, many of them professionals I would hear make sober presentations about ancient chariot roads or rock art, who practically launched themselves across the table to share their pleasure in McGovern's work. Was he the star or was the star his subject, ancient beer and ale? It was hard to separate the two.

Some of these people had drunk with him at a seminal beer conference in Barcelona in 2004; others were local brewers, or even old colleagues, unsteady on their feet from age, not drink. One pushed her student at him, a young man doing, she said, some impressive work with the archaeology of distilled spirits. I felt like I was sitting with Elvis, as bashful and aw-shucks as Elvis himself was reported to be. As we sipped and chatted in the interludes, McGovern confided that when he runs low on one of his brews, Dogfish Head sends more. Nice perk!

I scrounged us another round, scavenging a plate of cheese and pastries from the ravaged appetizer table, and we nibbled while another archaeologist and fan stopped by to chat about hops. I edged a book close to the fan's hand. "Ah, I'd love to buy one," the archaeologist confessed, taking the hint, "but I don't have any money on me." "So send him a check when you get home," I suggested, plucking one of McGovern's cards off the stack and sticking it in the pages of the book. McGovern, or as the people at Dogfish Head Brewery call him, Dr. Pat, signed the unpurchased book and tried not to look alarmed as his valuable commodity walked out the door. McGovern didn't hold the rash act against me. We shook hands and he thanked me for assistance in "his hour of need." (Later, he sent me an e-mail, wondering if I had taken down the name of the archaeologist who had left without paying. I hadn't, but fortunately a check soon arrived for McGovern—even tipsy archaeologists, apparently, remember their debts.)

And as suddenly as that, the gallery was cleared and the archaeologists and archaeology fans had scattered. All that was left were empty bottles.

PIG DRAGONS

How to pick up an archaeologist

🐚

SAME CONFERENCE, different bar. The enthusiasts had long since gone home, so the serious business of archaeology could begin. The line of archaeologists snaked around the reception room in the Philadelphia Marriott, waiting patiently for their rations. Soon they would be celebrating colleagues who had made significant contributions to their field, but first they flocked to the back of the room. *Pop, pop*, the caps were flipped on bottle after bottle, then each archaeologist dove into the appetizer table, juggling a beer with a plate of cheese cubes and grapes.

The lovely older woman in line ahead of me joked as we watched the bartender serve an endless stream of beer: clearly, we agreed, beer is the international beverage of archaeology, cheap enough for students and shovelbums, and if you made it to awards night at the conference—free! It was her turn to order. White wine, please, she said. My sister in libation! We bonded over our glasses of sour house wine, made a dip over the dip table, and settled in beside each other for the program.

Her name was Sarah Milledge Nelson: early eighties, snow-white Wellesley pageboy. She wore sharp pants and jacket, a jaunty scarf, and Merrell Mary Janes. She had a way of gathering her hair up and airing her neck, as if she were out in the hot sun. I might have dreamed her up.

I floated a clumsy pickup line and tried to guess where she had excavated. Style, gravitas, easy banter. . . . I imagined that she headed for Greece, or somewhere else in the Mediterranean. Wrong. She said her spot was China, particularly in the Northeast, near Mongolia, where one of the earliest life-size statues of a woman had been found. China was not a place where you'd expect to find large clay statues of women, certainly not five or six thousand years ago, but there one was, in pieces, at the evocatively named Goddess Temple in China, along with a variety of other sculptures, including many jade pendants with pig heads—"pig dragons," as the pendants were called.

And this is what happens when you strike up a conversation with an archaeologist. Soon you are talking about bone grease . . . or pointy-headed babies . . . or pig dragons. No matter how many times I've heard about these sculptures since, or said the words *pig* and *dragon* together in my head, I still get a kick out of that combination of the homely and the exotic. Even the refined Nelson, I saw, also relished saying the phrase "pig dragon."

The Goddess Temple had been Sarah Nelson's site to dig. She was the first foreign archaeologist allowed to visit it in 1987, and won two American grants to excavate there, and though she squeezed the grants to last over seven years of frugal summer trips, the permit from the Chinese to break ground didn't come through until after her funding ran out. What does an archaeologist without a permit do? On one visit, she did ground-penetrating radar with a handful of students; on another, she measured the temple's alignment with the sun, the stars, and the planets, studying the site's archaeoastronomy. Recently, she applied for another grant to excavate the Goddess Temple but was turned down, she suspected because of her age. Here was something I hadn't considered: that an archaeologist could focus on a

site for years and never get to break ground. Besides endurance, stubbornness, and hard work, it seemed that an archaeologist also needed
luck. And I had not imagined that the desire to dig might still be
burning into one's ninth decade.

I sat next to this woman, thwarted in her attempt to do hard physical labor in remote China, but still serene as she listened to the tributes
made to colleagues who succeeded in acting on their visions: the man
who received the gold medal for notable contributions to archaeology;
the woman who won the teaching prize that three of her students had
already won—an act of tribute to the ancestor that seemed fitting and
possibly overdue. And, in my ignorance, I felt sorry for Nelson.

We traded business cards and went our separate ways, and I
found myself caught up with an assortment of other archaeologists,
but Nelson stayed on my mind. She might have been disappointed
in her efforts to excavate the Goddess Temple, but it turned out she
was a recognized authority in the archaeology of Asia, particularly
of the remote places and cultures beyond the Great Wall, in the
region once known as Manchuria. "Those of us who have had the
opportunity to work in Asian archaeology," one American scholar
wrote, "are constantly impressed by the amount and intensity of
research undertaken in the region, and by how little of that work
is visible in the western-language literature." The scholar pegged
Nelson as a key figure in interpreting Asia, particularly China and
Korea, to Western archaeologists.* The more I read about Nelson,
the more I got the message: I had picked up a pioneer.

In addition to her work in Asian archaeology, Nelson has also
written and edited a whole shelf of books on gender; she is an outspoken voice for women in their efforts to join the boys' club that is

---

*Sarah Nelson wrote the first key English-language text on archaeology in
Korea, and one of four key texts in English on Chinese archaeology. She also
taught at the University of Denver for most of her career and won the highest
faculty award.

archaeology, and to study not just the men and objects of the past but the women, too. How do you do groundbreaking archaeology when almost everything conspires against it? By the time I caught up with Nelson a few months after we met, at the Society for American Archaeology's annual meeting in Memphis, and once again we sat with our wine in a sea of beer drinkers, I needed to hear her story.

Nelson set the stage for me. She graduated from Wellesley in 1953 with a degree in biblical archaeology, and married a Harvard man. She spent some years in Germany where her husband, Hal, a doctor for the Army, was stationed. By 1961, they had three sons. They moved often, but Nelson didn't mind as long as they lived in stimulating places like Europe or San Francisco, but postings in small towns in the southern U.S. were stifling. "At one point," she said, "I was so desperate for something meaningful to do that I convinced a friend to ride bikes with me in the scorching sun with our babies in seats on the backs, looking for Indian mounds that were marked on the map of the [Army] post. We never found the mounds, but later I learned that they were on the firing range, with targets propped up against them. Off limits." She vetoed an assignment to Fort Bragg, in North Carolina. My turn, she told Hal.

At age thirty-six, Nelson won a spot in archaeology graduate school at the University of Michigan; she had interviewed in pearls and heels. She found herself a student again, a mother of three trying to fit in with the hippies. Most of her professors made it clear that training women was a waste of time. Even after her time in Asia, she said that reentry to the university had been the worst culture shock of her life.

When her husband accepted an assignment to spend 1970 and 1971 in Korea, "unaccompanied," as the Army delicately put it, Nelson planned to take the children and a tutor to Taiwan to do research for her dissertation. While camping at her sister's house in California with her entourage, Nelson's plan collapsed; she couldn't get visas for her children for longer than thirty days, and "we couldn't be flying to Hong Kong every month," she says. "Anyway, what kind of mother would take her children off to the wild?" There she sat in a house in California with her three sons, her sister's five young children, and eight cats. "I had to get out of there," she said. So she improvised a plan to spend the year in Korea, off the base; at least there she and the children could visit her husband every other weekend. She didn't know much about archaeology in Korea. There was nothing in the literature in any of the languages she spoke (English, French, Spanish, German, or Chinese), so she began to teach herself Korean.

Never mind the complex grammar, or the characters in both Korean and Chinese. Nelson was studying with nine-, twelve-, and thirteen-year-old boys running around. Korean is a subtle language. The meaning is hard to pin down, which is maddening to a scientist; it's "more adapted to nuance than to straightforward declarative sentences," she wrote in the introduction to one of her books. "When reading Korean with various native Korean tutors, I would ask exactly where in the sentence it said such-and-such. 'You have to catch between the lines,' they told me. And sometimes even my tutors could not be sure they had caught it right. . . ." Within a year, though, she was reading the language.

Then one of her tutors introduced her to a local archaeologist who offered to collaborate with her on a survey of sites along the Han River. The archaeologist provided the permits and the tools; Nelson wrote up a plan using the new methods of surveying she'd learned in graduate school, and also provided the team with access to American cigarettes and beer from the military commissary.

Nelson enlisted the extended Army community for help with the survey. "The area we lived in was full of women who had nothing to do because they were there with their husbands, so I organized them into a very nice field team. Some had husbands who were very helpful. One got detailed maps from the U.S. Navy, one did helicopter photography—he would go up and take pictures of the Han

River. One woman had a very nice car, and a driver, Mr. Oh, who wore little white gloves and took us on many expeditions—and then Mr. Oh would dig with us." She is still delighted at the way people pitched in. "Something new and wonderful had dropped in my lap," she said. The survey of Neolithic sites along the Han River became the topic of her dissertation, and at forty-one, Sarah Nelson became the second woman awarded a Ph.D. in archaeology from the University of Michigan. She returned to Korea multiple times, twice as a visiting scholar. At sixty-two, more than two decades after her first improvised appearance, she wrote *The Archaeology of Korea*. "This book has been written in the hope of placing Korea on the map of world archaeology, from which it has been conspicuously absent," she states on its opening page.

I imagine her story as material for musical comedy, with sporty Army wives sifting soil and singing on the Korean riverbanks, and Mr. Oh in his proper white gloves, the calendar pages flying by, and, ultimately, the triumphant book. But there are glimpses in the book's preface of what exactly it meant to bridge this culture: the fact that someone's name could be spelled Lee, Li, Rhee, Rhi, or Yi—"and sometimes the same author has used several alternative spellings of his name"; or how to cover North Korea archaeology when "archaeological reports from the north have been difficult to obtain, and at one time were illegal to own in the Republic of Korea." And, oh yes, she told me, there was that one time they were digging too close to the DMZ and someone fired a warning shot.

Nelson lifted her hair and cooled her neck. We had snagged one of the tables in a hotel lobby across from the Memphis convention center. Archaeologists shouted and clinked glass bottles around us. Because Nelson's left eye "is all gone but around the edges" from macular degeneration, she has trouble recognizing faces, but she still seemed to know everyone. She introduced me to a parade of colleagues who had spent time with her in China or on fellowship in Bellagio, Italy, and we chatted above the noise, taking turns buying rounds of wine in convivial rhythm. Some of her stories were like scenes from exotic novels, full of shamans and warriors. While teaching a class in Seoul, she and her students would sit on the rocks above the walls of the city and watch female shamans, called *mudangs*, at work; once, the women beckoned them down, and they got to join a graceful ceremonial dance. And Lady Hao of the Shang dynasty. Had I heard of her? Nelson wondered. She had been buried in China with her servants, all of whom were beheaded except for one who had been cut in half at the waist!

In her seventies, Nelson looked back at her scholarly work, including the books about ancient queens, goddesses, and shamans, and decided to have some fun with what she had learned in Korea and China—not just the stories of big clay statues of women and other exotica, but the whole scene: the collision of East and West; sex in the field; sexism in the field; looting and drinking; jealousy. She began writing archaeological novels from her home in Denver. "Teaching novels," she calls them, with real artifacts and discoveries as the grist. Nelson is well aware that "we don't know a lot about some of these periods," but says that "everything we do know makes it into the books," including pig dragons, a status symbol for the Hongshan people who built the Goddess Temple, and oracle bones, bones with prophecies carved into the surface—northeast China is apparently littered with these.

The novels gave Nelson another way to work out archaeological puzzles, another tool to imagine variations on the distant past. The excavation of a Korean dwelling with a rare double hearth, for instance, inspired one of these novels. Why two hearths? Nelson remembers a male archaeologist speculating that it belonged to a chief with two wives, a presumption that bothered her. The chief might have had two mates—but what if the chief were a woman? "A lot of evidence in East Asia suggests that women had leadership roles. If you look at historic times, important women ruled in China," she said. The largest burial mound discovered in the ancient Silla region of Korea contained a noble woman in a spectacular crown, though written histories mention only kings. Lady Hao was not just buried with the accoutrements of a warrior; according to the inscriptions on oracle bones, she had led men in battle. "There's so much we can never know," Nelson said. "We do know that so much has been pushed under the rug or misinterpreted."

In typical pragmatic fashion, Nelson breezed by the frustrations of the difficult publishing market and founded RKLOG Press, with the intention of publishing her fiction and the fiction of other archaeologists, too. RKLOG? "Say the letters aloud," she said, laughing. She didn't lack for readers; fans who had read her scholarly work on goddesses made sure of that.

In one of Nelson's novels, an older professor is asked about his future plans. " 'Retiring soon,' he said. 'But I have so many ideas to write up that I may never be really retired.' " I thought of that scene from her fiction when Nelson and I caught up via Skype. She was about to turn eighty-two. She was packing for a conference in Jordan. She had visited ten foreign countries the previous year, from Mongolia to Morocco, including a trip to Australia to witness the total eclipse of the sun. Direct injections to her eyes were controlling her macular degeneration ("I know!" she said, "but thank goodness for modern medicine."). She was working on six different papers she had agreed to deliver, planning three more novels, and finishing a draft of a memoir "about being a woman in a field that was proclaimed to be a 'band of brothers.' " The manuscript began with her quoting a famous male archaeologist on the divisions in the profession—not between men and women, but between "the hairy-chinned" theorists and "the hairy-chested"* field-workers. Neither hairy-chinned nor hairy-chested, Nelson made it clear that the hardest battles she had to fight were the ones for the respect

*In Nelson's *Gender in Archaeology*, she credits archaeologist Alfred Kidder with the dichotomy of hairiness.

of her male colleagues. "My archaeological writings presume that what women did in the past is recoverable and interesting," she wrote.

And interesting. That she felt the need to add that phrase was telling. To some extent, archaeologists find what they're looking for, and if you never look for evidence of powerful women, even if the hills and valleys are full of queens and warriors, they'll be invisible.

Art Gallery Interlude

SERENDIPITY RULED MY chance meeting with Nelson, and serendipity led me, the year after we first met, to spot a gallery ad in the *New York Times* for Hongshan Late Neolithic Chinese Jades. I thought Hongshan was an overlooked culture, but here were the objects from Nelson's beloved Goddess Temple, on display, and apparently for sale, in Manhattan. You'd have to travel from Seattle to Florida to see two pig dragons in the United States; there are perhaps four altogether in American museums. But I had only to take a short train ride into New York City to find a cool dozen or more on display in the midtown art gallery. I signed in with a guard at the desk. Inside someone took my coat, offered me tea, and left me free to roam in a big room filled with treasures, while soft Asian music set the mood. Was a secret camera following me, in case I was the sort who pocketed pig dragons? I didn't see one. After a circuit of the whole room, and even after seeing the "hooked cloud" plaques and horned owl pendants, I had to admit that the pig dragons stood out. The term *pig dragon* is misleading in English. A pig dragon has no scales or long tail; it is a piece of jade shaped like the early Chinese symbol for dragon, a curved C. The C is smooth and the top of it ends in a carved pig face. The objects range in size from fat little rings to large paperweights, and in color from dark-green jade to the palest green and even yellow. From what I could see, each pig face was different.

All but one, I noticed, had been sold. Never fear, there were more where these came from. The dealer, who told me he had a deep personal collection, brought out six or seven more for me to drool over. Are their faces really pigs? He thought they might be bears. Here's a fine one, he said, nudging me toward a large chunk of dark carved jade that had a price of ten or eleven thousand dollars. But for me— only $8,500. I asked him if a purchase included papers. Ah yes, he said, each piece had been authenticated by three experts. Naively, it hadn't occurred to me that they might be fakes. No, no, I said. How do I know they're legal? How can I be sure they haven't been looted? "Ah," he said. "These are, how do you say it, *stray finds*. The farmers pick them up in their fields. I declare every one and pay duties and taxes on them, but . . ." Then he shrugged.

He invited me to take cell-phone photos of my pig dragon, and gave me an official photo with its dimensions and description, and then he made me a gift of the handsome gallery catalog, a seventy-five-dollar item. I usually identify myself as a writer, but somehow, though I signed my real name into the guest book, I never found the right time to share this fact. I was a cultural prospector, and not a fellow collector, like the suited gentleman and smartly dressed women who browsed knowingly by my side. The dealer and I parted ways as fellow lovers of an ancient art form. Perhaps he is still waiting for me to return with my credit card.

The gallery's catalog was not as coy as he was. "Most of the jades of the Hongshan Culture were unearthed from medium and small scale tombs," I read on the first page, then I studied helpful photos of what a grave looked like *in situ*, in the ground, and how an unearthed grave of the period looked with its skeleton decked out in jade. The text even told us to expect "three to nine artifacts per tomb." While they last.

When an object is looted, as any archaeologist would tell you, it loses its archaeological meaning. "For years art historians thought the Hongshan jades were from the Shang dynasty, because they didn't have any context," the heroine of Nelson's novels declared pointedly. Three thousand years separated the Hongshan from the Shang dynasty. Pig dragons, once looted, are still beautiful, even in the hands of a dealer, but they can't be dated, they can't illuminate a place, and they can't tell a people's story. Looted objects lose the power to speak.

MY LIFE IS IN RUINS

Jobs and other problems

❧

LIKE MANY professionals dedicated to the careful study and preservation of our cultural remains, archaeologists find that work that pays a living wage is scarce. A snapshot of the profession shows salaries and wages lower, on average, than those of artists. One source estimated fifty percent unemployment in the field. In 2014, *Forbes* identified "Anthropology and Archeology" as the #1 worst college major, "based on high initial unemployment rates and low initial earnings." At the SAA conference in Memphis in 2012, a gathering of more than three thousand archaeologists, I stepped into the room designated "Employment Service Center." Only five full-time jobs were posted. Archaeologists could find temporary fieldwork through cultural resource management (CRM) firms, which handled compliance issues for developers, but permanent positions were harder to secure. I mentioned those five lone jobs to John Shea, and told him how much I admired the stubbornness and humor of his fellow professionals in light of their brutal economic prospects. "What does this tell you?" he said, almost grimly. "It tells you how much we love this work." Not romantic love, bathed in hopeful illusions—something fiercer, that costs dearly.

At the same conference, one of my archaeological guides took my elbow and urged me past the rooms of Mayans and Africanists, past the exotic "Ethnoarchaeology of Fire Features in Fiji." "I think you'll be interested in this," she said, leading me into and through the labyrinth of the conference center to some forgotten rooms far from the action. There, the Committee on Museums, Collections, and Curation had packed a room with the beleaguered. The next year, the federal sequestration and government shutdown would introduce the rest of Americans to the cutbacks in government support, but these professionals were old hands at austerity. They had been in crisis for a generation.

In the room, archivists, curators, preservationists, and archaeologists, all keepers of collections of artifacts, discussed their challenges as the stewards of rooms full of excavated material that had not yet been inventoried. The *stuff* of archaeology, the material, was burying them.

"We are *not* encouraging our master's and Ph.D. students to stop digging—*and we must*. Look, we don't have room to put everything you're digging up!"

"This collection is going to be out in the trash dump! We can't be asked to fund this storage! We just had the third worst year in a row!"

"Do we really need to dig more 1880s farmhouse sites?"

"Tell them to slow down the digging!" one called, and the voices chimed back: "We've tried!"

There was no funding for volunteers to help catalog the collections that piled up. The professionals felt "lucky even to be paid," one said. Everywhere there were collections orphaned because the cultural resource management firms that excavated them had gone out of business. The federal Save America's Treasures program was one of the largest and most successful grant programs "for the protection of our nation's endangered and irreplaceable cultural heritage," I learned, but it was not funded at all for that year, so the National Park Service, which administered it, was no longer accepting applications. The federal Advisory Council on Historic Preservation would not even talk about collections. Every six years, the National Historic Preservation Act of 1966, which was created to fund this work, was renewed at smaller and smaller margins.

In this room, the archaeologist who directed the curation and management of archaeological collections for the U.S. Army Corps of Engineers said, mournfully, as if he were a farmer during the Great Depression and the last crop had just blown away: "National historic preservation is a first-generation job. I began when that legislation came through, as so many of us did, and we are the first and perhaps the last people to be employed our whole lives in this field. We've had too many warnings that this is not popular legislation, though, and too many people are blissfully unaware of the consequences. We are keeping our history alive, but if that legislation goes down and we are all gone, there will not be a ripple on the water for the loss of this discipline."*

Two rays of hope: the National Endowment for the Humanities (NEH) continues to breathe life into the storerooms of artifacts with an average of eighteen grants awarded each year, giving archivists and museum guardians some tools and support. And archaeologist Giovanna Vitelli reported that she had just been funded by the Andrew W. Mellon Foundation to direct the "University Engagement Programme" for the Ashmolean Museum at Oxford, charged with dreaming up new ways for teachers to engage with its collection. "I have a ton of money and a bunch of postdocs," she said, inviting everyone to network. "I'm in a sandbox with a bunch of toys."

She was the only one who did not seem to be wailing and rending her garments.

I followed several of the Cassandras of archaeological collections to the next panel—on the access and preservation of archaeological

---

*This was Sonny Trimble, who is trying to get funding for military veterans to help sort and preserve these materials.

information—and watched them confront the elegant and affable John Yellen, who heads the National Science Foundation's powerful grant program that sends many archaeologists into the field. NSF archaeology grants are made only to scientists with plans for long-term preservation of their data, such that it could be accessed by other researchers. But "after they have the money," Yellen allowed, "there's not a lot we can do." How long should an archaeologist have exclusive access to the data?—this was a burning question. There is a limbo between excavation and publication that some archaeologists never got out of—a limbo where intellectual work stalled and the artifacts and information gathered were out of reach, invisible to other researchers.

Yellen said that the National Science Foundation, too, "is being pushed by Congress to save money. Our travel budget is down fifteen percent. We have panelists come to advise us and review applications, and we do not have money to buy them refreshments. At the same time the number of proposals is increasing enormously."

Was it any wonder the noise in the hotel lobby that night was deafening? In the roar of the late evening's libations, the archaeologists shouted across tables, sat perched on the lip of the fountain outside, laughed at the gods. The field archaeologists, the lucky ones, would soon be heading to Turkey or the caves along the coast of South Africa or the Peruvian desert or Washington State or Dmanisi, Georgia (nice *Homo erectus* skulls!), or they'd be spreading out across the countryside, ahead of the bulldozers, chasing history. The graduate students roamed in packs, lean and hungry. The assistant professors counted their crumpled bills and compared travel grants. The keepers of the collections muttered into their beer.

IN THE SUMMER of 2011, Grant Gilmore had warned me not to wait to come to St. Eustatius, and I soon learned why. The shiny job he'd enjoyed for so long, directing the independent archaeology center on Statia, had tarnished somewhat by the time I met him.

His unusual temperament, the combination of fierce energy and equanimity, had worked well for doing the demanding work of archaeology in the tropics, on an island where nothing happened quickly. Gilmore helped found SECAR with the locals in 1997, and though it was not funded until 2004, its creation had been nothing less than, as even he said, "astounding." Gilmore's old teacher, Norman Barka, who first began charting the island's role in the global economy of colonial times, had told him, "If Statia gets an archaeological center, I will eat my hat." As the years passed, local support waxed and waned, and the recent election of fundamentalists to key political offices did not augur well for the center. Then, the month before I arrived, two female volunteers were assaulted, a first for SECAR. The young women fought off the drunken locals and reported the attack, but the police declined to follow up. Gilmore demanded a meeting with the chief and objected strongly to the casual dismissal of the case. Soon after that, the old car the volunteers drove was impounded, and Gilmore himself was stopped several times; he began to feel unwelcome.

I remember bouncing in the Land Cruiser over the charming cobblestones in Oranjestad, and Gilmore snorting. "Completely inauthentic. This road was in terrible shape. The original stones are underneath. I told them they should just uncover the junk on top of it. But that wasn't in the plan." He stopped at the waterfront one morning to loan out Matt, the perpetual volunteer, this time to act as SECAR's eyes, keeping vigil over a dredging operation to expand the harbor, to make sure the dredgers didn't destroy the remains of the old warehouses that had sunk when the wharfs were burned. When I asked what Matt was doing, Gilmore said, "He's watching them destroy our archaeological heritage." Barka, his mentor, had lasted twenty years in the islands, long enough to become "a jaded pessimist—that point that I would get to," Gilmore said wryly. And as their children approached school age, he and Joanna took stock and decided that they needed a fresh context.

So my first, revelatory visit to Statia happened as his own time there was coming to an end.

Neither Grant nor Jo had another job, but their plan was to head to the U.K., the U.S., or the Netherlands, trusting they would find work before their savings ran out. This was a terrible time to find archaeology jobs, but Joanna had a master's degree, experience working with museums, a calm disposition, and an indefatigable will, while Grant was strong, personable, and confident, a font of knowledge and resourcefulness, with a Ph.D. and seven years' experience running his own archaeology center. Both had studied at University College London, which, according to the *Guardian*, edged out venerable Cambridge University as the top-ranked archaeology school in the U.K. Gilmore would leave with "a lifetime of stories" and plans to write at least three books rooted in Statia, including an encyclopedia of Caribbean archaeology.

I STAYED IN touch with Grant and Joanna via Skype, where Grant's profile pictured him grinning in a T-shirt with the legend, MY LIFE IS IN RUINS.* I met up with them in June, seven months after their departure from Statia. They had taken up temporary residence at Jo's mother's house a few hours north of London in Lichfield, the beautiful old city in England's West Midlands, but as the seasons changed, as Grant turned forty, as their almost-five-year-old daughter started school, and their two-year-old son preschool, one job interview after another failed to yield a paying position. Gilmore was a finalist for a number of these jobs, but that didn't change the tally: 190 applications, zero jobs. Jo had stopped keeping track; she'd applied for perhaps thirty. "We psych ourselves up, and it's a tremendous lift to do well in the interview. Then there's a period of hope. Then . . ." She shrugged. "We start all over again."

Grant and Jo were still on Caribbean time and late picking me

*Gilmore's Twitter handle is @Dig_or_Die.

up from my hotel in Lichfield. We piled into the little yellow car they had bought from her mother, Grant squeezing between the empty children's car seats in the back, and headed off to see the sights of the charming and ancient city. Their children were in school all morning for the first time, and the hours stretched ahead of us, a recess for adults.

We wandered through the medieval Lichfield Cathedral under the soaring eaves and the stained glass, and lingered in a side room off the chapel, where major archaeological booty was displayed: the eighth-century Lichfield angel, unearthed from beneath the altar, and some of the priceless Staffordshire Hoard, the bounty of gold and silver weapons uncovered in a nearby field in 2009. The woman in charge of the exhibit couldn't figure out how to illuminate the display cases, so Grant helpfully trotted off to find a guard who could decode the lighting panel.

We piled back in the car—this time I took the spot between the car seats—and drove through bucolic country to the old Roman wall where Jo first learned to dig, a crumbling ruin set in a vivid green landscape. We were in a fantasy of English countryside, rolling hills cut by stone walls, green lanes out of Thomas Hardy. "It's gorgeous here," I enthused. Jo and Grant exchanged an amused look. "This is the first time the sun's been out in six weeks," Grant said. "We did have that nice week in March, remember?" Jo added.

Jo remembered digging ferociously along the historic wall after having been told how scarce jobs were in archaeology. "I *will* be an archaeologist; I *will* be an archaeologist." The week before I arrived, she and Grant found her old diaries in her mother's attic, full of her archaeological obsession and her first experience of Statia, when she headed there to study with Gilmore. He had chosen her to be his graduate assistant because she was serious and dedicated and she had the short fingernails to prove it. "Archaeology. Love it. Hate it. Can't live without it," as she summed it up. "What a conundrum!" Gilmore had never considered being anything else; his parents (his

father is a prominent marine biologist) pegged him as an archaeologist when he was four or five and already collecting fossils and
stones. Jo and Grant were in thrall to a profession that couldn't sus-
tain them.

We drove to their modest brick house—Jo's mother had recently married and moved nearby with her new husband—and Jo
ran to pick up the children. They came in hiding behind her legs;
Elias, named for Elias Ashmole (whose priceless collection is now
housed at the Ashmolean Museum at Oxford), was sneezing and his
nose was dripping. Both he and Amélie had been sick much of the
English spring with viruses and infections, and were just getting
healthy when Elias licked a train window and fell ill again.

The original plan for the afternoon was to whisk Grant to phys-
iotherapy for a knee injury he sustained digging in clay on an old
excavation, while the rest of us spent the afternoon at Beaudesert, a
fourteenth century estate where the Gilmores had been volunteer-
ing, but the children didn't want to cooperate. Because Grant had
flunked the British driving test, figuring out the logistics of the afternoon was as complicated as a typical day on Statia, juggling consultants and volunteers, multiple sites, and one vehicle.

The easiest course was for Jo to drive Grant and take Elias, and
for Amélie to stay behind with me. The four-year-old and I colored
companionably for an hour. "I was scared of you," Amélie admitted
after we covered the table with bright drawings, and I realized with
a start, Wow, they just left their kid with me. But all was fine, and
we laughed about it later; Grant and Jo were working on being more
guarded in England, but their relaxed island habits died hard.

The Caribbean approach served them well in the storm of children's moods. These parents were so calm! Grant was in the middle
of telling me about the guide to colonial artifacts he had been working on when Elias had a meltdown. It was contagious; soon Amélie
fell apart, too. One whimpered in Jo's arms, one howled in Grant's,
and Jo gave me a little smile. "It's like this every day," she said. The

weather hadn't helped, and even this sunny day had turned gray and drizzly. "Last week was so bad and stormy, we saw no one," Grant said. "We might as well have been in Statia." "Except for the grocery store," Jo countered. So many choices! Even the marked-down, days-old produce was fresher than what they could get on the island. And in this age of streaming video, they had been at a disadvantage in Statia, almost the last place in the Western Hemisphere to get broadband. I mentioned a documentary, and Grant looked blank. "Did it come out in the last thirteen years?" he joked.

It was time for *Mister Maker* on the BBC, and that was how we all wrapped up the afternoon, watching a rubber-faced Brit make little aliens with three googly eyes out of modeling clay and pipe cleaners. The little aliens in the living room in Staffordshire watched, entranced, and the adults smiled over their heads. Jo's mother and her new husband were on their way, to free them for an evening of wine and Indian food and, best of all, talk of archaeology.

There was no question in their minds they made the right decision. They were glad to move on, even into difficulties, and I realized that, in spite of everything, they were cheerful. Even when Jo said, "It's like this every day," about the meltdown, she was smiling, and Grant—where was that self-mocking almost bitter tone that underlaid everything he had said in Statia? He was bitter-free. The upside of not working, they freely acknowledged, was that they got to spend this time with their children. And Statia had simply become untenable. A friend who escaped the island to live in the Netherlands had decided, on retirement, to return to it, and Grant was mournful recounting this. "You know that Dutch phrase, *dat is verkeerd?*—that is just wrong? Well, I told her, *dat is zo verkeerd.*"

He shook his head, then began to outline a big idea he and Jo wanted to float past the International Committee on Archaeological Heritage Management (ICAHM): a registry of archaeological sites and monuments on Google Maps. Anyone could list a site via iPad. An archaeological directory for the world!

In 2013, almost a year after my trip to Lichfield, Joanna posted on Facebook, "My hero of the day is Grant Gilmore, for never giving up." Grant found work in a bike shop for a while, and reported that he was getting in shape. Later in 2013, two years after he left Statia, he won a six-month teaching position in the Department of Archaeology at the University of Sheffield. That signaled the beginning of the end of his professional limbo. *The Encyclopedia of Caribbean Archaeology* that he coedited was published in early 2014, and soon after, he landed a plum job in Charleston, South Carolina, another cradle of historical archaeology, as director of the Program in Historic Preservation and Community Planning at the College of Charleston. His mission: to introduce more archaeology into the curriculum. "Yes, we have had champagne," he told me at last after the thirty-month test of his commitment and character. "We cannot believe this is happening—I think over three hundred job applications has resulted in the perfect job."

ROAD TRIP THROUGH TIME

Our partner, heartbreak

❧

Much important history has been lost forever. I thought of that line from one of Grant Gilmore's reports as I went out in my dusty gray-and-brown trail shoes, a copy of *Ethnic Oasis: The Chinese in the Black Hills* in hand. Spurred by the book's coauthor, archaeologist Rose Estep Fosha, I was looking for the last piece of the Chinatown of Deadwood, South Dakota. The town was hardly big enough to have a separate section with *town* in its name, but during the gold rush years of the late 1800s, hundreds of Chinese had lived and worked around lower Main Street. The street was mud and muck in those days; now it was quaint brick, restored to a pretty period of history, not quite to its ugly roots. I walked down Main Street, past the Masonic lodge and the Franklin Hotel with benches along its broad porch and Charlie Utter's place and Kevin Costner's joint and the open doors of T-shirt shops and casinos, pop music and *ka-ching, ka-ching*, the music of money falling into local pockets, at least some of it marked for preservation. The desire to rescue its crumbling buildings was what brought the gaming industry to Deadwood.

The weather had been unseasonably warm for September, and all day long the ozone had been building up as clouds stacked above the hills. Late afternoon, a broody, purplish sky hung over the historic and half-historic buildings, tourists snapping one another's pictures or milling around slot parlors. I reached the newer, rawer part of town dominated by the innocuous Hampton Inn and the Tin Lizzie casino on one side of the street and a series of shallow-graveled parking lots backed by eroded ravine walls on the other. I could see exposed tree roots and the occasional crumbling foundation in the walls. Signs strung on chains broke the parking lots into sections: FOUR ACES CASINO & HAMPTON INN PARKING; VALET PARKING; GUEST PARKING ONLY. A trashcan sat next to a large interpretive sign about Deadwood's Chinese population, not far from a blue Dumpster parked by an old retaining wall. This was all that was left of the city's Chinatown.

The day before, I had hiked up the steep hill to Mount Moriah Cemetery, where Wild Bill Hickok and Calamity Jane were famously buried. The altar where the Chinese laid their burial feast offerings had recently been rebuilt, using bricks salvaged from the last piece of Chinatown, the Wing Tsue Emporium of Fee Lee Wong. In the early decades of the twentieth century, he had been the most prominent Chinese merchant in Deadwood, the link between the white and Asian populations. Like a bright-white miniature temple, the altar rested on the side of the hill over the old and crooked tombs, just up the path from Bill and Jane, the wild and the calamitous, and the stark white cross over the Civil War tombstones worn almost smooth, and the Jewish section where piles of stones commemorated the ancestors. Brand new tombstones nearby memorialized the *Infant of Fee Lee Wong, born Deadwood, died January 30, 1895,* and the *Child of Fee Lee Wong, born Deadwood, died March 20, 1899.*

The story of the Chinese in Deadwood was a story of resourcefulness; chased off the potentially lucrative claims for gold, they became merchants, launderers, and restaurant owners in Deadwood and catered to the daily needs of the miners. Even when the claims yielded nothing, the miners needed food and clean clothes. Few of the Chinese had emigrated with their wives; after the Chinese Exclusion Act of 1882 banned further immigration, the mostly male population dwindled. Fee Lee Wong had had the good fortune to bring his wife, and though two of their children died, eight survived.

His descendants had met in 2004 and gathered on lower Main Street in front of the establishment that their great-grandfather and great-great-grandfather had built. A memorable photo was taken. Then, before they left town, the descendants of Fee Lee Wong visited the mayor and lobbied to save the building. Everyone wants to save the building, the mayor assured them. The owner had been specifically instructed to preserve the building when he got permission to demolish the unstable structures on either side. But somehow, on Christmas Eve 2005, the owner and his sons began the demolition, and when it was over, the Wing Tsue Emporium—the final architectural vestige of Deadwood's Chinatown—lay in rubble on the street.

Archaeologist Rose Estep Fosha's voice was tight with emotion, recounting the story of the demolition. "I couldn't talk about it for eighteen months without tears. It was a wonderful piece of the history of Deadwood." When she and her husband, archaeologist Michael Fosha, told me about the Deadwood dig, they struggled to keep their composure.

The story of the demolition wasn't the only sad thing I heard from them, or from other archaeologists, for that matter. The sites that get written about and become heritage destinations and tourist sites often incorporate a story of loss and destruction; think of the Parthenon, or Pompeii. But how many sites get destroyed altogether through carelessness or venal intent, whose treasures get plowed under or sold on eBay? Rose Fosha had been focused for years on the dwindling and threatened remnants of this particular part of Deadwood; she had supervised digs into the foundations of Chinatown, and after endless polite requests, had finally persuaded the owner of Wing Tsue to let her make a record of the interior of the building, if only for an hour. That was a request modest enough to entertain; the owner let her in, and for an hour she snapped and snapped and snapped pictures—just one floor, no more, one hour, no longer. "I have a presentation I give on it that is . . . I don't know that I could do it without tears, still," she said.

Mike Fosha listened intently to his wife in the back room of Botticelli Ristorante in Rapid City, an hour from the empty lot in Deadwood. His passion was tracking down mammoth sites, looking for places where humans had cut and flaked mammoth bone into tools. "Fresh mammoth bone works just like stone, only better," he said. Looking for evidence of human culture in North America that was older than 13,500 years ago—pre-Clovis, the archaeologists call it—he thought it was a good bet it would come from a mammoth butchering site in the West. "Pushing back human entry into the New World is fun because it is hotly disputed," he said. He found a site in Brookings, South Dakota, that would have passed the stringent requirements for an undisturbed site, and sent the broken mammoth bone samples from it to two labs for dating. "There's only one critter that can break up mammoth bone and that's a human." The labs dated the bone to roughly 14,500 years ago, a thousand years earlier than the oldest Clovis points. But before he and his volunteers could finish excavating and recording the layers, a county highway crew destroyed part of the site. It was a mix-up, or maybe it was a turf issue. There was no poetry in the story, and no sense either, for the likes of me. "All you can do is laugh about it," he said.

In spite of the disappointments, the Foshas could not imagine a different life. Rose, in her mid-fifties, now worked for FEMA, the Federal Emergency Management Agency; Mike, four years younger, worked for the state of South Dakota—"I work for the people," was how he described it. Even on vacation, they find sites to visit, if not excavate.

Late-afternoon light filtered through the windows of the restaurant. Rose and Mike shared a panini, their heads bowed toward each other, hers blond, his balding on top and combed neatly to below his ears. She had a flowered shawl draped over her shoulders; he wore a tidy vest and collared shirt. Rose said she had wanted to be an archaeologist since fourth grade. "I told my teacher I wanted to dig up—I didn't say dead people, but I wanted to dig up people who were here before the people we give names to." Her teacher said, sweetly, "Why, you want to be an archaeologist." Rose was thirty-four years old, the mother of two, before she was able to go to college; she commuted for years to the University of Kansas from her home in Kansas City. Mike was the assistant director of her first field school, where they met. He had a gift, she said, for looking at the landscape and figuring out what it was like eons ago. He knew instinctively where the first shovel should be placed at a site—it's a combination of training, sensitivity to the soil, and knowledge of geomorphology, how landscapes evolve through the ages. Mike called what he did "taking that road trip through time."

Rose's first husband, the father of her children, visited her near the end of that first field school, on a day when she found a decorated pottery rim. "It was larger than usual, and we had the neck and the rim," she said. The decoration was crucial, Mike pointed out, because "it showed who made it and when it was made." "I was just so thrilled," Rose said. "I still have chills talking about it!" She called out to her husband to come see her great discovery. "And he comes over and he says, 'Rosie, what are you doing out here in this heat, getting so excited about something broken? You must be crazy.' And I thought, 'One of us is.'" Divorce was perhaps inevitable, and eight years after the summer of the field school, she and Mike married.

So, how long had they been together now? "Fourteen years," Rose said without hesitation, and Mike shook his head. "I was afraid you'd ask. I deal in thousands," he said, laughing.

I envied their ability to see sites and artifacts in the landscape, and told them about the invisible effigy mound in Wisconsin. Mike and Rose laughed and said they knew plenty of people, including archaeologists, who couldn't spot features.

"It's so much better to walk with someone who knows what they're looking at," I said. "Somebody who can see the mound, or notice a glass bead on the ground." I was thinking of the blue glass beads of St. Eustatius.

"And ask where this glass bead came from," Michael said, picking up my image and looking at Rose.

She locked eyes with him and whispered: "Shipwreck."

I had already been bitten by the archaeolo
initial request for an interview. "I am glad
rine archaeology and its difficulties," sh
possible for you 'to observe the tea
not release our unpublished intel
the same person who had po
that existed for scholars
Marine Archaeology
tions, or data from
does so has viol
for infringen
bull, wit
her o
re

"I'M
final
room in a
Complex.
maritime

around at the neat piles of paper and maps, the yellow plastic kitty-litter bucket filled with tape measures and twine and waterproof clipboards. Empress of what exactly? And then she showed me where her treasures are buried: the harbor where America's biggest fleet of sunken Revolutionary War ships rest in their watery grave.

I settled into the passenger seat of her rumbling van. It suited the marine archaeologist: aging but functional, even jaunty, a seventeen-year-old Pontiac Trans Sport with more than 80,000 miles on the odometer and three lit-up warning lights on the dashboard. Abbass's beautiful square face was framed by flyaway white hair, most of it bundled into a topknot of curls; her eyes were ocean blue and sharp. The driver's seat was pitched back to accommodate a spine damaged by osteoporosis. Abbass warned me that Diva, her Pekingese, who was riding in the back, had recently been cured of fleas but might have them again; Abbass had been bitten by a flea last night. Was she trying to scare me off? It wouldn't work.

gist herself, after my
to talk to you about ma-
he responded, "but it is not
n from the shore,' and we will
ectual property to you." This was
sted a notice on Academia.edu, a site
to share their work: "The Rhode Island
roject and I will post no reports, publica-
our research on this website. Anyone else who
ated our non-disclosure policy and is at risk of suit
ient of our intellectual property rights." She was a pit-
a Pekingese sidekick. To ride shotgun, I had had to join
ganization ($25, a bargain) and supply her with a personal
erence from Grant Gilmore, and because her office was located on
a naval base, I also had to send my Social Security number and get
security clearance. But I was determined to see her in context. In
a profession of loosely affiliated tribes—of academics, government
archaeologists, and archaeologists-for-hire—Abbass had, like Gilmore, created an independent archaeology center. She had done this
with almost no money and in the shadow of gilded Newport Harbor, with the famed shipwreck explorer Robert Ballard ensconced
at the University of Rhode Island. Never mind the crowded pond;
she had made news herself and promoted archaeology along the way.

Abbass pressed hard on the pedal, moving us past the offices
of the Rhode Island Marine Archaeology Project (RIMAP) on the
grounds of the naval base, and out onto the lovely boulevards and
vistas of Newport. The empress had another warning: "I bought
this van used ten years ago," she said. "It's not worth fixing, so
when it dies, I'll leave it by the side of the road." Duly warned—in
addition to the other hazards, we might end up on foot. On an overcast fall day, out we chugged past the armed guards at the gate of
the naval station in the possibly flea-ridden, rattletrap van, heading

toward the mansions of Newport and the harbor waters that hold the historic fleet.

The treasure of Abbass's empire consists of thirteen ships, sunk deliberately by the British in 1778 to prevent the French from sailing to the aid of the Continental Navy and relieving Newport. Who knows what would have happened to the course of the war if the French navy had been able to stop the British there? All by itself, this sunken fleet was a historic prize; some of its ships had been used to run weapons and soldiers to fight the rebellious colonies; some held prisoners-of-war. Abbass claimed that one of those ships had a previous life as the *Endeavour*, also known as the *Endeavour Bark*, the first vessel to carry the British explorer James Cook around the world. If Cook meant anything to most Americans, he was just one more eighteenth-century adventurer, but to the rest of the world, he was the king of explorers. His voyage on the *Endeavour* put Australia and New Zealand on the map; the *Endeavour* was Australia's *Niña*, *Pinta*, and *Santa Maria*, and maybe its *Mayflower*, too. Cook's international reputation was why Abbass had more than the usual dose of archaeologists' paranoia. "You can't imagine the number of folks who contact us who only want to pirate our information about the search for Captain Cook's *Endeavour Bark*," she confided. Imagine, a naval archaeologist worried about pirates.

Abbass, now in her late sixties, has spent fifteen years circling Newport Harbor, doing what she could to safeguard these sunken ships while preparing for a clean excavation; but "we're nowhere near ready," she told me. "We have a number of years of work yet to do." So the ships continue to lie submerged in open water, at risk from natural disasters and looters. "There are people anchored out there right now," Abbass admitted, but she refused to be hurried. Among the things an archaeologist needs in order to perform an underwater excavation the right way, she said, is a place to study and conserve what you find. Everything that came up had to be conserved, an ongoing responsibility that seemed formidable enough if you were talking about changing the water in the jars that held the fragile artifacts and were small enough to fit on a shelf, but multiplied in difficulty when the object to be conserved was a submerged ship, much less a fleet. And whatever you touched, you were going to disturb—in fact, you were going to wreck the site for future archaeologists. So you better be damn sure you know what you're doing.

THE FUTURE OF archaeology lies underwater. The experts formed a chorus here. "If you want to have an impact as an archaeologist," one of my sources said, "learn to scuba-dive." Back in landlocked South Dakota, Mike Fosha had geeked out when our conversation turned to the oceans. "Water has risen three hundred feet since the glaciers melted," he said. "That landscape under there, that's going to tell the story of the earliest occupants. *That's* where the early sites are." Although Fosha hadn't specialized in underwater archaeology, he follows its developments avidly, from excavations of the earliest English settlement in Jamestown, now partially flooded, to the discovery off the coast of England of more than forty submarines from World War I, some with their crews still inside. What looks to the untrained eye like murk and slimy stones and lumps with fluttering seaweed were keys to the deep mystery of our past.

Kathy Abbass didn't start out focused on shipwrecks or flooded archaeological sites. "My particular career path was not traditional," she said, an understatement. She was an Air Force brat who grew up all over the world and landed at Southern Illinois University. While still in college, she married into "Arab royalty," the son of a former Iraqi ambassador to the United Nations who was teaching at the university after a coup. She majored in anthropology, figuring she would end up in the Middle East and find work at a museum in Beirut or Baghdad. One of her teachers, the influential archaeologist W. W. Taylor, told his class that there was no room for women in archaeology. "Today, of course, he'd be brought up on charges," Abbass said dryly. She learned early to persevere without encouragement.

Abbass didn't know port from starboard when she pursued a fellowship at Harvard; she wanted to figure out how early horses and cattle and pigs were transported to the Americas from Europe. She imitated the professor, a British marine archaeologist who wore a monocle: "'My dear, that's one of the most important topics that has ever been addressed.'" (The effort! The mechanics! The colonial mind-set!) Wondering how pigs and horses got to America led her, naturally, to ships, which she turned out to have an aptitude for. She left a tenured teaching job at an all-black university in Virginia, took scuba and sailing lessons, and went to work for a ship surveyor in Newport. "I ran away to sea," she said cheerfully. "I was the first woman in the country to do marine surveying. I'd go into yards where I was set to inspect something and they'd show me the stereo system. I'd say, 'Open the bilge. I want to see the engine.'" Her grounding in the working mechanics of ships is an advantage that she still wields.

Abbass and her husband divorced amicably (no children, and she kept her married name, which means *God*, and also *grim*, in Arabic). She ran the Museum of Yachting in Newport for a year, then found herself unemployed—too senior for entry-level jobs, not senior enough for the big-time positions, and "not this dewy-eyed little thing that's going to do what I was told." She had her own goals. She knew she wanted to work on water.

One day, Abbass joined an archaeologist from the Naval War College on a trip to Lake George, where sport divers had discovered a submerged warship from the French and Indian War, a type of boat called a *radeau*. The crew had permission from New York State to investigate as long as an archaeologist supervised their work. But when their archaeologist took off after a day, Abbass leapt into the breach, choreographing the excavation of the oldest warship project in North America.

Abbass was commuting regularly from Newport to Lake
George by slow bus to study the *radeau* when the state archaeologist of Rhode Island suggested she do that kind of work for her
own state. Rhode Island had tons of wrecks. The state archaeologist was responsible for the preservation of Rhode Island's heritage, but though much of that heritage was on or under the water,
he had no staff and no expertise in this field. According to Abbass, "They didn't even have an inventory of what was here in the
state. They didn't know what had been lost, what might be found,
except for the occasional bits and pieces." The Rhode Island Marine Archaeology Project was born in 1992, at Abbass's kitchen
table. "That's the first thing we did, the inventory," a database
that continued to grow. She trained volunteers to document the
marine history of the state and to help survey its underwater sites.
She and her colleagues offered museum workers, sailors, teenag-
ers, retired people—almost anyone—courses in history, diving,
excavating, and conservation. Many of her students went on to
graduate school in the field. RIMAP also provided field experience for the graduates of programs in maritime history and marine archaeology. Most, she had found, "don't know beans about
boats." She wanted to foster a public that understood and appreciated the significance of the historic ships in the sunken fleet,
and she also wanted to train a cadre of archaeologists who knew
firsthand what they were excavating.

In the beginning, Abbass supported herself and covered her lab
fees by working as a cleaning lady in some of the beautiful houses of
Newport, the houses that I watched out the window as we puttered
around in the old van. The "fairly wealthy women" whose homes
she scrubbed "knew I was building this nonprofit. You'd think
they'd give you a tip or a little donation. But no. I still run into
women who say, 'You were the best, I miss you. I can't get anyone
who cleans as good as you.'"

Hold on. This archaeologist was telling me she was a great cleaning lady? Exactly. Abbass said, "I think if you're good at something, you're usually good at other things as well."

Kathy Abbass would have quit underwater archaeology ten years ago and "taken a job selling insurance in Illinois or something"—except that she figured out what happened to Cook's *Endeavour*, and that, as she promised to elaborate for me later, was "the career maker."

Abbass maneuvered the van into a parking place in a historic neighborhood of Newport and I waited with Diva while she ducked into the print shop. "What's up?" I asked the dog, and Diva scratched herself with a hind leg. She had been twice rescued, once by Abbass's friend after the death of her owner, and again when Abbass's friend died. "It takes them about a year to realize their owner isn't coming back," Abbass told me. Diva looked unperturbed now; her future as a mascot to underwater archaeology was secure.

Abbass emerged with a man wheeling a dolly laden with boxes of brochures, which he loaded into the back of the van. "Now, this is for our series on Revolutionary War sites in the state," Abbass explained. "Our office generates a lot of gray literature. You know what gray literature is, right? Research, reports, even books that aren't commercially published." RIMAP's gray literature includes a five-volume history of Rhode Island during the Revolution that Abbass had written.

On the back of the flyer about Revolutionary War hospitals, RIMAP was described as a volunteer organization that trained members to do fieldwork and invited them to participate in historical research. "Want a thrill?" was the way she put it to me. "You can be the person who found it, handled it, archived it!" She had not been too shy to add on the back of the flyer: "RIMAP needs: An artifact conservation, storage, and display facility that is easily accessible to the public."

"I'll show you the old Revolutionary War hospital at Hammersmith Farm," Abbass said, and we embarked on a tour that reminded me of others I have taken with archaeologists, vivid with history (the colonial house where a Revolutionary War spy lived; Doris Duke's mansion), but also full of ghosts—archaeologists can't help pointing out where history had been demolished. Abbass's tour included the phantom eighteenth-century piers, torn up by urban renewal projects. "Marine archaeology also takes place on land," she pointed out.

The old Revolutionary War hospital at Hammersmith Farm is now occupied by farmers who breed obscure livestock strains for Tufts University and the Campbell's Soup heiress. In the groomed countryside, the farm had some mess and mud to it, with goats, possibly the rare breed called Tennessee Fainting Goats, milling around.

Touring Hammersmith gave me a glimpse of Abbass's social life. She told me about someone named "Yusha," who lived elsewhere on the Hammersmith property, Yusha being the nickname for Hugh Auchincloss III, a former diplomat whose step-siblings included Gore Vidal and Jackie Onassis. "You gauge your closeness by whether you can call them by their pet names," Abbass said, laughing. Did I know the reception for Jackie and JFK's wedding took place here? Abbass went to the occasional dinner party at the "cottages" of Newport—"Yes, I have makeup and nice clothes"— and pictures of her in a velvet vest holding a cocktail have appeared in the society pages. "I'm their trained monkey," she joked, adding that none of the Old Guard has money anymore; she meant relatively, compared to the assets of venture capitalists; they all had heaps more than she did.

"Cultural chameleon" is how one archaeologist I met had described herself, but the phrase fit them all, none more than Abbass. She was an expert in material culture, someone who could assess the worth and fitness of a yacht, who laughed at the McMansion among the great homes—"You can tell the difference, right?"—but who chose to live with few possessions herself and traveled in a failing van through patrician neighborhoods where she had been both cleaning lady and dinner guest.

The member of the Old Guard of Newport with the most invested in Abbass's archaeology institute is Commodore Henry H. Anderson, Jr., known as Harry, the former director of the New York Yacht Club and a patron of sailing and sailing education. In his nineties, never married, he was considered an eligible bachelor in Newport. He had introduced Abbass to potential donors and sometimes squired her around town, and it was his seed money that got her to London to figure out what happened to the *Endeavour*.

THE STORIES HAD persisted for years, that Cook's *Endeavour* had been retired after its famous voyage and rechristened *La Liberté*. While delivering whale oil to the colonies, it was said, she ran aground in Newport. Pieces of *La Liberté*'s timber, scavenged and identified as pieces of the *Endeavour*, were displayed in the Newport Historical Society and also in the Australian National Maritime Museum, where the *Endeavour*'s stern post is a major icon, "even though it's this old, worm-eaten crummy piece of wood."

But in 1998, while Abbass was trying to identify the fleet of British transports in the harbor, she got a letter from two Australian amateur historians who believed that the ship had been misidentified. Those alleged pieces of the *Endeavour* displayed in the museums, they thought, really came from another of Cook's ships. Along with the letter, the Australians had enclosed an article they'd written, ending with a sentence that had tantalized Abbass: "It said, 'Nobody knows what happened to the *Endeavour*, but she was carrying troops out of London under the name *Lord Sandwich* in the 1779 edition of Lloyds Register, and she drops out after that.'" As it happened, one of the ships in Abbass's Revolutionary War fleet was named the *Lord Sandwich*. "It didn't take a rocket scientist to say, 'Aha!'" she said. The *Lord Sandwich* was already an important historic vessel; if it had also been the *Endeavour*, there was a world-famous wreck submerged in Newport's waters.

A friend in Whitby, England, where Cook's ships had been built, gave Abbass a plane ticket to London, and a friendly historian who had dived with Abbass and knew about her research offered her a couch to sleep on, around the corner from the Public Record Office.* In the course of one scholar's dream week, Abbass turned Harry Anderson's five-hundred-dollar donation into photocopies that traced the history of a collier (a ship that hauls coal) named *Earl of Pembroke*, chosen and outfitted by James Cook and Joseph Banks for their history-making first voyage circumnavigating the globe, and renamed *HM Bark Endeavour*. This bark, or small sailing ship, became the first Western vessel to sight New Zealand and the eastern coast of Australia; once back in England, the ship was sold and rechristened the *Lord Sandwich*. Her next owner offered her services to aid the British in the war overseas, and after undergoing repairs, the *Lord Sandwich* transported Hessian mercenaries to Rhode Island, then hung around the Newport Harbor to serve as a prison ship for captured colonists. When the French fleet sailed in to aid the revolutionaries, the British ordered their own ships, including the *Lord Sandwich*, sunk, to block the French from the harbor and to keep the ships from falling into French hands.

"I found the documents that disproved one story and showed another. That's the career maker," Abbass said with satisfaction. Now came the suspenseful part: Is the *Lord Sandwich* ex-*Endeavour* still submerged beneath the silt of Newport Harbor? Is anything left of it? Will RIMAP be able to prove it? Will there be anything to display? If so, will a stream of international tourists come to Rhode Island? Abbass threw her plan to retire to Illinois overboard. She will never retire now.

---

*The Public Record Office in London is now known as the National Archives.

She loved the fact that Cook was a farmer's son from Yorkshire, England; like her, he came up through the *hawespipe* (in nautical slang, "from the deep nothing to the top of the heap"). He was "the nobody who explored and mapped and discovered more than anyone in the history of the world! He's a really big deal," she told me. "And he was killed and eaten in Hawaii, which makes him even more glamorous," she says.

"He was eaten?" I asked.

She answered in a stage whisper. "Shhh! We don't say that very loud, but that's probably what happened to him!*

"I keep saying to the Newport tourism people, 'Yeah, the mansions are here, all these wonderful eighteenth-century homes, but there are better, bigger mansions elsewhere in the country. What Newport has that nobody else in the world has is this boat stuff associated with James Cook. There's no place else in the world!'" Abbass just has to persuade Americans, and particularly Rhode Islanders, that this international figure should mean something to them, too. She is formidable in her passion, a scholar with a marketing plan. Perhaps she can track down Johnny Depp and persuade him to make a movie about Cook?

Our tour of Newport ended down by Fort Adams on the waterfront, where cones had blocked off a parking area on the promontory. "I'm with the archaeology crew," she said to the guards, and the cones were promptly moved with a wave for our van. We pulled right up to the harbor, splendid even on a gray day. Abbass pointed out Goat Island, once a place where pirates were hanged and buried; a Hyatt now stood on their remains. Imagine a rectangle from Goat Island to just above the Claiborne Pell Bridge and east toward the shore; that was the two-square-mile portion of the harbor where the Revolutionary War fleet was sunk.

---

* According to the Captain Cook Society website, Cook was not eaten by Hawaiians, only boiled to retrieve his bones.

In a sly political move, Abbass arranged for the symbolic "arrest" of those two square miles of the harbor, to claim its bounty on behalf of the state. "Salvage law is older [than preservation law]; it's stronger and more established," Abbass explained. The idea came from her colleague Kerry Lynch, who said, "Why are we bothering with preservation laws if salvers are the ones who have the goods?" Abbass ran with the idea, and RIMAP and the state's attorney general went to federal court and won the right to claim all nonmotorized wooden vessels within that two-square-mile area on behalf of the state of Rhode Island. Because of their audacity and political maneuvering, the state of Rhode Island now holds custody and title to the *Lord Sandwich* ex-*Endeavour* and a few other frigates as well, and federal marshals can arrest anyone trying to disturb the wrecks.

Abbass's crafty use of salvage law to make a claim on behalf of the state has been a model for other marine archaeologists. Her often-cited article, "A Marine Archaeologist Looks at Treasure Salvage," begins in rip-roaring style: "Not all lawyers are toadies to wreck-raiders hell-bent on ripping glittering treasure from glamorous shipwrecks. Not all archaeologists are effete intellectual snobs determined to keep important historical sites closed to the public."

The waters of Newport Harbor are brown, not blue like the Caribbean. A RIMAP diver recalled visibility so bad on one local dive that "we had to tie ourselves together." Advances in technology, particularly in side-scan sonar, can produce wonderful pictures of the bottom; but, still, Abbass said, "A lot of the local geography looks just like shipwrecks." What, I asked, could possibly be left from a wreck over two hundred years old? A pile of ballast stone that "stands proud" (appears upright), protecting planks and other ship debris under the silt. To the untrained eye, pictures of a ballast pile from a historic ship look like any other pile of rocks on the harbor floor; even to the trained eye, the piles can look ambiguous, and have to be investigated in the process archaeologists call "ground truthing." "We spend a lot of time ground truthing," Abbass said.

And underneath the silt, wouldn't the remains of wooden ships be rotted and useless by now? No, if undisturbed, the silt creates an environment free of oxygen, and the organic remains of wrecks won't start disintegrating until they're exposed to air.

"If you buy me lunch, when we go back I'll show you textiles and leather and other things that came off these ships that are still here," Abbass said. "There's a lot more out there." Until the 1960s, even archaeologists doubted that underwater excavations could yield information and artifacts worth the effort of collecting. Those doubts are gone, but conservation methods in use even a few years ago are already inadequate. This is another reason for Abbass to take her time excavating; the technology gets more sophisticated every year. Other archaeologists say the future is underwater; Kathy Abbass says the future is in materials science and conservation. Preserving what you find is the hardest part, and she's tired of "hero/explorers who think finding a famous shipwreck is the point. That's only five percent of it!"

So I bought her lunch. We settled in a booth at Bishop's 4th Street Diner, an aging silver zeppelin on the rotary outside the naval base, grungy and stuffed with Betty Boop tchotchkes in the windows. The waitress greeted Abbass familiarly and promptly took her order: a hamburger, rare, and fries.

Abbass had trained several replacements for RIMAP, but could any of them work as hard as she did and live as frugally, on less than $1,000 a month? (This income included her Social Security check from ten years of teaching.) "It's hard to ask people to do that who are young and want to raise a family. I keep telling my students, 'You think you're going to earn sixty thousand a year? Who told you that?' Even thirty thousand. It's not real. I had more disposable income when I was a graduate student!" Abbass is scathing about most graduate programs in archaeology and anthropology; she feels they "perpetrate frauds on a public that doesn't understand there is very little chance for graduates to get a job."

She pointed a french fry at me and drilled me with her sharp eyes.

"Now, it's taken me six hours to get you to the point where you understand why it's taking so long, but do you see? We did our first remote sensing, looking for the Revolutionary War fleet, in 1992 and 1993. That's twenty years!

"People say, 'Well, why haven't you found it, Dr. Abbass?' Do you understand what a big deal this is and how difficult this is? It's a multifarious, multi-site study. Technology is improving, which is a big help, but this is a big project, and all being done by volunteers with no money."

Dreamed up by someone with a vision, willing to scrub floors to realize it.

SIX MONTHS LATER, I returned to Newport for an all-day course in marine archaeology. To prepare, I had studied the three pounds of nautical instruction Abbass had sent home with me, the maritime vocabulary and sketches of schooners, the code of ethics, "A Fisherman's Guide to Explosive Ordnance" (there was still stray ordnance from World War II to be encountered in Newport Harbor), and "A Note about Scientific Integrity, Primary Evidence, and the Control and Protection of Data: The Non-Disclosure Policy." Geekery beyond geekery, but for a fifty-dollar tuition fee, I could spend the day with divers interested in archaeology, and listen to Abbass, who, as I already knew, was an effective teacher. She had sworn I wouldn't have to put my head underwater to get into underwater archaeology; there were maritime sites on land, and there was lots of conservation and classification work with artifacts aboveground.

The class was supposed to start at 9:30 a.m. in a conference room of the handsome Newport Library. I arrived on time, but Raul, a diver who studied at the New York Maritime College (located, romantically, under the Throgs Neck Bridge), and I were still chatting in the conference room at ten when a RIMAP volunteer finally showed up, rolling a dolly with two big file boxes and bearing bad news: a few hours earlier she had driven Kathy Abbass, screaming with pain, to the hospital. The doctors thought it was kidney stones. The volunteer, Debby Dwyer, had caught the other students outside. Now she gave Raul and me a pound or two each of handouts and announced, with effusive apologies, that the class would be rescheduled. Dwyer was heading back to the hospital; and, yes, she said, I could follow her.

We drove through the winding one-way streets of Newport and arrived at the emergency room just as Abbass was being wheeled back from a CT scan, her white hair gathered into a bundle of curls, and beaming when she caught sight of us. I wanted only to see that she would be all right, but Abbass was pleased to have company, and feeling much better since the painkillers had kicked in. "Pain meds! They work!" she said. For the next hour, Abbass held court while we waited for her test results, a sultana resting on her pillows. She had news of her ancient van, which finally sputtered and died. Now she commuted by bus from her home in Bristol to Newport, which wasn't a problem—it was that two miles from the bus stop to RIMAP's office on the naval base that were tough. Dwyer and other volunteers conspired to keep Abbass mobile, taking turns driving her to the grocery. "She's like my second mom," Dwyer said. (Eventually one of the volunteers sold Abbass a beat-up Mercury for one dollar.)

The ER nurse interrupted to ask Abbass to rate her pain level. "Much better, six or seven," she said agreeably, so the nurse prepared another injection and asked us to step outside. "No, no, they can stay," she told the nurse. Abbass had just begun telling us the improbable tale of the visit of the Earl of Sandwich and his wife to the RIMAP offices, and continued the story while she got sedated. It was slightly more complicated than the usual Abbass story, and decidedly more wacky.

The guy who supposedly invented sandwiches—that is, the

fourth Earl of Sandwich, in his capacity as Lord of the Admiralty of England, had sent James Cook around the world. Naturally, Abbass has been tracking his descendants since her discovery of the *Endeavour*'s ties to Newport. She began corresponding with the son of the present earl, the eleventh Earl of Sandwich. The son, who has no title, is the U.S. director of the Earl of Sandwich fast-food franchise. "Dine with the new royal couple, Avocado BLT and Pastrami Reuben," trumpets the banner on the company's website. "Join the Upper Crust."

When Abbass got word from the son of the eleventh earl that his titled parents were coming to the United States for the opening of the newest shop in the chain, she swung into motion. She wrote to the earl himself, "Give me a day." And so, on the last afternoon of their trip to the States, the Earl and Countess of Sandwich—John and Caroline Montagu, as they are otherwise known—found themselves at Newport Naval Base, visiting the offices of RIMAP. Abbass showed them copies of documents she'd dug up in the Public Record Office linking Captain Cook's *Endeavour* with the *Lord Sandwich* and the Revolutionary War. She also shared the few artifacts taken from the sunken ships, things "floating around that might have been seen or stolen," including the fragment of an old teapot. "They're interested in the search for the *Endeavour*," Abbass reported happily. She was already plotting an Earl of Sandwich restaurant in the as-yet-unbuilt RIMAP museum and conservation facility. "Shops and restaurants are the way museums make their money. We want the earl to be our British patron. I don't know whether this is going to work, but it's not going to be for lack of trying."

By the end of their visit, rain had drenched Newport, and the Montagus were hungry before their flight, but—"Where do I take an earl and countess to lunch? And in such weather?" Abbass wondered. She drove them through Burger King. "They split a hamburger," she confided. "They shared everything. They're very thin." And then, she added, "I hugged the Earl of Sandwich goodbye."

"But wait," I said, "you drove the earl through the Burger King?" and there we were in the ER, laughing about this clash of worlds, when the young doctor arrived. He was a diver, too, and wanted to hear all about her work as an underwater archaeologist, so he was invited to visit RIMAP to take a class. He then wrote Abbass some prescriptions and cautioned her to make a follow-up appointment (Abbass had no intention of following up), and released her. She insisted she felt well enough for lunch, though, so the three of us went to Bishop's 4th Street Diner, where she grandly treated us to sandwiches.

Later Abbass wrote me:

I haven't had health insurance for the 20 + years of RIMAP. There just isn't enough money, either to pay a policy for the organization or to pay me enough of a salary so I can pay for it myself.

The reality of being the working poor is pretty grim in the US, and being well-educated doesn't help if you pursue (like I do) a career that doesn't pay a living wage. Part of what we discuss in the Intro class is the reality of the profession, what it takes to become qualified, what the chances are for employment, and what other nonmonetary costs you have (like the embarrassment of being considered "indigent" in order to have "charity care" at the hospital). But it was my choice to continue with RIMAP rather than go and get a "real" job.

And in the end it has turned out that so many who chose what appeared to be a more economically viable path have since lost their retirements in the recent financial scandals, or have seen their wealth crumble with the downturn of the economy, or have been fired and replaced with lower-paid, younger folk. So who is in worse shape—

the one who mostly followed passion and knows how to live on a shoestring, or the one who continued in a drudge job for elusive economic security and is probably deep in debt, too?

Abbass emphasized that this was her choice. This was an adventure that she herself had orchestrated, from England to the South Seas and Australia and into Rhode Island waters. Difficulties be damned.

She credited her determination and growing enterprise to a surprising source, the League of Women Voters. As a young person in the sixties, she wanted to make a difference, but "those were the days when university students were rioting and burning things down." Joining the League, Abbass thought, was "a way to be politically active without being destructive." When her husband, a new American citizen, went to Vietnam "to do his duty," Abbass threw herself into running the local League in Norfolk, Virginia. She learned how to lobby politicians and use the law. "People laugh, but those old broads—like I am now!—they were the ones who taught me how to survive graduate school. Once the mayor has yelled at you at a city council meeting, whatever your professor says at grad school is nothing." They also taught her that "If you want to overturn the law, you have to get politically active. Archaeologists are few, and we tend not to be the hardball, bare-knuckled types that you have to be to change things." Her greater ambitions for RIMAP are fueled by the spirit of civic responsibility fostered by the League, and by her belief that, if a thing is worth fighting for, "Well, gird your loins and go to war for it."

I recalled an earlier visit to RIMAP, when Abbass and I sat on opposite sides of a desk, enjoying a companionable Diet Coke while she assembled stacks of gray literature for me. I made notes, and Diva dozed at our feet. I tried to imagine what I would do for fun if I poured my life into marine archaeology and lived in voluntary poverty with a rescue dog in a wealthy yachting community. I figured

I'd go for malicious pleasures. On a hunch, I asked Abbass if she read murder mysteries. She didn't hesitate a beat. "I'd marry Lord Peter Wimsey right this minute if he walked through this door." Then she gave me a mysterious Dorothy L. Sayers half-smile. Of course she loves a good mystery. She put herself right in the middle of one.

THE CLASSICS

EXPLORERS CLUBS

Classics of the ancient world and Hollywood

❧

T HE AUDIENCE at an archaeology lecture is ancient. I watched
them stream in, drawn to slides of artifacts and talk of ruins:
snowy-haired, with canes and sensible shoes. They listened with
hunger. It is a common by-product of aging, to find yourself reaching for the unreachable past, longing for the residue of bygone
civilizations. The man next to me in the New York University
auditorium—we were attending a conference called "Performing
Memory in the Ancient World," sponsored by the NYU Classics
Department—leaned forward to concentrate. He was in his sixties,
on the younger side in this room, a retired writer. He showed me
his marked-up schedule for this conference, with other lectures circled. He was tearing himself away to run uptown to the Center for
the Ancient Mediterranean at Columbia University to hear an Italian scholar talk about Pompeii. Would I save his seat? He figured
he'd be back at this conference at NYU by lunchtime, and so he
was, slipping into the same chair and opening his notebook.

"Did I miss any handouts?" he wanted to know. He pored over
the one I showed him, then sprang up to scavenge his own copy.
"It has a bibliography," he explained, happily. He was eager to hear
about one particular talk he'd missed, the one by Joan Breton Connelly, the classical archaeologist and recipient of a MacArthur "ge-

nius" award. I described it in detail and with a little too much relish and his shoulders slumped. The avid consumer of lectures on the ancient world had gambled and lost. You don't want to miss a Joan Connelly talk.

Connelly's book, *Portrait of a Priestess: Women and Ritual in Ancient Greece*, is both scholarly and engaging, a bold look at the role of women in ancient Greece from the late Bronze Age to the fifth century A.D. Although commonly characterized as invisible during this era, ancient Greek women, on the contrary, wielded considerable power in the realm of religion, which was woven into almost every aspect of life. The book got me excited about the classics. I sought out stories about Connelly's excavation at Yeronisos, off the coast of Cyprus, where she had, since 1990, been digging a temple built—by Cleopatra's court, Connelly suspected—in homage to Apollo. I couldn't find anything personal about Connelly herself. For someone in the public eye, in the age of social networks, she had cultivated an impressive privacy. Her Wikipedia entry did not even furnish her birthday. She dedicated *Portrait of a Priestess* to four female mentors. The acknowledgments contained not a hint about anyone "without whom this volume could not have been written." Instead, it evoked a vast network of scholars, cloistered archives, exotic locations, and, in the only personal touch, the "epic summer road trips to Brauron and Eretria with Lilly Kahil in her Citroën DS." These were wisps out of time, as insubstantial as the fragments of pottery and bits of carvings from which Connelly had teased out her history of Greek priestesses. It was foolish to read anything into them, but I imagined she lived in a cool, orderly sanctuary.

The head of the NYU Classics Department introduced her with a flourish: Connelly had studied at Bryn Mawr, Princeton, the Field Museum, and no fewer than four of the colleges at "a little university in the middle of England you might have heard of called Oxford." The MacArthur grant given to her in 1996 was mentioned, and other honors, too. Connelly took the stage smiling, petite and pretty enough to stand out, not just among the scruffy folks who wandered into a free program in New York City, with free coffee and bagels, but also among the undergraduates serving as maiden attendants for this classics program, in flowing hair and Grecian dresses that bared a shoulder. The other speakers—the Frenchman with the corona of hair who sounded like Inspector Clouseau, the bow-tied professor, the woman in the sweater-set—showed you the crowns of their heads as they read their scholarly papers. Connelly, too, read from a text, but with a performer's confidence.

The screensaver on her laptop projected the image of a pair of high heels and a shovel, poised to bite into a Mediterranean beach, drawing laughter from the audience. Unlike several other presentations that day, Connelly's worked without a hitch, opening with a photo of an empty auditorium—"On November 26, 2010," she began, "twenty-seven hundred people paid the equivalent of five hundred Canadian dollars to hear Tony Blair and Christopher Hitchens debate whether religion was a force for the good, in which Hitchens declared, 'I could not live without the Parthenon. I don't believe any civilized person could . . . but I don't care about the cult of Pallas Athena, it's gone, and as far as I know it's not to be missed.'" Not to be missed? Connelly begged to differ. She evoked the days of the cult of Athena and demonstrated persuasively how vital it was to the Parthenon and to Athens. Then she spun an argument for a reinterpretation of the narrative on the pediments of the Parthenon: it was not a parade to honor the city, as some had claimed, but to save it, by sacrificing one of the king's daughters. When Connelly waved the remote control, a beautiful slide of the Parthenon appeared, glowing at the top of a hill against a night sky lit with stars, particularly the constellation known as the Hyakinthides, which rose in the sky during much of the summer and was clearly visible above the Parthenon's eastern porch. Some said it represented the three daughters of Erechtheus, one of whom had been put to death, and whose sisters then leapt to their deaths in solidarity. Connelly recounted the story, using the figures in the Parthenon's frieze. Then she had us imagine a circle of Greek maidens dancing in worship as they remembered these sisters—and the ancient pile of stones that was projected over our heads shimmered with ghosts. Religion was not something to be brushed aside, Connelly insisted, and certainly not dismissed out of hand. Religion had power. Indeed, the Parthenon, beautiful as it was, was nothing but a dead ruin without it.

There was something masterful and timeless about her presentation. She might have been a scholar from any era—save for the technology and another odd piece of her public profile: she was one of the experts featured in the 2008 History Channel documentary *Indiana Jones and the Ultimate Quest*.* Our cool, sophisticated professor had put herself in the hands of the same team of producers and directors whose credits included *American Idol*, *Girls Next Door*, and *Ancient Aliens*.

"The extraordinary accomplishment of the Indiana Jones series is taking something that is the life of the mind and turning it into something action-packed and heroic," she had declared in that documentary. And later, between noisy clips from the movies in the franchise—Harrison Ford as Indy galloping at reckless speed through a desert excavation, pits of writhing snakes, painted natives preparing to deep-fry Kate Capshaw, not to mention the director of the Center for Ancient Astronaut Research—Dr. Connelly had intriguing things to say about the risks archaeologists face in the field, in particular about the excavation she directed on an island off of Cyprus: she talked with animation about having to get in fishing boats every morning and fight strong currents to get to the island. Then the fishing boat had to land amid big rocks. Then she had to climb a twenty-one-meter cliff, just to get to the site.

---

*Connelly also appeared as an expert in the History Channel's *Star Wars: The Legacy Revealed*, as well as in *Secrets of the Parthenon*, from Nova and PBS.

And once the boat capsized! This thrilling story was immediately drowned out in the History Channel documentary by Indiana Jones sputtering, "Nazis. I hate these guys."

Connelly's moments onscreen exhibited more range than Harrison Ford's. She could be campy, shuddering over snakes and noting that the venom of a snake native to Cyprus can kill its victim in twenty-five minutes (her team worked more than half an hour from the nearest hospital and did not keep an antidote on site). She could also be passionate. "The illicit antiquities trade [is] third only behind drugs and weapons, six or seven billion dollars a year. . . . Let's say a coin is found, they take a coin out [of the ground]. That coin could have dated an entire now-missing building. You've just destroyed a part of history by taking it out. You may think there's nothing there, but there's never nothing there."

Watching the documentary, I had to stop to replay that part. *You may think there's nothing there, but there's never nothing there.* That was a line that bore engraving in stone, the freeze-frame moment at the center of the rowdy romp.

Connelly had waved off Indiana Jones's questionable archaeological practices, his tendency to yank things out of context and run. "I believe that if he was working in 2008, Indiana Jones would be a great proponent of cultural heritage protection and he would be on the front lines, helping law enforcement stop the trade in illicit antiquities," she said, erring perhaps on the side of generosity. The Indiana Jones movies had been deliberately set in the thirties, precisely so that its archaeologist could be a swashbuckling snatcher of treasures. This meant he practiced (movie-style) archaeology before the real-life rules changed—before, for instance, the Convention on the Protection of the Archaeological Heritage of Europe, the Native American Graves Protection and Repatriation Act, UNESCO's Cultural Heritage Protection Act, and The Hague Convention of 1954 for the Protection of Cultural Property in the Event of Armed Conflict. Indiana Jones operated free from the current expectation that ancient artifacts and treasures should remain in the country where they were excavated and that those artifacts already taken, years before, should be returned.

If Indiana Jones were a contemporary archaeologist, he'd be on his knees, marking off test pits, brushing the soil, tweezing bits of bone and broken pots in baggies, then spending hours washing these fragments and analyzing them in a laboratory—not quite as cinematic as galloping through an excavation on horseback, grabbing the girl and the gold and streaking past the villains. Indy's job was acquisitions, not science; he was all about snagging the stuff. He collected golden, bejeweled objects for his university's museum, or big-ticket items like the Ark of the Covenant or the Holy Grail. He collected them by any means possible. "Professor of archaeology, expert on the occult, and, how does one say it? Obtainer of rare antiquities," as one character described him in *Raiders of the Lost Ark*.

These days, Indiana Jones would be considered a looter.

So what was Connelly doing in a documentary about Indiana Jones? Apparently, George Lucas, a friend of hers, was a distributor of it, and Connelly trusted that he would "do this well, as he does everything." And, more importantly, she knew he would also let her get her message out about the terrible toll that looting took on the world's cultural heritage. She promotes archaeology with a passion. But she's not alone in her regard for Indy and her appreciation of those movies. The character has been used as a foil in serious academic work, as one British archaeologist did in a paper titled, "Why Indiana Jones is smarter than the post-processualists" (*post-processualist* being an unpronounceable name for archaeologists who believe that, in spite of all the science, their work is subjective):

> In an admittedly rare classroom scene during that memo-
> rable biopic *Indiana Jones and the Last Crusade*, our hero is seen
> addressing a large class of adulating students. The theme:
> nothing less than "The Nature of Archaeology." After com-

menting that the discipline is 95% library work (an assertion which the rest of the film makes no attempt to support, if we except the scene where Indiana and his attractive assistant are engaged in skullduggery beneath a library floor), Professor Jones throws out a culminatory aphorism: "Archaeology is about Facts; if you want the Truth, go next-door to the Philosophy Department!"

Every archaeologist I interviewed worked Indiana Jones into the conversation, usually with affection, as if mentioning a daredevil older brother. Wherever they happened to stride, archaeologists absorbed his swagger. Grant Gilmore told me, "It's tongue-in-cheek, but if you scratch any archaeologist, deep down inside they want to be him, one way or another." Battered Indy-style hats bob across the archaeological landscape, among the bandannas and keffiyehs (Arab head wraps) and baseball caps. Archaeology department costume parties double as Indiana Jones conventions. "For whatever reason," one female grad student confided, "the guys all own fedoras and whips."

Archaeologists get a kick out of the envy they excite. Do orthopedists get a poster boy? Do book editors? Who is out there making the dental hygienists cool? Archaeologists are so grateful for Indiana Jones that the AIA not only appointed Harrison Ford to its board of directors, but also awarded him its first Bandelier Award for Public Service to Archaeology. Ford's service, of course, consisted of being a perennial advertisement for archaeology; he was the profession's superhero recruiter. Before presenting the award, the executive director of the AIA acknowledged the field's debt to his character: "I can't tell you how many archaeologists have come up to me and said, 'I never would have become an archaeologist had I not seen these films.'" The year was 2008, just before the release of the fourth film in the series, *Indiana Jones and the Kingdom of the Crystal Skull.* Coupled with a timely cover story in the AIA's *Archaeology* magazine on crystal skulls (a fraud perpetrated in the nineteenth century, as the article made clear), the Indy tribute offered both an endorsement of the franchise and a meaningful thank-you. A sheepish Harrison Ford accepted his award via video feed. "He's a good guy," one source told me. "He auctioned his whip for archaeology!"

As in most things, archaeologists take the pragmatic approach. Where would complaining about this character get them, anyway? Of course they embraced this promotional gift from Hollywood, even though it was pure fantasy. They weren't deluded. They understood that crouching in a fetid hole and teasing out bits of ancient garbage had nowhere near the enchantment of snatching glittering artifacts and dodging the Nazis, any more than clouds of mosquitoes evoked pits of giant, writhing snakes, or impoverished indigenous people resembled bloodthirsty cannibals. But, aside from the cinematic exaggeration, as Joan Connelly knew, archaeologists happened to be engaged in the same business as Indiana Jones in all his B-movie adventures: the heroic search for a glimmer of the past; the continual test of one's fortitude, endurance, and ingenuity; and the exotic, gutsy, authentic alternative to the tamed and packaged life.

JOAN BRETON CONNELLY (call her "Indiana Joan" at your peril) led me on a private expedition to the Explorers Club one hot summer afternoon. The Manhattan headquarters of the international club is an extravagant piece of real estate, a monument to the adventurer's life tucked improbably on a manicured street on the Upper East Side. Generations of mountain climbers, divers, astronauts, explorers, and, yes, archaeologists have dropped their gear at the front desk and clomped through its nineteenth-century rooms ahead of us. The club didn't admit women until 1981. Connelly, who is comfortable walking into male enclaves—she was a member of the third class at Princeton to admit women—joined the Explorers Club in 1990.

"This members' lounge used to be a great old, dusty, authentic place," Connelly said in the barroom, pulling down wineglasses and pouring us diet iced tea from her cooler bag, "and then they decided to refurbish it. Now it's the Explorers Club bar as designed by Ralph Lauren." It looked authentic to me—the narwhal horn perched over the lintel of the bar, the tusks framing the fireplace in the next room—but then, I've never seen a narwhal in the wild. We finished our refreshments, then left the bar to climb the creaky wooden steps. Archives, map rooms, and trophy rooms snaked randomly off the central staircase, with photographs of adventurers like Thor Heyerdahl and Buzz Aldrin and Ernest Shackleton and Roy Chapman Andrews and Reinhold Messner and Jim Fowler of the old Marlin Perkins wilderness show and Sylvia Earle, the great underwater explorer, all gazing down at us. Connelly pointed out Richard Wiese, host of the ABC adventure show *Born to Explore*. He had explored the world, skied to the North Pole, collared jaguars, and lived with pygmies. He had also dug on Yeronisos and declared that Connelly was "the best expedition leader I have ever explored with."

We tore ourselves away from the walls of fame and climbed farther. Connelly led me into one room—"The single explorers used to meet here on Sunday mornings back in the nineties, and we'd make pancake breakfast together and hang out. Those guys! So much fun!"—and then into an elegant ballroom, and out onto a spacious terrace. "I used to hold the fundraiser for my dig in Yeronisos here every year," she said, "but then they started charging thousands of dollars to use the space. It's the problem with clubs like this. The people that it's for can't really afford it. And then ideas and customs change, and it's not really politically correct to have stuffed animal heads on the walls. . . . " The explorers had held fast to their trophy room and its contents through changing times. They kept it "as a shrine to our founders, and to Teddy Roosevelt in particular," Connelly explained, but she approached it with trepidation, worried that some of its treasures might have disappeared or been changed while she was out of the country. Were the jaguar, the lion, and the whale phallus still here?

Stuffed animal heads covered the walls of the trophy room and filled the deep window ledges. Lions, bobcats, gazelles—props for an old-fashioned movie about explorers. She pointed—"That is what we call the 'canoodling sofa,'" she joked. But where was that whale phallus? We explored the whole room, and just when it looked like the strangest trophy of all had gone the way of the dodo, Connelly found it, tucked into a window well, mounted on wood, petrified, a termite's nest rising to a bony point, about four feet high. It was a magnificent specimen, the sort of thing you really want to see in a natural history museum but almost never do. Connelly stood beside it while I snapped her photo with my cell phone; then she photographed me, beaming by the towering whale member—souvenirs of our hunt.

Downstairs, by the fireplace framed with tusks, Connelly pulled out her laptop and files and the lesson she planned to give me in stratigraphy to help me visualize the way soil and rock get layered through time; she also pulled out a plastic ginger-ale bottle, sturdy and lightweight, which she'd filled with a fizzy, summery white wine. She had taken the subway uptown to the club, and worried that a wine bottle might break in the crush. Now she poured it into wineglasses from the Ralph Lauren bar. My expedition leader had thought of everything.

Convent-educated in Toledo, Ohio, Connelly grew up spending Saturdays with her beloved Irish-American father. He'd take her to the art museum in the morning for drawing lessons (there were riding lessons, too); then they'd visit his construction sites. He taught her how to use surveying tools, lay a foundation, talk to workmen, keep a project on task. Her dual education meant she felt comfortable anywhere, in museums or lumberyards. She spoke a basic workman's Greek, picked up while working on excavations at Nemea. She is not married and has no children, and that surprises her; her mentor, Dorothy Burr Thompson, had both a great career and a family. Thompson was seventy-four when they met, "and how long do you think you have with someone when you meet them at that age? But she lived till she was a hundred and one. I had her wisdom and experience for twenty-seven years," Connelly said wistfully. Someday she hoped to write about Thompson, after she finished her next book, about the Parthenon.

We were deep in conversation when the receptionist warned us that the club was closing in ten minutes. "In the old days," Connelly confided, "some of the members used to slip the guy at the door a fifty- or hundred-dollar bill to keep it open. And he would!" Ah! A glimpse of the swashbuckling life! She had seen Thor Heyerdahl and Sir Edmund Hillary preside over these rooms. In the 1980s, she told me, she had traveled alone through Egypt, Syria, Jordan, Turkey, and Kuwait, staying in old legendary hotels "before they were refurbished," communing with "the glamorous past." As an archaeologist, Connelly did not simply appreciate that past; in a room with tusks framing the fireplace, she conjured it with flair.

FIELD SCHOOL REDUX

The earth-whisperers

T HE COOL, orderly sanctuary I had imagined for Joan Connelly when I first heard her speak was a product of my imagination. She lives in NYU faculty housing, and her apartment is hers only until retirement. "Then they'll ask me to leave," Connelly said. "I know I ought to buy a place somewhere, but I haven't." She also has an office on campus, with a huge window overlooking the Washington Square Arch, as well as a combination conference and storage room, a veritable fiefdom in New York City. Then there is her claim to the Explorers Club. But the real estate with the grip on her heart is in Cyprus; in particular, on the tiny island of Yeronisos, off the west coast of Cyprus. Its cliffs hold aloft a table of cracked Mediterranean earth the length of three football fields. Over the course of twenty-three years, Connelly has dug trench after trench there, assisted by teams of NYU students. Gradually, she has pieced together a compelling story of this spot that suggests that Yeronisos was once developed to honor Caesarion, Cleopatra's child by Julius Caesar—the heir Cleopatra hoped would unite the empires of Egypt and Rome, the East and the West.

In her conference room at NYU, Connelly has assembled a shrine to Yeronisos that includes a wall of twenty-three artful photos, one from each year of the ongoing dig, featuring members of her

various expedition teams posed around a piano perched incongru-
ously on a bluff, the photogenic island of Yeronisos shimmering in
the background: attractive students in dressy clothes, sometimes
with a famous archaeologist or even a *famous* famous person—a
sunburnt, grinning Bill Murray, for instance—or someone wealthy
who thought archaeology sounded fun and was willing to donate
$10,000 to the program for a week in the field.

I joined the dig team for a more modest donation, and set about
trying to cram what should have been months of physical condi-
tioning into a couple of weeks. Connelly was adamant about visitors
to Yeronisos being able to swim. She envisioned someone sinking in
the waters off the island and taking her beloved program with it. I
remembered her mentioning the cliffs her team had to climb that
were twenty-one meters high (nearly seventy feet!); how would I
hoist myself up something like that? Along with swimming lessons,
I signed up for a climbing class. The second time I fell off the practice wall, the instructor offered me my money back. The swim lesson went better; I made it across the pool.

The day before I left for Cyprus, Connelly e-mailed: she was determined to decorate the hills and patio for her annual dig party
with sand candles but had been unable to find paper lunch bags on
the island. Could I bring as many as possible? I managed to stuff a
hundred bags into my carry-on, and during my layover in London,
I even hauled them through the British Museum. Before they held
flickering candles on the hills of Cyprus, those brown paper bags
basked in the presence of the Elgin Marbles.

YERONISOS GLEAMED OFF the coast of the little town of Agios
Georgios. It looked as if it were only a few hundred yards from
shore, easy swimming, if swimming came easily. This turned out
to be deceptive. Each daybreak, we met at the town harbor and
climbed into the *Nemesis*, a boat run by Valentinos, a handsome
local fisherman. We huddled on the deck floor, smashed up against

each other in our bright life preservers: Joan Connelly and her two archaeology partners, Richard Anderson and Paul Croft; one grad student, ten undergrads, one local hired hand (Yanni); and one interloper (me)—a flock of strange orange birds herded into the Mediterranean. The waves might be gentle, so only those with delicate stomachs felt queasy, or the waves might be brutal—but I tried not to think about that ahead of time.

My first day, the waves were not gentle. It took half an hour to cross that seemingly short distance and loop around to the island's south side, and I could feel myself turning green. Connelly's graduate assistant, Talia, coached me, "Keep your eye on a fixed spot, and breathe in and out with the swells." Then we waited patiently, the fishing boat bobbing in the water, to disembark in shifts into a small dinghy, which Valentinos pulled, via rope, to the landing. The whole operation consumed another hour and was fraught. Valentinos steadied the dinghy and delivered orders, a cigarette tucked in the corner of his mouth, and the chain of Croft, Anderson, and Yanni steadied us as we staggered out of the wobbly dinghy across tires and planks—a jerry-rigged dock—to a cluster of boulders—the shore.

After we were safely on land, the more experienced crew formed another chain, and Valentinos passed up the backpacks, the equipment, the bags with breakfast, and the jugs of water (there was no fresh water source on the island). We threw our life jackets in a pile at the foot of a sheared cliff and began to climb, single file, up crumbling and ancient steps—steps!—to the top of the island, an elevated plain of rock and ruin, circled by gulls and surrounded by the sea. We emerged at the top of the cliff near two huts with stone foundations and wooden frames, their walls open to the view. These *khalifis*, set up above pilgrims' huts from the sixth century, made our base camp shady and picturesque. We arranged ourselves on the stone benches in the larger *khalifi* and got our trench orders, our digging assignments, while the seagulls wheeled overhead, shrieking. Across the channel, Agios Georgios's little Byzantine gem of a church twinkled in the early morning sun.

For the first two years of this island project, 1990 and 1991, Connelly directed an ecological assessment of the island that tracked its flora and fauna and prescribed ways to minimize the destructive impact of the excavation. "Our ecologist suggested only earth tones [for equipment] up here, so we wouldn't disturb the birds," Connelly said. "Our buckets, you notice, are earth- and sea-colored, not red and orange." She recalled going to Machu Picchu and looking out over the breathtaking specter of mountains and ruins. "And then it started to rain, and out came these plastic ponchos in millions of colors—yuk!" The ecologist made numerous other bird-friendly recommendations that Connelly incorporated into her vision of the place. "We have an early and short season so we don't interfere with their nesting. And the *khalifis* are not covered in ugly corrugated metal, but thatched with sticks and brush."

For Connelly, who was part of the Art History Department before she joined the Classics faculty, directing an excavation also meant art-directing it. Her field books are hand-bound "by a little old man in Limassol," and filled in by hand, complete with illustrations of found artifacts. "Some digs give everyone an iPad, but we have no power source on the island. We use trench books that go back and forth in waterproof bags. Narrative on left, trench number, date, supervisors' initials, weather, initials of everyone working on it, space for photos, trench drawings, objects written in red"—the classical approach to a classical dig.* Even the clothes Connelly worked in were earth-colored, for stepping lightly on the earth: beige linen shirt, snug green cords, canvas boots. (None of us wore red or orange, in deference to the birds.) There was an aesthetic element to everything. One day, Yanni reinforced a concrete wall near the staircase by slapping on more concrete. It was func-

---

*The dig team's computers and databases are kept on shore in Agios Georgios.

tional, but that wasn't good enough for Connelly; the next day, he recemented the wall, artfully.

YERONISOS, MEANING "HOLY island," was first occupied 5,800 years ago, then abandoned. What interested Connelly this particular season was its brief occupation in Hellenistic times, when for several intense decades during the first century B.C., vast wealth poured into the island. An elaborate cistern was built to collect water, and numerous buildings were erected on huge ashlar blocks of native limestone. A circular floor was built in the open air and filled with tons of marine silt laboriously brought up from the seabed—a dance floor dedicated to Apollo, they conjectured. Connelly and her crew had found quantities of small amulets, and many small cups, miniature bowls, strainers, and writing tablets. Slowly, they began to speculate that Yeronisos was the site of an ancient boys' school, equipped, it seemed, by someone with vast wealth, ambition, and is a gift for symbolic spectacle.

"Good archaeology fills in the blanks of history. It tells the losers' story. It teases out the history that falls between cracks," Connelly said. She thought this site told a story of Cleopatra VII and her son Ptolemy XV, called Caesarion, two of the great losers of history. The island was visible off the coast to travelers sailing between Alexandria and Rhodes, a convenient stop on the trade route from Egypt to Constantinople, and very near Paphos, the traditional birthplace of Venus, whom Caesar claimed as his ancestor. It was an ideal place to build a temple to Apollo and make a claim for the child of a Roman emperor and an Egyptian queen. Connelly and her team had found bronze coins minted during the joint reign of Cleopatra and Caesarion. They'd also found Egyptian artifacts; in addition, the buildings on Yeronisos were constructed to Egyptian measure. The dates fit. "And who besides Cleopatra had those kind of resources?" she asked rhetorically.

In 30 B.C., after the battle of Actium—"the turning point for the rest of history," Connelly declared—and the death of Cleopatra and Marc Antony, the money stopped flowing to Yeronisos. An earthquake in 15 B.C. left the island something of a ruin. Then, in the fourth century, a series of massive earthquakes took down the sides of the cliffs. Later, a major Christian complex was built on the island, then it once again fell into ruin. In 1980, it was targeted to be the site of a casino, but an archaeological officer in the Department of Antiquities and later Cyprus's director of antiquities, Sophocles Hadjisavvas, turned over enough ground to see that something ancient had once stood there; he and Cyprus put a stop to that development. Connelly, who had dug in nearby Paphos with Hadjisavvas, learned about Yeronisos from him. There she found the piece of real estate on which to make her archaeological stand. Each year she has to demonstrate tangible progress to the Cyprus Department of Antiquities to renew the license to work there.

Connelly would do almost anything for Yeronisos. During a week in which she and her crew excavated on six of the seven days, she also delivered four separate lectures to outside groups (among them the European Union, on the subject of ecological partnerships with local communities); threw her annual party to thank a hundred or so locals; and hosted numerous guests, including Richard Wiese and his camera crew from *Born to Explore*, four visiting high school students, including her nephew, and me. She did all this short-handed, after two graduate assistants had been called home on family emergencies. Connelly had just celebrated her fifty-eighth birthday, and though she wore her years lightly and had the build of an athlete, I wouldn't have believed her stamina if I hadn't been a witness. Every day, the woman hurled herself off a metaphorical cliff and swam through choppy water with tools in her teeth, then donned a fancy outfit and charmed her way around both humble and influential circles. She got little sleep. Sleep? She ran on adrenaline.

The first day, I knelt by my assigned trench as Connelly leaned in to demonstrate the art and skill of excavating, close enough to reveal a thin layer of foundation on her face, a nod to the network cameras. "Make a two-centimeter pass, then go back to the beginning," she directed. "The rule is, you always remove the most recently deposited layer and think about it. If you see something blue-green, it could be bronze—that's what it looks like when it ages. Iridescence? That could be glass. We have found lots of ancient glass here." She peered up to make sure I had been following her. "You're in deep trouble if I start seeing fresh breaks. The edges of the pottery you find should be dirty." She was interrupted by an undergraduate who thought he had found a coin, but it was clear to Connelly that it was a fractured piece of bedrock. "It is the right size, but not the right weight," she explained to the student. "When in doubt, ask," she said and sent him back to his trench.

"We backfill much of this each year," she told me, which is to say, they carefully refilled the trenches they dug with the excavated dirt, to protect the walls and other features they uncover. "I'd replace this dirt at the end of the season, and I'd think, 'I know you, hairy blue earth! I know you, purple-y earth!'" I could only imagine what hairy blue earth looked like, but Connelly spoke the poetry of excavation. "An archaeologist has to be like an earth-whisperer," she said.

I started my study of the baked earth side by side with her students, using hand picks to loosen the topsoil; then we took our trowels and, with a chopping motion, broke up the dirt, our eyes sharp for anything—a bit of pottery, a glint of glass, a land snail (we were also collecting land snails for a scientist). There were plastic bags at the top of each trench to organize the finds. I was slower than all my trench mates, who were digging in sleeveless shirts and seemed to thrive in the scorching Mediterranean sun, while my face turned red and my hair bushy. Later in the afternoon, Connelly went through my little pile. "This is pottery, a part of a roofing tile," she told me. "This is a Chalcolithic shard. My students call it a Chalcolithic biscuit. Good!" The rest—mere rocks.

Each afternoon, we repeated the complicated boat drill in reverse and then the action shifted to the apotheke, the picturesque headquarters on the bluff opposite Yeronisos—essentially a huge storeroom and offices with a plaza, thatched and covered by grapevines. There artifacts were washed and logged, a late, hearty lunch was served, and Connelly lectured on pottery, or a visitor shared some research from his thesis. Then the students went for a quick swim in the Mediterranean or a run in the late-afternoon heat, though, as Connelly fretted, "It takes three days to recover from dehydration!"

At eight at night, we gathered on the patio of a restaurant half a mile from the apotheke to eat french fries and Cypriot dishes with pork pieces, or plain pasta with tomato sauce (that one went quickly), or the lovely vanishing lettuce salads. Complaints about the food made Connelly bristle; this was what the Cypriots ate, and when in Cyprus . . . She had eaten this food herself for more than twenty years, but her doctor had recently put her on a low-carbohydrate diet. So she got a simple plate of grilled chicken and fresh steamed vegetables—and looked weary when anyone pointed at her plate and said, "Can I have that instead?" She wanted to talk about the excavation, about Cyprus, about the European Union, about what to do for her colleague Paul's birthday the next day, about our *souls*. Anything but fuss over the daily menu, hers or ours.

One night I wrapped a piece of bread in a napkin and slipped it in my purse. Nothing was open in town when we took off each morning, there were no stores, and I had run out of protein bars. "Are you sneaking bread?" Connelly asked. Caught red-handed! I laughed and told her, "No, I am forgoing the pleasure of eating this bread until later," and the moment passed. (Indeed, though I had expected to be on my own for most evening meals, Connelly had invited me to dine with the group every night.) I did regret my bad manners, taking that bread. Writers are hungry. Archaeologists are hungrier. Underlying their hunger is the tough economics of practicing the slow work of archaeology in a world that demands speedy returns. I learned this lesson regularly, about how close to the bone archaeologists live, and how much it cost them simply to do their jobs. For instance, Coca-Cola Hellenic Bottling Company donated soda and bottled water to the Yeronisos dig, and one night the team forgot to bring that evening's allotment to the restaurant. Connelly sent someone back to fetch it. She had negotiated a price for their dinners that didn't include beverages, and "two euros here, five euros there—our budget is simply too tight to squander that money when we already have the drinks." But then she decanted it all into picturesque pitchers—thrift, served with grace notes.

Connelly's solution for the celebration of her colleague Paul Croft's birthday was ingenious: she ordered a bundt cake from the restaurant, and instructed the cook to stuff it with Nutella. The neatly baked cake, collected before dawn, transported in a snug plastic container and passed hand to hand via two boats, over the rocks, and up the crumbling stairs, was festooned with little cocktail flags instead of candles and cut with gleeful ceremony after breakfast.

Croft, the burly expat archaeologist from Cambridge University, "who does all things well" in Connelly's view, wore a keffiyeh and a Las Vegas T-shirt. I asked him how he liked Vegas, and he looked surprised. I pointed at the shirt and he pulled it away from his chest. "You mean this? It's whatever was in the bin at the used clothing shop." Of course, I realized; this man who lives on nothing in Cyprus doesn't goof off in Las Vegas. He was someone who uncovered a wall, and said, "Now we have the responsibility to conserve it," then he mixed up some mud and straw and plastered the wall with care. He repaired the ancient stairs and improvised a landing. All of them, they make do, and, like most archaeologists of good faith these days, they leave part of each excavation untouched for the people who will follow them, with greater knowledge, superior tools, and maybe more funds.

What made this classic archaeology dig different from, say, a dig on a sugar plantation in the Caribbean? For one thing, Connelly stood over our trench chatting about Apollo, Cleopatra, and Homer, as though they were old friends. On the boat leaving the island, Valentinos led the students in a goofy Greek chant that sounded like *Emena me lene pagoto!* ("My name is ice cream"). Talia, Connelly's graduate assistant, told those of us huddled in the stern the story of Menelaus dragging Helen by the hair. We were mesmerized. "Have you written about this?" someone asked, and Talia admitted that she had written a thesis on that very topic, titled "From Beauty to Booty." Hilarity in the boat. Paige, a theater major, said, "I can show you how to drag someone by the hair onstage," and when we disembarked and shed our life preservers, she pulled one young woman aside and demonstrated. "See? I hold my hair in a bunch at the top and you grab my collar. I wheel away, screaming, 'No, no!'"

I was right on top of them, and I swore it looked real.

THE APOTHEKE WAS bustling the Saturday afternoon of the party, with ten toned and tawny NYU students toiling to hang outdoor lights and trim shrubbery and, with candles and sand, turn all those paper lunch bags I'd brought into lanterns. The students had each paid handsomely for the five-week dig* and like students in any field school, were expected to sweat and suffer, haul buckets of dirt, and scrub pieces of broken pottery with old toothbrushes. But these students had also been called upon to stage an elaborate party for the local Cypriot community and perform for the attendees. After their yard work, trimming the bushes and hanging the lights, they set up the lanterns—"Not that high up the hill!" Connelly called—then practiced a native folk dance and a local song

---

* As with most field schools that students can take for college credit, most of the cost goes toward tuition, in this case, about $5,000 for NYU credits and about $2,000 for room and board.

in Greek. Squeezing in another day of excavation on Yeronisos cut into party preparation time, but our leader couldn't resist the combination of placid seas and sunny days to seize the opportunity, and now things felt a little frantic. This was a planned invasion—Connelly and her team were eager to connect with the locals and celebrate Cyprus's past and present—but nevertheless, a hundred people were dropping by soon and we weren't ready.

I looked around at the unswept terrace and grabbed a broom. Nothing made me happier than to pitch in as part of Connelly's team, and sweeping was something I knew how to do.

"Now we'll set up the photo," she directed, and we all trooped to the bluff where the piano had been rolled out. It was a stage set out of a colonial past, an effort to re-create the glamour of the great era of exploration, though this project and the party to celebrate it were the opposite of colonial. Connelly stood at her tripod with the expedition camera and composed the shot: one of the two handsome young male students was designated the "wounded warrior" and stretched out, head propped on his arm, in the foreground. Talia sat in the slingback chair. Connelly's two colleagues, Paul Croft and Richard Anderson, stood attentively beside the piano, and Connelly's nephew and a local twelve-year-old, Andreas, a performer who taught the students their dance moves, crouched at the foot of the bench where Connelly would sit. I stood beside two of my trench mates, Yeronisos over my left shoulder. We would return to these spots in our party clothes for the official shot.

Everyone scattered to the two rental houses that served as dorms to dress up and hurry back to finish the photo session. Connelly was teaching us how to race from dirty dig and sweaty cleanup to sparkling party in twenty minutes flat. "The extremes! I love the extremes," she exulted as we swapped boots for heels. "What I hate is the boring middle!"

Richard Anderson, an architect by training with a permanent sunburn who could talk knowledgeably about any subject, especially Byzantine churches, walls, and ruins, had changed into a jaunty plaid jacket and looked as if he had been born to host the steady stream of guests: the wealthy residents of Cyprus, the American ambassador and his family, Baroness Betty Boothroyd (the first and only female speaker of the British House of Commons), Valentinos the fisherman, a masseuse, an elderly local woman who read the future in coffee grounds, the tanned ABC film crew with fashionable stubbled cheeks, and a coterie of monks. Connelly, in pale peach silk and vertiginous heels, swirled around the patio in generous welcome. Everything looked stunning in the soft night air, the lobster lights twinkling above the arbor, the gorgeous ruin of Yeronisos in the background.

I chatted with the bearded and black-robed monks, who showed me how to eat the grilled *haloumi* cheese with my fingers. Connelly swung by and said, "You monks are the greatest!" The students' transformation from grubby diggers to groomed and gracious American hosts was impressive, and they smiled and laughed throughout their spirited folk dance. Connelly, dancing later with one of the guests, twirled expertly on those tippy heels and lifted her arms to snap her fingers. I remembered her telling me about falling one icy night on the Upper East Side of New York while wearing little Italian boots, shattering her ankle. She did physical therapy diligently for a year. "I did not want to be a limping old lady on Yeronisos!"

I left, changed into sneakers behind the apotheke and walked back to my apartment on the midnight-dark road with the aid of a tiny flashlight. The party, I heard, went on for hours. Most of us took Sunday off to recover, but Connelly and her nephew spent the day on a boat with Boothroyd and some prominent Cypriots, cruising the sea. Just thinking about that made me ill. I went swimming in the Mediterranean with Talia, who had to save me only once.

MY TRENCH MATES were clever students, good sports, and good company through the long hot hours. They liked to play a guessing game, where one thought of the name of a person they all knew, and the rest peppered her with questions: If X were a kind of makeup, what kind would X be? If X were a type of chair, style of music, archaeological tool, etc. Their wordplay amused me. If one dubious subject were cheese, they were told, he'd be "fake cheese"; if coffee, "instant coffee." They guessed immediately who it was. They were stumped by another, though. "Okay, if he were a George Marshall Peters accomplishment, what would he be?" one asked. They all laughed. I thought they were referring to an explorer, but no, it seemed George Marshall Peters was a former student on the dig whose accomplishments were legendary. He did everything, from finding significant artifacts to illustrating them with talent. He had even decorated the dig house.

Not an hour later, when we took our break for breakfast, Connelly, as if she had heard the guessing game, mentioned George Marshall Peters, and the students swallowed their giggles. But what she said quickly sobered them. The little foghorn that Peters had donated years ago to the dig, the one used every day to summon us from the far corners of Yeronisos for breaks or the end of the day or emergencies, had been stolen.

We weren't isolated on Yeronisos. Every afternoon, we heard the tour boat docking nearby, the clear strains of "Saving All My Love For You" floating up, or we'd glimpse the Pirate Cruise boat gliding past. An odd collection of stacked rocks beyond where we dug turned out to spell "I love you" in Russian, clearly a modern incursion. Yeronisos was a cultural monument owned by Cyprus, and no law keeps people away. But it was also fragile land, so fragile that although tours of Yeronisos would be a natural thing to offer at the annual party, the project couldn't risk it, particularly with that rocky landing dock. In the long run, Connelly wanted to restore Apollo's circular dance floor, bring Andreas and the local boys who danced together to perform out here—"bring my village." But this was a dream, the happiest possibility for a distant and by no means certain future. And now here was this unwelcome news, the missing foghorn, the first theft in the history of the dig.

In Valentinos's dinghy, Connelly brooded about the changes to Cyprus that she had seen, the concrete buildings and subdivisions that have sprung up across Cyprus, the bulky generator on the beautiful shoreline that runs constantly to provide electricity to a snack shop. "I gave this talk at the new Acropolis Museum, called 'Building Partnerships in Eco-archaeology: Lessons from Yeronisos on Cyprus,' and I start it off by showing how from the beginning we had done floral studies and bird counts. I showed them 1992 aerial photographs that I took from a helicopter of this whole area. At the end of it everyone was like 'Wow, wow,' and then I said, but this year I returned to this. And I showed these horrible developments, and the whole auditorium gasped. It is shocking. In one year, its character is destroyed. All this really happened in a year. Bad stuff trickled along, and then in one year, boom!"

More invasions. I was standing in the trench dumping buckets of dirt in the wheelbarrow when a couple in flip-flops and bathing suits emerged at the top of the staircase and walked onto the site. Connelly swooped down and engaged them in conversation, then they wandered over to the lip of the quarry, a giant hole that separated the sites where we dug and the *khalifi*s from the eastern cliffs, where the seagulls nested and where we ducked when we had to pee (the archaeologists speculated that it was the place where the early people of Yeronisos quarried limestone and a chalky white clay called *marl*). What were they doing here? The woman stood at the top while her friend clambered down, and after a while they headed back down the stairs together and chugged off in their boat. "What's geocaching?" Connelly asked when they left. I tried to explain what I knew—geocaching was a scavenger hunt run from a website; caches and clues were hidden in the real world and participants used GPS to find them. Connelly said there was a clue apparently hidden in a plastic container at the bottom of the quarry, which was what the couple was looking for. She wanted it removed from Yeronisos. I worried that if its coordinates were listed on a website, people would come looking for the cache, whether it was at the bottom of the quarry or not; I promised Connelly that I'd find the website and send a note of protest. I had nothing against the sport—it seemed to me like a neat way to explore the world—but geocachers should not be traipsing through archaeological sites. (A few weeks later, the geocache website responded to my note and took down the listing).

Connelly's distaste for the sport was visceral. She hated fake explorers, contrived adventures, virtual games. "There is so much real adventure, real engagement. There's so much to be done!" she said. "These people are playing at exploring." The difference between her team and the geocachers was obvious. She said, passionately, "We're not playing!"

I was digging in the trench next to her nephew when Connelly came to observe our technique. We both met with her approval, though I didn't squat in the classic archaeological pose, but instead sat on a foamy kids' pool float and saved my knees. I was swaddled against the elements, a bandanna moistened and tied over my mouth and nose to keep me from inhaling the swirling dirt. First I chipped rhythmically across my section of the trench with the pick (my two-centimeter pass), then scraped with the trowel, then swept up the debris for further inspection. I chiseled around protuberances and kept the surface dusted and the edges straight—"This is your workspace," she had told us. "This is your laboratory. Keep it clean!" Her nephew was doing a beautiful job, brushing around the top of an amphora he had found. Connelly turned to me and spotted a piece of pottery with a fresh break where, no doubt, one of my tools whacked it. I wanted to sink into the quarry and curl up in shame.

Instead, I asked her about the skeleton of the woman her team found several years earlier, and Connelly glowed telling us. "It was a woman, found near where the dance floor to Apollo is now. She was dated to the first or second century A.D. We have nothing from that era here on the island, no artifacts at all, so Yeronisos was a ruin then. She was buried facing east, so apparently she was Christian. Her diet reflected wealth—mostly protein—and she had both hands positioned at her waist. Perhaps she was holding something. She was old for those days, into her fifties. Was she an early Christian holy woman, a hermit? Could be. The Church didn't stop women from participating as elders, deaconesses, and priests until the fourth century. And her shoulders were drawn up high. Can you guess why?" I couldn't. Even my imagination was stumped.

"From the winding cloth," Connelly said. She gestured toward Apollo's dance floor, part of its wall exposing the particular beauty of historic ruins, and looked down at her nephew. "When I die, I'd like to be buried where she was found," she told him. "Or if that's too complicated, maybe my heart could be buried here." I couldn't see her face, partially obscured by her canvas hat, and she had the light behind her, what she called "a raking light," casting shadows at the edge of the trench.

When I brought this up later, the touching idea that she might be buried one day on Yeronisos, Connelly was all brisk scientist, and laughed off her momentary romantic impulse. Surely the Cyprus Department of Antiquities would have something to say about that, not to mention the laws of this country. She was an honorary citizen of the local village, but that didn't come with any privileges. Her relatives might have trouble with it, as well. Really, I should just forget it!

But I tagged along on a tour of Yeronisos that Connelly gave one day to the visiting high school students, and when she got to Apollo's dance floor and the place where the pilgrim had been found, she lay down on the ground to show them how the woman had been buried with her shoulders hunched. She closed her eyes and lay very still. The students and I stood transfixed. The gulls whirred and cried overhead. Again I heard the echo of her words: *We're not playing.*

CONNELLY WAS SENSITIVE to the expression of religion over the centuries on Yeronisos, and she had located women's power in ancient Greece in the realm of religion. She satisfied her own spiritual hunger with long, philosophical conversations with the Orthodox monk, Father Neophytos, an imposing figure with a black beard and a probing intelligence. "Perhaps because I am Catholic, I'm enthralled by the Orthodox Church and their talk of the soul," she said; "I know some of my friends on the island look at the Church differently, but . . ."* She has an annual Clergy Day on the dig and credits the bishop of the local monastery with unearthing the inscription that linked Yeronisos with Apollo. On New Year's Eve of 2000, Connelly decided she wanted to celebrate in a place that had been around for a thousand years. "I couldn't manage that exactly, but I felt that the Monastery of St. Neophytos was as close as I could get, having been founded in 1159." She flew to Cyprus and spent New Year's Eve with ten monks and their abbot at the monastery, cut into the rock face of a mountain above Paphos. She attended services, sang, talked about the spiritual life, watched fireworks from their balcony, and drank French champagne. "And then we watched *Star Wars* and the segment with Yoda teaching, and Father Neophytos demonstrated to us how Yoda's words are based on the teachings of the Egyptian Desert Fathers of the fourth century A.D.!"

I was charmed by this whole story. I pictured her in the depar-

* Among its extensive holdings in Cyprus, the Orthodox Church owns the land on which the apotheke sits; the Cyprus Department of Antiquities owns the building.

ture lounge at JFK airport, an explorer, a pilgrim on a pilgrimage, and I wondered what her island would look like with a shroud of New Year's mist.

When the season was over, and New York swallowed us all back up, I found that, by virtue of my time in Cyprus, I had gained admittance to a rarefied club, the Friends of Yeronisos. Connelly met me near NYU in her low-heeled walking boots, wearing noise-canceling headphones to block out the din of city traffic. We laughed and gossiped about archaeology and publishing. The students from the dig were sophisticated adults in the city, appreciably taller here. How could that be? Perhaps because we were always crouching in a trench in Cyprus.

I followed Connelly to a conference on cultural heritage in Ohio and listened to another of her lectures about the international trade in illegally acquired artifacts and its harm to communities, cultures, and our bank of knowledge. Her cheerful tone with just a hint of sass was engaging and convincing. The Elgin Marbles, for instance, which now sat in the British Museum in pieces, separated from their context on the Acropolis, were an absurdity to Connelly. "We have the situation where Poseidon's shoulders are in London and his 'six-pack' is in Athens," she said to appreciative laughter. She showed a slide with a picture of the Acropolis at night. It looked like an island floating above Athens, a cluster of lights in a sea of purple, and I realized with a start where I had seen that same shape: a photo I took of Yeronisos rising out of the Mediterranean just before sunrise. I thought of a Spielberg movie, not one of the Indiana Jones adventures, but the more mystical *Close Encounters of the Third Kind*, in which people are drawn to a place with a particular shape, one seen in their dreams. They sketch and sculpt this shape until one day they find it: a mountainous structure with a flat top; a raised platform; a place where cultures separated by time and distance meet.

ARCHAEOLOGY
AND WAR

THE BODIES

Who owns history?

❦

T HE MOST important archaeological site in the United States
might well be a wooded lot on a battered commercial stretch
of Route 9 in Fishkill, New York. So says Bill Sandy, a seasoned
contract archaeologist who has had his hands in its soil. Sandy
would have shown me the place himself and pointed out its graves,
but he was tied up on an emergency excavation in the Bronx, so I
drove alone to Fishkill, about sixty miles north of New York City. I
parked on the gravel behind the Maya Café and walked across the
side road to get a look at what its owners called "the Crossroads
lot" and what Sandy claimed was "inch for inch, the most important site in the country." I saw no marker or trench, only a collar
of trees in waist-high grass, a scrubby parcel of ten or so acres, between the café and a Hess superstation and across Route 9 from a
ghost mall—a significant archaeological site disguised as a wooded
lot. Two signs faced the side road. One sign said NO TRESPASSING,
the other, partially obscured by leaves, NO DUMPING.

In 2007, while assessing the land for development, Sandy discovered seven graves in the lot. Based on their size, the condition of the
bones, and the residue of rusted-out coffin nails, he concluded that
the bodies belonged to Revolutionary War soldiers. Sandy believed

he had located the burial grounds of the old Fishkill Supply Depot, on land the owners bought to develop as a strip mall.

Who ever heard of the Fishkill Supply Depot? You could turn blue looking for a mention of it in history books, though the place served as the Continental Army's largest supply center, as well as the quarters, staging area, and mustering grounds for two thousand or more troops for seven and a half years, almost the entire length of the Revolutionary War. George Washington had overseen its secret operations, directed the construction of its barracks, ordered troops, provisions, and military supplies moved in and out of Fishkill, and corresponded frequently with his generals about its security, the inoculation of soldiers against smallpox, and the hanging of traitors. Though battles were fought in the area and the British burned the encampment at nearby Continental Village, the Fishkill Supply Depot had not been compromised or captured. It stayed a secret during the course of the war, and has remained secret, more or less, ever since.

Most of the land I could see from the edge of the lot had been part of this seventy-acre military city. What was once an almost treeless stretch of high ground about five miles from the Hudson River* was now a mix of woods and patchy commerce. I was on a weedy stretch of Route 9; looking north, with the Maya Café at my back, beyond the Hess superstation (a Blimpie, a Nathan's, a Godfather's Pizza), and just before the ramp to Interstate 84, I could see the lawn of the Van Wyck Homestead, the only surviving Revolutionary War structure on the Depot grounds; the former headquarters for Washington's generals was now a modest museum. Across Route 9 sprawled the remains of the Dutchess Mall. Only a drive-through McDonald's and a Home Depot survived; the rest was hulking buildings and graffitied windows, with a big apron of pitted asphalt, detritus from the seventies. All of this constituted the grounds of the historic Depot: armory, barracks, parade grounds,

---

*The Hudson River was then known as the North River.

stables, blacksmith, jail, hospital, everything but the general's headquarters invisible now.

I stood on the edge of the lot and thought about all the trouble that finding bodies can cause.

The discovery of the graves was not a complete surprise. Although no burial grounds had been marked on Washington's map of the Fishkill Supply Depot, there had to be a graveyard. Disease had been rampant here throughout the war, and in 1777, a smallpox epidemic had raged through the barracks. Sick and wounded Continental soldiers from elsewhere had been shipped by Washington north to Tarrytown and, as he directed, "from thence in boats to Fish Kills Hospitals." Residents recorded seeing bodies "piled up as high as cord wood" in the streets of the village. And local historians knew that a black marble monument to the war's dead had stood on this lot at the edge of the road for the better part of a century. So many speeding cars had sideswiped the marker that it had finally been relocated to the front yard of the Van Wyck Homestead. I walked along Route 9, cars and motorcycles whizzing past, and a quarter-mile north I found the monument, a large, dark headstone. The Daughters of the American Revolution (Melzingah Chapter) had erected it in 1897. The engraving read:

1776–1783. IN GRATEFUL REMEMBRANCE OF THE BRAVE
MEN WHO GAVE THEIR LIVES FOR THEIR COUNTRY DURING
THE AMERICAN REVOLUTION AND WHOSE REMAINS
REPOSE IN THE ADJOINING FIELD.

I imagined the phrase *in the adjoining field*, separated from its original context, floating north on gasoline fumes.

Other archaeologists had looked for the bodies in the 1960s and '70s. Although they found no bodies, only the remains of barracks and numerous artifacts, their efforts led to the depot being placed on the National Register of Historic Places. This was an honor—official recognition that the depot was "archaeologically sensitive"—not an order of protection. So when the owners of the land between the Maya Café and the Van Wyck Homestead decided to develop it as a commercial property, the town of Fishkill and the New York State Historic Preservation Office required them to hire an archaeological team to determine if the proposed construction would disturb any fragile and important history. That survey turned up nothing. "The archaeologist dug a hole every fifty feet, which is what archaeologists did in the nineties, and he didn't find anything," explained Bill Sandy. The final report found "no evidence of Revolutionary War activities. . . . We can now confidently state that additional testing is not necessary and no further work is recommended."* The evaluation allowed construction of the Hess gas station and permitted a mall on the Crossroads lot; but by the time the owners were ready to move forward with the rest of their plans, a public petition persuaded the town's leadership to make one more effort to see if construction would disturb irreplaceable history.

If the owners had built promptly, Sandy and his crew would not have been in that lot on Halloween in 2007, jittery with thermos coffee. Sandy worked for the same cultural resource management (CRM) company that had dug the test holes in the nineties without finding anything; this time, a backhoe fitted with a special blade would be used: "It's what archaeologists do when we're removing topsoil but we want a nice clean cut." He figured if there were burials, they'd be lined up to the road, so "when I do a survey like that, I go at a forty-five degree angle to the street."

Sandy, a tall, shaggy-bearded guy in his fifties, "brilliant and eccentric," according to my archaeological sources, stared at his hands as he remembered. I knew there were bodies at the end of

*From Greenhouse Consultants Inc., Stage1B Archaeological Survey of the Touchdown Development, Town of Fishkill, Dutchess Co., NY, Prepared for Battoglia Lanza Architectural Group. P. C. July, 1998.

this story and I pressed him for details. "We were ready to work at eight a.m., which was fine, except the backhoe wouldn't fit unless you cut down a few trees. So we had to wait while a construction guy came and chainsawed the trees." He remembered someone from Godfather's Pizza coming out and offering them free pie; old slices no doubt, but Sandy was delighted. "They weren't fifty years old, so we fell on them." Did he remember what was on them? Pineapple, he recalled.

Finally, at about three p.m. that Halloween afternoon, the backhoe was maneuvered through the trees and carefully began cutting a trench fifty or sixty feet long through the top layer of the ground. "Right away, we found two graves, one as clear a grave as I've ever seen," Sandy said. "Once you've seen a bunch of graves, you know." Two dark rectangles lay under the backhoe. The owners of the lot leaned over them; a local activist hovered nearby ("I had to ask him to leave," Sandy recalled. "I cannot discuss the site with anyone when I'm working on a job."). Then Sandy realized he wasn't through with this trench. "So I started to dig backwards, to take off an extra inch. And guess what? I find another grave—there's another, another, another, another, maybe another." At the end of the day, there were seven, perhaps eight large dark rectangular shapes in the soil, the signature of adult graves.

The owners called it quits until further notice. Sandy and the other contract archaeologists were "trowels for hire," as he put it; they packed up and went on to other jobs, until the owners called them back to finish their evaluation.

CONTRACT ARCHAEOLOGISTS, ALSO known as compliance or salvage archaeologists, have a tricky job. They are hired by owners and developers, but their responsibility is to the site and its archaeological resources. If, in their judgment, a proposed construction project will harm those resources, then the project has to be modified or moved, or the archaeologists must shift into emergency mode and record and rescue what they can—they "mitigate." In lower Manhattan in 2010, archaeologists were stunned to find an eighteenth-century wooden ship in landfill. While the construction equipment idled, they mitigated, scrambling to get the giant timbers, disintegrating as they were exposed to oxygen, hurried to a laboratory for preservation and study.

Any archaeological find is a mixed blessing when a construction project is looming, and the last thing any archaeologist wants to find, it turns out, are human remains.* As Bill Sandy wrote in his notes after finding the graves on the Fishkill Supply Depot, "I have some experience with cemetery projects. . . . As often as not, they tend to be controversial. [They] get a lot of publicity and can ruin a successful archaeological company. And they can turn professionals and/or companies against each other."

Bill Sandy's experience with cemetery projects had been alongside his old friend and colleague, Ed Rutsch, a contract archaeologist beloved by coworkers and clients. Sandy remembered Rutsch saying, " 'You love me now, but you are going to hate me when I find a body.' "

In 1991, Rutsch had been chosen by a long-time client, an engineering firm working for a federal agency, to survey a swatch of property for development in lower Manhattan that had appeared on old maps as a "Negroes Burial Ground." Rutsch suspected that burials would

* I was told this by the first archaeologist I interviewed. "Have you heard of NAGPRA?" she said. The Native American Graves Protection and Repatriation Act was a belated effort to stop archaeologists and museums from collecting and displaying sacred relics, particularly the skeletal remains of tribal people. "You've heard of Kennewick Man?" she said. "That was a nightmare for everyone involved." The remains of the nine-thousand-year-old skeleton, found in Washington State, were in legal limbo for eight years, with both scientists and Native Americans suing for its custody. The bones are now under the control of the U.S. Army Corps of Engineers, held away from public view in the Burke Museum of Natural History and Culture, visited by both scientists and Native Americans. Skeletal analysis suggests ties to Asia; recent DNA analysis found his genes had more in common with Native Americans.

still be found there, and wrote up a plan to test the ground before construction, but he wasn't given time to execute it. When his team, including Bill Sandy, started finding bodies, more bodies than even Rutsch had estimated, he insisted on excavating by hand. He had uncovered the African Burial Ground, where both slaves and freedmen had been interred with dignity in the seventeenth and eighteenth centuries. Rutsch called it "the 'Plymouth Rock' for Black Americans." His engineer employer and the General Services Administration pressured him to speed up the mitigation process, then quit honoring his invoices. The archaeologists found themselves at odds with the GSA and with the construction workers, and soon were the focus of daily protests staged by a suspicious public, particularly African Americans, who saw predominantly white men and women digging up black graves. Rutsch and his team were replaced by a larger CRM firm, in partnership with a team from Howard University, and soon after, a Congressional oversight committee shut down the excavation. "We were vilified," Sandy said, simply.* He still flares up whenever he reads an article claiming that the bodies from the African Burial Ground were discovered accidentally, by construction workers.

Sandy's specialty, which he employed on that job, is microflora, paleoethnobotany. His eye for the tiniest finds is extraordinarily sharp; one of his colleagues told me that Sandy could walk into a field, reach down in the grass, and pluck out a crinoid bead (a Native American bead made from a marine fossil a fraction of an inch long). Sandy's work at the African Burial Ground required him

---

*The GSA's account of the excavations are available at http://www.gsa.gov/portal/ext/html/site/hb/category/25431/actionParameter/exploreByBuilding/buildingId/1084. The New York Preservation Archive Project's account of it appears at http://www.nypap.org/content/african-burial-ground. That account states: "Although the HCI [Rutsch's firm] found a 1755 map that showed an African Burial Ground two blocks north of City Hall, archaeologists reasoned that 19th and 20th century development would have destroyed any remains." This was *not* Rutsch's conclusion.

to assess the smallest artifacts—seeds, fish scales, insect parts, bone fragments—so he took samples of earth from the burials and forced water through the dirt using a set of fine screens. He wrote the preliminary "flotation report" on the African Burial Ground, and still maintains that the official body count of 428 is far too low. He thinks there must have been many more burials. He found too many tiny baby teeth in his screens.

And this was another reason for Sandy's conviction in 2007 that he had located the military cemetery in the Fishkill Supply Depot: family graves of the colonial period are full of infants and children. What were the odds of finding seven adults out of seven burials? "One percent," he said flatly.

IN NOVEMBER 2007, Bill Sandy got the all-clear from the owners of the Crossroads lot to return to the site and excavate one dark rectangle and verify its contents. He alerted the coroner, then gathered the crew at the lot in Fishkill. He knelt in the fallen leaves, an orange watch cap on his head. He focused on the grave that showed most clearly after the initial cut. Some of the graves "had nails on the surface base of the plow zones, typical of the coffin, maybe a tiny bit of cardboard-like wood adhering to the nail. We went down, and it was typical of a site that old. If a grave is always wet, or always dry, that's good—either of those conditions are good for preservation. But if a grave is [alternately] wet *and* dry, it's shit. And these were shit. The bones were in very bad shape. We exposed the leg and arm bones, part of the cranium, then I made the decision we're not going to go in anymore.

"Archaeologists hate to [pull back], and I've rethought it a thousand times. Respected professionals asked if I shouldn't go back in and look for regimental buttons. I felt if we kept working, we were going to literally destroy this burial. This site screamed 'significant.' It was seventy-five yards from where the [DAR] monument [had stood]. The button wouldn't make a difference. I said we didn't need any more proof."

He and his crew reburied the skeleton with American flags, including flags of that era, "although most of those guys probably never even saw one," Sandy said. "We had our own ceremony before we closed up the site, paid our own respects in private, and we wrote something and put it in a plastic bag. Some of my students might go out there in the future, send a robot in to get DNA samples. What they'll know in ten years will put us to shame. . . ." He sat quietly, a tall, rough-bearded man in flannel and jeans.

"That must have been emotional," I said finally.

"No, no. In the field, you have no emotions," he said emphatically. "You're just doing your job. How that all plays out is not something you're thinking about. Sure, in the African cemetery, we could tell people our opinion, *It's tremendous, worth saving*, but our job is to answer the question, *What is this?* and write it up. It's up to the state historic preservation people to get emotional." He hesitated. "A little bit later as you thought about it, you'd think, 'Not even a marker. They didn't even have a marker.'"

THE TENSION BETWEEN keeping a site secret so it won't get looted and publicizing it so it can be preserved and appreciated is a constant in archaeology. Almost forty years after the Fishkill Supply Depot was added to the National Register of Historic Places, my copy of the nomination from the National Park Service arrived with a cover page that warned: THE LOCATION OF THIS PROPERTY IS RESTRICTED INFORMATION. Inside, directions were redacted for each of the depot's features and the longitude and latitude of the depot was blacked out; never mind that I could read through the black marker. The first thing I learned upon joining online archaeological groups was not to discuss publicly the specific locations of archaeological sites or anything else that might compromise a site's preservation. But how can you save or even appreciate something you don't know about?

Bill Sandy could not discuss the excavation of the graves with outsiders while he was in the employ of the CRM firm; but after the report on the Crossroads was filed with the state, he was no longer bound to keep its secrets. "You do your job, you're changed a little by each and every one, and you move on. Unless you get side-tracked," he said. He himself wasn't a military veteran, but the loss of his uncle at sea, torpedoed off Greenland during World War II, had shadowed his childhood. His freedom and identity were gifts from veterans like those he found in Fishkill. "I owed it to those dead people," he figured.

The Register of Professional Archaeologists' Code of Conduct committed its members to "actively support conservation of the archaeological resource base" and "to represent Archaeology and its research results to the public in a responsible manner." When Sandy got a call from a local organizer whose petition had led to the successful search for the graves,* he described what he had found and agreed to talk to her and her fellow activists. He got permission to take them onto the property. "The owners let you?" I asked, and Sandy said of Domenico Broccoli, one of the owners of Crossroads: "Sure. He loves his country, like everybody." And so began Sandy's pilgrimages to the lot, sponsored by the newly formed Friends of the Fishkill Supply Depot. "I can't separate it from going to a memorial," he said. "It's just the next thing I did." He started showing anyone who was interested where the bodies were buried. He got sidetracked, as he put it, at Fishkill.

ON REVOLUTIONARY WAR Weekend in September 2011, I found Sandy sitting at a folding table in the yard of the Van Wyck Homestead. Boy Scouts, a blacksmith, several women in colonial dress baking apple fritters, and a reenactor in a tricorn hat on a horse mingled as Sandy talked to curious people stopping by. Three times

---

*Mara Farrell is the local organizer who was involved in early efforts to preserve the site.

a day he led a tour to the graveyard that began at the monument. After a few words about its significance, Sandy accompanied anyone with sturdy knees down the shoulder of Route 9. He carried an archaeological measuring rod (with black paint marking every thirty centimeters) like Moses' rod in his hand. Three Boy Scouts positioned themselves at intervals across the side road so we could safely cross at the gas station.

In the fall woods, with an eager band of several dozen listeners around him, Sandy took a deep breath and began speaking in his Jersey twang, telling the story of the early efforts to locate the graves, the unlucky archaeologists who had missed the bodies, and of his team's historic find. Sandy hid his emotions behind his full gray beard and wraparound sunglasses, a billed cap pulled low on his shaggy head. He twisted to the side as he talked, using a cupped hand for emphasis, as if he were scooping words out of the air. "We removed about a foot, foot and a half of soil with the backhoe. Took the brown stuff off, saw the yellow soil. Then we started to see these features, each the size and shape of an adult coffin . . ."

Sandy kept his eyes on the ground, where a depression a few yards long was still visible—the remains of the trench he had excavated. Except for the sound of traffic through the trees, there was no noise in the clearing. His listeners stood rapt in the overgrown grass.

"Now, archaeologists are skeptics. We don't believe anything. You can tell me three stories that your grandfather told you and I'd be very interested to hear them, but I'd take them with a grain of salt. We are looking for ground proof. We are looking for proof in the ground that what we say is so."

After Sandy and his team obtained ground proof of the burials, they filed their report with Fishkill and the State Historic Preservation Office. The owners had hired a second CRM firm to identify the limits of the area that could potentially contain unmarked graves. That firm's archaeologists, using ground-penetrating radar "identified," in the words of their report, "an area [with] hundreds of anomalies consistent with the previously identified grave shaft." This was not just a burial ground, Sandy told us. It might well be the largest cemetery of Revolutionary War soldiers in the country.

Sandy had a gift for this kind of folksy talk, powered by the conviction that he was doing something important, speaking for the first veterans of our first war. He testified about the conditions in the Continental Army, not for the generals who were housed and clothed, whose lives were recorded and whose bodies lay in church graveyards, but for the ordinary state militiamen, conscripted for a year or nine months and marched to Fishkill, where they would have slept in shifts and scrounged for food. Wood was scarce in those days; local people complained that the soldiers were tearing down their fences and burning the planks to stay warm. He mentioned the "naked barracks," a building set aside for men with not enough clothes, and quoted a letter from Major General Israel Putnam to George Washington about a regiment "unfit to be order'd on duty, not one Blanket in the Regiment— very few have either a Shoe or a Shirt . . . several Hundred Men are render'd useless merely for want of necessary apparel—"

Sandy called the depot the "Gettysburg of the Revolutionary War." How had we not known about this place? A high school student in the group said that even his teachers didn't know about it, but he planned to tell them so they could network and spread the word. "That's how it has to be," Sandy agreed. "People don't know. If they knew, we wouldn't be standing in a clearing on the site of a bunch of unmarked graves for those who died for their country 235 years ago."

Before he led our little band along the busy road back to the Van Wyck Homestead and the monument to the Revolutionary War dead, Sandy tried to answer everyone's questions, but there was one that stumped him: Why had the land the graveyard rested on not yet been protected? The price tag the owners put on it was $6 million. There was no federal money to purchase such a site. The National Park Service's American Battlefield Protection Program protected battlegrounds of the Civil War, but not those from the Revolutionary War; and, anyway, these were not battlegrounds. Sandy shook his head. "Senator Chuck Schumer has been working for years to change the bill so its budget could double from five to ten million dollars and save important sites from the Revolutionary War and the War of 1812." But having our first veterans lie in a lot that was still for sale years after the discovery of their bodies, that struck him as wrong. When historical or archaeologically important artifacts are found on private property in most provinces in Canada,* they belong to the public. Here, the private-property owner rules.

No matter what other project demanded his attention, Sandy was steadfast when it came to Fishkill. Months after the fall tours, he learned about the Wreaths Across America program: every year, on the second Saturday in December, at noon, volunteers place wreaths on veterans' graves all across the country. Here was yet another opportunity to remind people of their debt to the Revolutionary War soldiers. With the Fishkill Historical Society and the Friends of the Fishkill Supply Depot, Sandy mounted a last-minute memorial in December that drew forty or so hardy souls, including half a dozen reenactors from the Fifth New York Regiment. I joined Sandy and the others at the DAR monument in front of the Van Wyck Homestead, then we marched along the shoulder of Route 9, bearing wreaths.

We assembled in the clearing in the middle of the lot for brief, pointed speeches from local politicians. "Thank you all for coming," said one county legislator. "Today is a very solemn day. I hope when we gather next year that the work will have begun to properly attend to our soldiers." That was her entire speech: perfect and succinct.

A woman in colonial dress, complete with bonnet and cloak, laid a wreath, and military veterans followed: a total of seven wreaths were placed, one for each of the bodies discovered in 2007. The mil-

* All provinces, according to Parks Canada, except Ontario and Quebec.

itary reenactors spread themselves along the length of the trench scar, visible in the frozen ground. They wore long-skirted coats of brown and blue, festooned with buttons, and tricorn hats, though one was in shaggy breeches and a red knit cap with the crudely embroidered legend LIBERTY. They rested their muskets on the ground, hands crossed on top, and heads bowed, in a posture called "mourn firelocks"; one soldier on the end stood with his arms akimbo, as if to ward off the motorcycles that roared up and down Route 9, just a few yards away.

This was not long after the trashing of the remains of Iraq War veterans had come to light: the Air Force admitted that unclaimed and unidentified body parts had been incinerated and dumped in a landfill. Across the centuries, we felt the shameful lack of honor toward the dead.

The Fifth Regiment's officer gave the order to load and fire, and the first of a series of salute volleys thundered above us. More muskets failed than fired, a homely touch in the winter woods. The last time I felt this mix of momentousness and sorrow, I was walking behind a casket.

I CAUGHT UP with Bill Sandy two years later at an organic garlic farm in northern New Jersey, where he was running a summer field school four days a week. He sat on an old tire, sun-damaged hands wrapped around a homemade sandwich. His students at Sussex County Community College, where he is an adjunct instructor, were digging test pits and finding points and flakes from four and five thousand years ago on the hill above us. He was eight years away from Medicare, with diabetes and hypertension, but he had trouble finding time for doctor's visits; he hadn't taken a day off in months.

He was energetic, though, even exuberant, telling me about a young bear that had walked through these fields, right past him and his students—could I believe it? Sandy shared his Tastykake— "the pride of Pennsylvania"—and introduced me to his students, including one in her eighties; she was fulfilling a dream to go back to school and study archaeology.

What kind of place did he live in, I wondered. "A little house in the country, about forty minutes from here," he said. "You want to see?" After the students left for the day, we headed for our vehicles. "Wait, what if I lose you?" I said. He laughed. "You're in the country," he said. "You can't lose me."

I followed him for miles through black dirt and rolling green hills, and he was right: on a clear day, I was in no danger of losing sight of an old pickup truck with a load of screens and shovels in its bed. Before we got to his house, we made a detour. He stuck his hand out his window and pointed. I pulled in next to him in a small church parking lot. "You have to see this," he said, indicating the lovely white church with an unusual octagonal building next door. "During the Civil War, the congregation here was divided, so the Northern sympathizers met in the church and the Southern sympathizers met in the octagonal building." He stood there, marveling. Then someone shouted, "Bill! Bill!" Across the road, in a neat graveyard, a lean, weathered man on a mowing tractor was waving his cap. "It's Randy," Sandy said with pleasure. "Come on, you've got to meet Randy. He's the historian who surface-collects all the land around here. He found me the farm where my students are excavating. That's his legacy—he doesn't want the information to get lost." We strolled across the road and spent time with another man who honors the dead by tending a cemetery.

We stopped twice more to see historic sites before we made it to his house, a former fruit-and-vegetable stand on a county road in New York. Although Sandy has been in a long-term relationship with a community preservationist from a neighboring town, he lived like a bachelor, papers and books stacked high on every surface. There was a television but no reception. His books include various collections inherited from departed friends. Boxes of postcards—roughly 37,000 of them—filled the corner of the living room, each filed by subject and coded for sale. His childhood doll, a red-haired boy named Max, looked at me from a shelf. The 1936 Oldsmobile convertible that Sandy had inherited from his father, his prize possession, is locked in the barn with what must be a ton of vintage promotional literature and repair manuals from Oldsmobile, which he also sells as a sideline. The ancient cherry-red Olds required a shot of gasoline before it would start. He eased it out past the old pickup, and I hopped in, by the peonies, and we went rolling through the countryside in his antique car. With every breath, he exhaled another bit of local history.

JUDY WOLF WORE colonial dress, apron, and bonnet in all seasons—I don't think I ever saw her in modern clothes. She is a dogged historical researcher who helped identify some of the soldiers buried at Fishkill. Every month, she and Lance Ashworth, the president of the Friends of the Fishkill Supply Depot, comb through the Revolutionary War muster rolls. Then Wolf tries to verify the soldiers' deaths through archives, electronic databases, pension rolls, and doctors' journals. Valley Forge's military archives have been consolidated, but Fishkill remains an orphan; Wolf has had to range widely to find records about its troops. She was stunned when the archivist at the U.S. Army Quartermaster Museum, which specializes in supplies and logistics, and should be a central source for information about all the supply depots, admitted he had never heard of the one at Fishkill.

Knowledge of the Fishkill Supply Depot and its ghostly inhabitants has given Wolf a claim. "By the time I verify that someone died at Fishkill, I've spent so much time with them, these guys have turned into family. I feel very motherly and protective toward the soldiers," she said. "There are times, honestly, I think they are helping me. They want to be found."

By early 2014, Judy Wolf had identified an astonishing eighty-four Revolutionary War soldiers who had died in Fishkill and were, presumably, buried in that graveyard, among them a Canadian nurse and Captain Abraham Godwin, wounded in action and buried near his son, Captain Henry Godwin. The phrase "sick at Fishkill until he died" appeared with haunting regularity on the "rescued" roll call on the Friends of the Fishkill Supply Depot's website.* The pages memorializing the dead by name appear in black and white, "and will remain colorless until the day that we can announce the soldiers' burial ground has been acquired and preserved, once and for all."

While the Friends' group continued to research individual soldiers and conduct respectful ceremonies to honor them, the graveyard was trapped in a parallel universe of tawdry commercial real estate. County records evidenced petitions and suits involving GLD3, LLC, the owner of record of the Crossroads lot. Between 1998 and 2012, there were liens and judgments, leases and mortgages, ambitious plans and delinquent taxes involving a property reduced in price to $5 million and assessed by the county at $400,000. After the report of the second CRM firm was filed, the New York State Historic Preservation Office had recommended no construction on the lot without a major reconfiguration that skirted the burials. A stream and wetlands on the property already limited its building potential. Like millions of Americans, Broccoli owned a piece of real estate whose value was far less than what he had hoped. Now he wanted to sell it. And who else but a preservation group would want this land?

A FEW WEEKS before Memorial Day of 2013, heavy equipment appeared in the clearing, and bright-orange polyethylene warning fences ringed the grave site. Every few feet, the orange fence was broken up

*Friends of the Fishkill Supply Depot website: http://www.fishkillsupplydepot.org/

with signs: PRIVATE PROPERTY, NO TRESPASSING. A press release*
announced that yet another CRM firm—the third—was completing
a survey to "ground truth" the boundary of the burial grounds. The
press release included these provocative sentences:

> To date there is confirmed evidence of only eight graves in
> a confined area at the southern end of the property. . . . State-
> ments reported in the press claiming that certain named in-
> dividuals are definitively buried on this property are purely
> speculative. While there is some historic documentation of
> individuals being hospitalized and dying at Fishkill Supply
> Depot, this certainly does not mean that they were buried
> at the Depot, or that their remains were not removed at a
> later date and reinterred elsewhere. It is not even certain at
> this point whether the few graves found are those of Ameri-
> can soldiers, British mercenaries, or evidence of a previously
> unknown small family cemetery.

The statement ended with the reminder that the site was private
property, not open to the public.

Bill Sandy offered his opinion. "It is just a distraction." He told
me not to worry about the caution fence, either. Several Friends
had met with Broccoli, who told them that he, too, was eager to
preserve the burial ground; he assured them they would be able to
hold a Memorial Day ceremony at the site. "We're on a slow course
to intersect," said the president of the Friends group, Lance Ashworth. "He needs to sell the land, and we're the only people who
want to buy it. But there will be lots of gnashing of teeth and pain
along the way." No white knight has appeared with millions of dollars. The Friends group keeps a tip jar at the Van Wyck Homestead,
takes donations online, applies for grants, meets with representa-

* Press release by Greg Lane, Snook-9 Realty, Inc., May 6, 2013.

tives of land trusts and preservation funds, does the massive detail work that will one day, they hope, end in preservation.

By Memorial Day, the bulk of the tape and signs had been removed. The crowd had grown, too, no doubt alarmed by the appearance of bulldozers and that fiery press release. Twenty-six men-at-arms—military reenactors, one on horseback—and several camp followers in colonial dress led seventy others down the Albany Post Road, including several in contemporary military uniforms and three descendants of the soldiers identified as the Revolutionary War dead of Fishkill. Reenactors and politicians took turns solemnly reciting the names that the Friends had found in the archives. Abner Hill . . . Gift Freeman . . . Josiah Graves, Sr. . . . The archaeologist stood with his head bowed. The man on horseback held his reins tight as the muskets fired volleys into the woods.

Postscript

DOMENICO BROCCOLI DID not sell his 10.47 acres to the Friends of the Fishkill Supply Depot, or anyone else. He decided to develop the property himself. Behind that orange warning fence in May 2013, Hartgen Archaeological Associates had been digging ten trenches to try to determine the boundaries of the burial grounds. Three burials were discovered in one trench, but a semicircle of trenches to the north and east contained no human remains. Hartgen concluded that the burials were confined to the .4 acres in the southwest corner of Broccoli's lot.

While the Friends worked with the National Park Service to coordinate the archaeology and maps of the entire depot, Broccoli unveiled his vision for the development of "Colonial Commons" to the Fishkill Planning Board in June 2015. He proposed setting aside the .4 acre as a memorial to Revolutionary War soldiers, with interpretive signs and walking trails for public access; on the remaining acreage, he would build a ninety-room inn, two eight-thousand-square-foot retail buildings, and a restaurant—an IHOP, he hoped, with its staff in eighteenth-century costume. He would bring together "tourism, history, education, and commerce." He did not offer to set the .4 acres aside under a conservation easement, a preservation tool that would protect the land in perpetuity, and the Planning Board has not yet suggested this. Though in February 2015, Broccoli told a local radio station, "I'm very proud that I found the soldiers," his lawyers have questioned that the graves are indeed those of Revolutionary War soldiers.

Pressed by a local politician to clarify the number of soldiers buried on the land, the New York State Office of Parks, Recreation, and New York State Historic Preservation cautioned in a letter dated May 21, 2015, that its comments were advisory and that identifying and counting the remains was impossible without further intrusive excavation. "While this office has no doubt that there are burials on the site, we cannot assign a definitive number based on the evidence in our files." After noting the shortcomings of the ground-penetrating-radar study in identifying actual burials, the state preservation office wrote: "So the question of how many burials, how many graves (multiple burials), who is buried there (soldier or civilian), and what is the extent of the burial site remain unanswered in the material that our office has on hand. . . . The information extracted to date from the overall Supply Depot site combined with historic documentation and anecdotal references tell us that there is without question something of great importance here."

What will ultimately become of the property and the burial grounds? That chapter is unspooling now in Fishkill.

EVIDENCE OF HARM

Bearing witness

❧

ERIN COWARD was in Hawaii on September 11, 2001, and
woke up six hours behind the news. It didn't seem real to her;
the attacks felt like something that happened on television. When
she returned to her family home near Washington, D.C., she made
her brother drive her to the Pentagon so she could see where the
plane had hit. More than five years after 9/11, she saw a listserv
notice from the Office of the Chief Medical Examiner of the City of
New York: Archaeologists needed for a World Trade Center recovery team; experience with human remains essential. Coward leapt.
It was work, and the contract archaeologist always needed work,
but beyond that, she said, "I wanted to make it real. This was my
connection to those people."

Coward, an attractive, compact redhead with slate-blue eyes
and a direct gaze, reported for duty to a converted warehouse in
Brooklyn. There she was fitted in a hazmat suit with goggles and
boots. Thick rubber gloves were taped to the suit at her wrists. The
material she would be screening—six feet of topsoil from the area
around the towers and even debris from the sewers—was toxic; her
health had to be monitored regularly. Coward and her team were
instructed to look for artifacts, bones as small as a quarter of an
inch, and teeth. A baby's tooth, Coward said, looks like a pebble to

the untrained eye. All day the piles of debris came to her on con-
veyer belts. "We went through some ugly stuff—tampons, rats.
It smelled," she recalled. "Someone found a freshly severed finger
and we had to call the police. Trust me, you don't ever want to go
through anything from the New York City sewers." But that's the
job: "I get paid to look at people's trash."

She plucked evidence of harm from the conveyor belt. She found
ID cards. She found a child's wristwatch, its pink strap still fas-
tened. She found a baby's T-shirt with a bear on it, burnt around
the edges. "That was hard," she said. "I found it the day of the Virginia Tech shooting and called my friend and said, 'Can I come over
and just hold your baby?'"

Like the other "arkies," Coward tried to keep the grim business
from overwhelming her; endurance was part of the job. She lasted a
year. "You're standing there for eight hours a day, so they allowed
us to listen to our iPods," she said. "It was nice to look up and see
someone dancing. We were alive."

Archaeologists were not originally part of the rescue and recovery after 9/11. Archaeologist Richard Gould reported walking lower Manhattan weeks after the attacks, encountering
"fragmented human remains along with other debris in alleyways,
on top of Dumpsters, and on fire escapes." He and others volunteered their services but were told that power-washing teams had
already been dispatched and the priority was cleanup. With archaeologist Sophia Perdikaris and several detectives trained in forensic
recovery, Gould organized a team of archaeologists and persuaded
the medical examiner's office to let them excavate in a parking lot
outside Ground Zero. They found human bone.* Human remains
were still being found in 2006, when construction turned up scores

---

*Forensic Archaeological Recovery (FAR) was organized in response to the
WTC attacks. A nonprofit, volunteer organization, it has dispatched forensic
archaeologists in the wake of fires, plane crashes, and hurricanes.

of bones and personal effects. Soon after, Coward saw the medical examiner's call for archaeologists.

Five years after she had sifted its blighted dirt, Coward walked with me through Lower Manhattan. The new tower rose above us; ironworkers moved on an upper floor, filling it in. We got tickets to the memorial site and lingered near the reflecting pools built in the footprints of the Twin Towers. "Reflecting pools" sounds peaceful, but these were cavernous, with water roaring down into what looked like a black hole, black marble etched on all four sides with names of the dead.

Coward was almost forty, though she looked younger. She had spent five years in the Army and had "tons of cousins" who served as well. She had read and reread Ayn Rand, not *The Fountainhead*, but *Anthem*—"That message of individuality was so important if you were in the military, you know?"

Though she did not yet have a master's degree, Coward had eight years' experience in cultural resource management. "CRM work, that's where you see the worst burnout," she told me as we wandered the site. "Jobs aren't steady, you move around constantly. If you want to have a family, you can't. One week in Virginia, and then you're in southern California, and then you're in the Sudan." She had yet to marry. "I need to find someone who understands I might be gone six months out of the year." Coward had deliberately sought jobs in a variety of places, first in Maryland, Virginia, and New York City, "but the East Coast is mainly colonial archaeology," she said, so she branched out to Hawaii and the American Southwest. She was at her happiest in field school in the middle of the Arizona desert, where the entertainment was as simple as sitting around a campfire at night drinking cheap beer.

The attrition rate for this kind of work is high. "I know at least ten archaeologists that are out of it now; they've gone into the medical field mainly, because they needed money and more solid jobs. There are archaeologists I've talked to who go from job to job to job. That terrifies me. People with master's degrees and twenty years' experience—I had a B.A. and was just starting out, and we're working for the same pay. They got involved with CRM work when they were twenty. Now they're sixty and all they have is a car."

Because so much CRM work is done for legal compliance reasons, the paperwork can be daunting. "I tell people who want to be an archaeologist, go on a dig," Coward said. "See if you survive the paperwork. Everything has to be documented: beginning of the day, end of the day, end of the month. Then try writing a report about not finding anything." She's comfortable with the uncertainty: "You can't set out to prove something," she said. What, then, can the archaeologist accomplish? She can say: "Here is something we can reasonably say is true."

Coward's take on the work she did boiled down to one word: *professional*. That's what the World Trade Center recovery team had been looking for, *professionals*. She is tough on amateur archaeologists. Coward grimaced. "Don't do it," she said. "An amateur pulls a pot out of a dig—it's like telling a murder detective, 'Don't worry, I collected your evidence for you.'"

School for Forensics

I RODE SHOTGUN with a CSI team, cruising the back roads of New Jersey's Pine Barrens with a bundle of red pin flags, looking for places where a drug-addled felon might have dumped the body of his waitress-girlfriend. Our driver was Amanda, a crime-scene analyst in gritty Camden, New Jersey (two tours of Iraq, two young children at home). Squeezed in the back, next to the children's car seat, were Lorna, a Scottish Ph.D. candidate in toxicology (one layer of blond, asymmetrical hair over a darker layer, two bracelets with skulls), and Alex, master's degree from Bradford University (West Yorkshire, England) in human osteology and paleopathology, meaning she knew a lot about bones, especially old diseased bones (dark asymmetrical hair, skull necklace). All three were in their twenties, sharp-eyed and competent. What is it about attractive young women and forensics? Did Temperance "Bones" Brennan, hero of the novels by Kathy Reichs and of the television series now in perpetual syndication, anticipate this trend, or inspire it?

Amanda had been late that morning to the Rutgers Pinelands Field Station, where our class in Forensic Archaeology to Maximize Evidence Recovery met, because her GPS had led her to a dirt road a mile or two away. So when we received the police report on the missing waitress, along with a map showing her house, the bar where she worked, and the dump where her boyfriend was employed, Amanda had pointed down at the unpaved fire road where her GPS had led her, a possible route between the waitress's house and the dump, and said, "That would be a great place to bury a body." We knew from our morning's instruction that a killer who knows his victim is more likely to bury her close by; that if the body wasn't in the backyard under newly poured concrete, it was likely to be somewhere along the route the killer traveled from home to work; and we knew to look for a spot off the road, possibly behind a screen or barrier and near some kind of landmark, so the killer could find the spot again and keep an eye on it. There were exceptions, as our instructor, Kimberlee Sue Moran, pointed out, but criminals behaved in mostly predictable ways.

We had a plan. We pulled out in Amanda's car and drove onto the dirt road. We saw the other team—two more twenty-something women, a young male anthropologist, and a male homicide detective in his thirties—planting pin flags in the piny woods. "What do they see there?" Alex wondered. We spotted two places along the fire road where a car could pull over. One seemed particularly promising, by a trail with a big pile of natural brush to furnish a screen. In the wet, cold spring of 2014, much of the ground in these woods sprouted moss, but the area behind the brush pile did not; it was a darker color, as if it had come from a deeper layer, and it felt spongy underfoot. Alex pointed. "A piece of rope!" Amanda said triumphantly. Lorna planted several pin flags, then we continued cruising. We were a good team; we found another spot that also looked promising.

I was only a little freaked out by the morning's instruction. Kimberlee Moran, cheerful, attractive, thirty-five—this field was made for young, tough people—had emphasized that forensic archaeology was simply archaeology, conducted to a more exacting standard. You excavated and bagged artifacts systematically, but separately; you mapped and sketched and photographed at every turn; you guarded vigilantly against contamination; and you followed police procedure, logging every step in the chain of custody and making sure your methodology could stand up in court. No problem. Then: "Let's share case studies!" Moran had said to start the class, and she and her two assistants had proceeded to tell us stories about the bodies they had encountered and the challenges they faced gathering evidence. I learned some things I can't unlearn: human kneecaps look like rocks; bones when burnt, shrink and twist. Moran's assistant, Ani Hatza, though still in her twenties, had worked on more than a hundred cases. She recalled a woman who killed her husband, then burned his body and dumped his ashes in a trashcan. Hatza's team had had to excavate the trashcan, layer by layer; one person at a time in the cramped quarters. "We also found a cat in there," Hatza said. "Good times!" The box of doughnuts in the middle of the table went untouched.

Fortunately, I was not at one of the five body farms in the United States (one memorably described by Mary Roach in *Stiff*), where those who donate their remains to science are buried, excavated, then studied by law enforcement people and archaeologists. Instead, I was in a corner of the vast and creepy Jersey Pine Barrens where, as John McPhee wrote, "From a gang-land point of view, it makes better sense to put a body in the Pine Barrens than in the Hudson River. [A] state trooper said to me: 'Anybody who wanted to commit a murder—all he'd have to do is ride back there with a shovel. They'd never find that body. I always did figure there's a lot of bodies in there.'" New Jersey does not permit burial and excavation of humans for the purpose of training professionals in forensic skills, so the victim we were looking for, the hapless waitress in our dummy police report, was actually a four-hundred-pound pig, buried by Moran and her team a year earlier. Depending on the temperature and other conditions, a body takes a year to three years to skeletonize—but "we checked it a few months ago," Moran reported, "and it was still fleshed."

Unfortunately, neither of our teams had pinpointed the pig's burial site. Moran and her assistants, Hatza and Eric Young, took us out behind one of the outbuildings at the field station and led us down a sandy trail through the woods. We hiked a mile or so to a spot closer to a busy paved road than the fire road. There, in a clearing near a big cistern, was an obviously disturbed piece of ground, roughly rectangular and sagging in the middle; at a certain point, a buried body begins to collapse and the stomach ruptures, leaving a telltale slump in the soil. Moran also pointed out straight edges where a shovel had sliced into the earth. "There are no straight lines in nature, people," she told us. I maintain that our mistake was in overthinking our criminal's desire to conceal the body. He was no mastermind, just a panicked criminal; maybe it hadn't occurred to him that he could find better cover off the fire road than the highway. But what, I wonder, was buried in the sites we did find? We were there for only two days; we had no time to investigate the rest of the Pine Barrens, full as it might be of murder victims. The next day, we had to excavate the pig.

SOMEHOW I FOUND myself alone in the woods the second morning. There was only one restroom in the field station, and I was last in line. By the time I emerged, everyone was gone, but I wasn't worried; though the site was a hike from here, it had been easy enough to get to, and there was that big cistern nearby, an obvious marker. But the first trail I tried was a dead end and I had to double back. I tried another that felt all wrong. The sandy ground and piny woods looked the same no matter which way I turned, and the trails seemed to be multiplying. There are more than a million acres in the Pine Barrens; it covers a huge swatch of the map. Perhaps you remember the episode from *The Sopranos* where two mobsters, Paulie and Christopher, decide to dump the body of their Russian victim in the Pine Barrens. They drive to the vast, gnarly-wooded wilderness, pop the trunk, and fall into a horror story, Poe by way of Godot. The body is not dead; the mobsters are attacked with the grave-digging shovel and have their car stolen. Paulie loses a shoe. The men wander the woods in sharp coats and what's left of their shoes, shivering and bickering. I knew how they felt.

I found my way back to the field station, where two resident scientists finally steered me down the right path; deep in the woods, I ran into Moran herself, who had gone looking for her missing student. I'd needed three rescuers, a personal record.

Moran and I reached the pig burial site just after the others had marked off a generous area around the grave with yellow crime-scene tape. I pulled on my lightweight white Tyvek suit, with booties and a hood to keep me from contaminating evidence, then finished my outfit with two layers of latex gloves, and joined the crew. We looked like a platoon of astronauts, dispatched to a sandy semilunar landscape that was littered with little pine cones and dead leaves. First, we photographed and mapped the site. Then, inside the taped area, we lined up a couple feet apart and walked slowly, south to north, through the site, eight abreast, veering around trees, the cistern, and the grave. As we searched for shell casings or any other evidence, we used our pin flags to probe the leaves and soft ground, marking anything that looked like a human might have left it behind. Then we spread out and walked west to east across the site. Next we studied each of the flags and mapped them. "Why is this one marked?" Moran asked. "There's your shell casing," said the homicide cop, pointing out the shell camouflaged in the brown grass.

This excavation was a painstaking affair. We measured, photographed, and logged every step of it; checked the color of the soil against our soil charts; and ended up with a rectangular area four feet by eight, divided into quadrants, marked by nails at the corners; we tied string between the nails to mark the perimeter of the excavation. Eventually, as we took turns carefully troweling the surface to reverse the hasty burial, we started finding trotters and toes and lumps of fat covered with hair from the rotting pig; we also found water bottles and even a beer can and cigarette butts, all potentially powerful evidence. "Cigarette butts are great for DNA, and bad guys like to smoke," Moran noted.

Lucky for us it was a chilly spring; we were sweating in the Tyvek suits, and I could just imagine what ninety degrees and swarms of insects could do to make this more difficult. We were already afflicted by buzzing gnats. As the hole deepened, reaching into the center of the grave to carefully extract the dirt required a stretch that made my ribs ache. "Try excavating over your head," Moran said, laughing. "Try excavating on a steep slope!"

When she was twenty years old, a recent graduate of Bryn Mawr in classical and Near East archaeology, Moran had been so determined to work as an archaeologist that she took a job on a field crew for a CRM firm. "It was tough, physical work, all day, every day," she said. Safety was not a priority, so, not surprisingly, she suffered lead contamination working at a hazardous site. In the year 2000, she made $9.50 an hour, with no benefits. It was a punishing job, but it had one reward. When anyone asked her profession, she could say, with satisfaction, *professional archaeologist.*

"Here's a maggot," Amanda called, and Moran offered her a vial and a label for the white, grublike creature. "I'm surprised we haven't found more of them," Moran said. "Sometimes, you'll remove a layer of dirt over the grave and there will be a whole bed of writhing maggots." Maggots, the larval stage of various flies, are activated by heat. Moran described how systematic and careful attention to them could, like everything else in the realm of forensics, build a true picture and timeline of the scene and even help make a criminal case. Identifying which species of fly a maggot represented, for instance, can be correlated with air temperature and burial conditions and used to calculate how long a body has been dead. "It's one of the more accurate indicators of time of death," Moran said. She was fascinated by all the ways nature recycled its dead and an eager scientist of decomposition. "I have forty-five rats buried in my backyard to study," she said.

By mid-afternoon, we had excavated a foot deep into the grave and were stretched out on our stomachs to reach inside—five excavators radiating out from the hole, a star with white Tyvek points. I scraped and brushed in dirt from around the pig into the dustpan, then, still on my stomach, twisted back to dump it in a bucket, which others would screen. The smell from the emerging carcass rose like a powerful repulsing wave. I forced myself to breathe it in and tried to describe it, along with my fellow crime-scene analysts. Organic, foul as sewage or fetid water, but with a persistent, cloying density, it clung to my hair and clothes. When I got home later that night, my dog went crazy over the smell.

Moran's assistant Eric Young was about fifty, the oldest person at the gravesite besides me. Bald and mustached, he was a retired cop who had gone back to school to earn two degrees in archaeology. He stood over us, amused by our efforts to describe the stench. "You think *this* smells bad?" he asked, and began telling stories from his days as a detective. One involved the shotgun suicide of a man who never bathed. He told me he did forensic work "because somebody has to do it." His passion, it turned out, was Mesoamerican archaeology, circa 3,000 B.C.; he excavated, when he could, in Mexico and Guatemala. Next week he and

Moran would be in Austin, at the annual meeting of the Society for American Archaeology.

Since Moran had earned a graduate degree in the U.K., she had been promoting British advances in the applied science of forensics (inspired, in part, she is convinced, by Sherlock Holmes—"He really anticipated a lot of forensics."). She is an advocate for developing standard operating procedures for crime-scene analysis and for the past seven years, she has helped organize the SAA's annual panel on forensics. This year, she would be presenting a paper on her latest experiment, giving law enforcement and forensics professionals a chance to conduct a "full-scale post-blast investigation." This had involved obtaining a bus, filling it with dead farm animals, and constructing an identity for each animal, complete with personal effects like cell phones and jewelry. The final step was to simulate a terrorist attack during the morning commute and blow up the bus.*
"The animals were dressed in clothing," Young said appreciatively as Moran nodded. "Children's clothing!" The professionals participating in this exercise had to respond to the blast, secure the area, and process the site. They had to gather evidence, gleaning what information they could from the debris that could lead to the perpetrators. And they had to try to gather and properly identify each animal and its property—their duty to the survivors. Moran was proud of the results: every animal in the simulation (and fifty-eight of the sixty-one personal items she had planted) had been recovered and identified.

I looked at the huge, partially decayed pig, the stand-in for our waitress, and thought how much more difficult this would be with scraps of blue jeans or a T-shirt. And what if . . . ? Most of my fellow excavators here had already handled human remains, and reported

---

*Moran said she could not have pulled off this simulation without the help of her colleague Al Stewart, who was instrumental, among other things, in obtaining a bus that could be blown up.

for work each day prepared to encounter more. I breathed deep, in a kind of salute to their fortitude.

It was late in the afternoon. Moran regretted that we didn't have time to remove the carcass from the grave. Sometimes what was underneath a body was telling: a weapon, or footprints. "Or even dead leaves," she said. "If the killer dug the hole in advance and left it open, this could be a sign of premeditation." But the partially excavated pig would be reburied and left for another class to find. Young, Moran, and one of the students puffed on a few of Young's cigarettes, then threw the butts into the grave, along with some soda cans and water bottles—criminal evidence for future forensic students to puzzle over. We filled in the pit with screened dirt, tamped it down, and hiked back through the pines with our shovels and crime-scene tape and evidence bags.

Amateurs

SINCE WORKING FOR the medical examiner of New York City, going through the debris from the neighborhood of the Twin Towers, Erin Coward had decided to make forensic anthropology her specialty. While she applied for programs, she was staying with her mother near Washington, D.C. We arranged to meet one afternoon near the Capitol. Coward and her mother, Lane, picked me up at my hotel to whisk me off to check out an archaeological museum Erin had found online. "We never heard of this place," her mother said, "but Erin called and made arrangements for a private showing." How great is this? I thought happily, as her mother chauffeured us around the circles and loops of suburban D.C. and chatted knowledgeably about her daughter's archaeological career. "Did she tell you about finding a seashell in the middle of the desert?"

It was an adventure with lively and well-read companions. The bedtime story that Erin had wanted to hear each night in childhood had been *Beowulf*; now she consumed biography, travel essays, British novels, Stephen Jay Gould, Bill Bryson. Of Bryson's *A Short History of Nearly Everything*, Erin said: "I was prepared to be a skeptic—'I will take you down!'—but he was amazing on evolution."

The car climbed the hills above D.C. to the Palisades, a residential neighborhood of lovely homes on an old river terrace above the Potomac. We would never have found the Palisades Museum of Prehistory without GPS. We were running a little late, and Erin nervously chewed a nail while her mother drove up and down a road of pretty houses, all of us squinting at street numbers. There were no signs, no indication that anything commercial was happening here—and, as it turned out, nothing commercial was. The address was for the corner house on the big lot, with a grape arbor and an outbuilding and children's toys littering the patio. Our host, Doug Dupin, was a relaxed young dad, a skateboarder, who led us out back. We walked across the lawn to the outbuilding, an elaborate clubhouse with just enough room inside for four. "I've been working for a few years on this thing, and every once in a while people come through," Doug Dupin said. He had been digging the foundation for a wine cellar when he began to uncover layers of history: old medicine bottles, Civil War bullets, shards of pottery, and Native American points. While Lane Coward and I admired the decor, burlap walls with bark accents, and the posters he made and sold (Smoking Pipes of the American Indian, Stone Points of the Potomac Palisades), Erin gravitated toward the display cases of mounted Indian points. She and Dupin began speaking the language of stone tools.

Dupin's personal collection, and his determination to salvage what he could of the archaeology of the area, had deepened when a soccer field was dug in his neighborhood. He watched bulldozers churn up the earth, exposing all sorts of artifacts. He alerted the archaeologist who worked for the District of Columbia, but could not get him to halt the construction or gather the artifacts, so he and a couple neighbors began surface-collecting points and pottery in the evenings. He posted his finds on an archaeology listserv, only to earn a scolding from the local historic preservation office. "Look," he told us, "I'm happy to let the professionals take over, but if they aren't going to do their jobs, I will step in." Dupin began noticing how little actually got surveyed and mitigated in the Palisades before developers broke ground. So he decided to intervene on his own, collecting and cataloging artifacts for public display. He bought some display cases, fixed up his clubhouse as a museum, put together a website, and stepped into the cavernous gap left by the local professionals. He also started to document local violations of historic preservation laws, to create a record of the local history that had been found—as well as the history that had been erased.

He was driven by a connection to this landscape, the people who once inhabited it, and the next generation who would inherit it. "The river below is full of fish," Dupin said. "You can see why the Native Americans loved it. I take my three boys exploring in the caves in the bluffs, and we've found petroglyphs [rock carvings] and arrowheads."

Coward told him about her work in the Southwest, and they found common ground in their love of the Native American past. Both were frustrated by the lack of economic support for Native American cultural history. These days, Erin and Dupin agreed, funding went to colonial sites and African-American projects. The extraordinary record of Native American life that stretched back more than ten thousand years was going begging.

Later Erin admitted that, after she met Dupin, "I had to reevaluate my thinking toward amateur archaeologists." If they were as responsible as he was, she wouldn't mind seeing them train volunteers. Come to think of it, "teaching the public how to properly deal with accidental finds would be a huge help to a number of professionals." She was ready to put the man to work!

Before Dupin's sons got home from school, we headed to Erin and Lane's family home in Annandale, Virginia, where we cooked mahi-mahi and Erin talked about working on the Big Island in Hawaii. She remembered finding petroglyphs full of piko holes everywhere. Piko holes—tiny gouges in the basalt where natives once buried the stumps of their babies' umbilical cords for good luck.

Lane beamed at the daughter who could find such marvels in the world. But when Erin carried our dishes out to the kitchen, Lane leaned my way, the concerned mother harking back to the World Trade Center rubble, and whispered, "Did she tell you about finding the baby's T-shirt?"

ARCHAEOLOGY IN A
DANGEROUS WORLD
A historic alliance

❧

"**C**HAMPIONS, TAKE your seats!" I heard the bark from a hotel meeting room and was swept from the crowded corridor and into a folding seat. I had been wandering the halls at the annual meeting of the AIA, looking for a tantalizing place to land, contemplating the sign posted outside this room: "Cultural Heritage Preservation in a Dangerous World." I liked the sound of that dangerous world. Certainly it was a difficult world I entered, one where archaeology met the military and acronyms spawned more acronyms.* This was a meeting of CHAMP, short for Cultural Heritage by AIA/Military Panel,† a complicated name but useful, if only

---

* One of these acronyms is IMCuRWG, for International Military Cultural Resources Working Group; another, CCHAG, is an acronym for COCOM Cultural Heritage Action Group, in which COCOM is an acronym for COmbatant COMmand.

†CHAMP removed its embedded acronym in 2014 and became the Cultural Heritage by Archaeology and Military Panel. The parallel group for the Society for American Archaeology, which features some overlap in participants, is called MARS, for Military Archaeological Resources Stewardship.

so about fifty of us could be called to order with the words, "Champions, let's start!"

Who were these people? I looked around and noticed how many men wore suits and ties and sat coiled and alert: the military was here in force—the Army, Navy, Air Force, even Central Command,* not to mention multiple members of the National Guard and a man who identified himself as the Special Assistant to the U.S. Army Judge Advocate General for Law of War Matters—now there was someone I hadn't expected to see at an archaeology conference. Polite, with a steely, attentive edge, the military people introduced themselves, along with several dozen archaeology graduate students and professors from multiple countries, a 3-D digital archivist, the former president of the Archaeological Institute of America, and me.

What was happening here? The archaeologists were collaborating with the military to protect the world's cultural heritage from tanks, bombs, guns, boots, and sticky fingers. With the blessing of high command, archaeologists had begun to arm U.S. soldiers with enough cultural information to conduct missions, and engage in combat without destroying the world's archaeological treasures.

Soldiers and archaeologists had worked together before. The Monuments Men and Women of World War II famously and cinematically helped reclaim the artistic heritage of Europe after it was plundered by the Nazis. But the collaboration stopped there. Then, in 2003, the National Museum of Iraq was looted, an event that tarnished the military and traumatized the archaeological profession. American troops had stood by while it happened, we were told in news reports; some accounts had the troops firing on the museum and opening the doors

---

* The Marines cared, too; Marine Colonel Matthew Bogdanos, author of *Thieves of Baghdad*, about the hunt for antiquities after the attack on the National Museum of Iraq, was part of the group, but couldn't attend this meeting.

to looters.* Defense Secretary Donald H. Rumsfeld compounded the damage, dismissing the plunder with the memorable observation, "Stuff happens."

The shock waves from this event and its aftermath galvanized Congress to finally sign the 1954 treaty, The Hague Convention for the Protection of Cultural Property in the Event of Armed Conflict (called simply The Hague Convention). It also propelled some alarmed archaeologists and military personnel to discuss joining forces again. Though it's hard to imagine two more cautious, even paranoid, professions, their members shared a fervent desire to minimize damage to the institutions and artifacts that preserve cultural identity. The people behind CHAMP, I learned, had been working for the better part of a decade to create trust between the two groups and advance their mutual interests. Some of their contacts had never been to an archaeology conference.

After being told of the reasons CHAMP had been formed, we split up into working groups. I gravitated toward the take-charge woman in a leopard-print wrap dress and black boots who was organizing those interested in cultural heritage information. Corine (Cori) Wegener, a retired U.S. Army Reserve major and museum curator, had served as the Civil Affairs officer assigned to the National Museum of Iraq after its looting. She was the founder of the U.S. Committee of the Blue Shield†—not the insurance company, but the American branch of an international nonprofit organization dedicated to the

---

*Bogdanos, who led the Special Forces investigation into the looting, does a fine job of re-creating those days, and dismantling the early press reports, in *Thieves of Baghdad.* The museum was on the no-strike list, but he points out that in being used as a machine-gun position by the Iraqi Republican Guard, it lost its protected status; and in fact he claims General Tommy Franks used admirable restraint in not demolishing the museum after it became cover for gunfire.

†Blue Shield's symbol, a blue triangle atop a blue diamond, is one devised after The Hague Convention, and is used to identify important cultural heritage sites throughout the world.

wartime protection of cultural property worldwide, the cultural equivalent of the Red Cross. Now in her forties, she presided over the group gathered at this table with the mission to place crucial archaeological information into the hands of military strategists. Ah, information, as in intelligence! I settled into a chair in the outer row, a satellite, an eavesdropper, drawn by nothing more than the thought of archaeologists throwing their bodies on the treasures of past civilizations.

Wegener reported to us on the Blue Shield's response to the Libyan conflict in 2011. After civil war broke out there, and the UN Security Council approved a no-fly zone over the country, a colleague at U.S. Blue Shield called her and said, "What are you doing? We should be doing something." Wegener in turn called on Susan Kane, an archaeologist with experience in Libya, and the two began reaching out to their contacts. Their mission: to compile a no-strike list of Libya's important archaeological sites, museums, and libraries, and to get the list into the hands of those who, ultimately, designated the bombing targets. "After The Hague Convention, each country is supposed to be doing this for itself," Wegener said, working up its own list of its archaeological treasures, but few are able to. "Some sites are obvious," she noted, like the five World Heritage sites in Libya, "but then it gets to be like asking people to pick their favorite kid. And I need it in twenty-four hours. You're going to have to make some choices. This is why you want to do it ahead of time." Kane drew in British archaeologists who had also worked in Iraq and who were collaborating with their Ministry of Defence. Once the lists were consolidated and coordinates checked, the archaeologists grouped and ranked the cultural sites.

Putting together this list was one thing. Where to send it turned out to be the tricky part. "The military is not one monolithic organization," Wegener said pointedly. She sent it to her high-ranking military contacts—including two of the men now sitting next to her here at this table—and to several of her Blue

Shield colleagues in other countries, who shared it with their military liaisons.

One of Wegener's contacts was Richard Jackson, the man who bore a title too long for a business card, Special Assistant to the U.S. Army Judge . . . etc. He pointed out that no-strike lists of cultural sites were already part of military planning. "All the branches do the same thing in terms of intelligence preparation for the battlefield. We define the battlefield, including the cultural landscape. We have a joint targeting doctrine: public infrastructure is essential for civilians," so hospitals and schools are on their no-strike list. Churches, mosques, and protected cultural property sites are also off-limits. "There has to be a very high level of approval to override that list," Jackson added. "A general is only authorized to attack such places if [his troops are] receiving fire [from them]." When these no-strike lists work, they work well. "Garbage in, garbage out—if good information gets to [the targeters], we can have good results." He mentioned a sensitive archaeological landmark, the Ziggurat of Ur, which was located on the edge of an Iraqi airfield in the first Gulf War. The ziggurat (a pyramid-shaped temple), which dated back twenty-three centuries, had been on their no-strike list, even though "Saddam purposely parked aircraft there. We didn't target it because of collateral damage."

The archaeologists' no-strike list for Libya was, predictably, more extensive than the military's, and included sensitive information from professionals who had worked at sites around that country. They submitted it about twenty-four hours before the first NATO bombing runs in Libya. Did they get the list into the right hands? Had it made a difference? An International Blue Shield contingent that had toured the strike zone afterwards reported no significant damage to cultural sites, and none from bombing. So far, so good: NATO reports mentioned that the archaeologists' no-strike list might serve as a model for future operations. At this point, Wegener paused to look around the table. One of the suits, Timothy Melancon, of the U.S. Defense Intelligence Agency, cleared his throat and said, "It worked in Libya. We factored [the list] into the bombing."

There was a crackle in the air, the unmistakable sense that here, at last, was what the archaeologists had been working for since the Iraq debacle in 2003. They had succeeded in bringing the military to the table. They had rerouted those bombs. Melancon leaned forward. "Sites were not damaged," he confirmed, "and not by accident." He acknowledged that he and his team were the last ones to relay target information to the combatants taking aim. "I am the point of contact, yes. My shop—we focus primarily on stuff we don't want to blow up, and we continually feed that database worldwide," he said.

This was the first time that Melancon and Wegener had met. Like the others here, they were too professional to exchange high-fives and huzzahs, but there were knowing smiles around the table.

"We've been searching for you and we found you," Wegener said to Melancon.

"Is the journalist here?" asked one of the uniformed men, a cultural resources contact for the U.S. Air Force. What business I was in might be a matter of debate, but I squared my shoulders and raised my hand. Now what? But the man wanted only to make sure that I got it right. "You understand what's happening here?" These people had taken me behind the scenes of a world conflict, recounting and reliving their roles as first-time collaborators. They had made a difference. The man in the suit gave me a nod: witnesses were welcome. Before the archaeologists had gotten involved, the Department of Defense had perhaps thirty cultural sites to protect in their database for Libya. Afterwards, the list contained 242. And after seven months of bombing, the sites survived.

Other archaeologists had tried to share their knowledge to keep the bombs from destroying cultural heritage. I learned later that during the first Gulf War, a professor at the Oriental Institute in

LIVES IN RUINS

Chicago had been sending information about archaeological avoidance targets to the Department of Defense,* but his warnings had not reached the right agencies and went unheeded. The challenges involved in penetrating the military bureaucracy are formidable.

But persuading archaeologists to cooperate in compiling a massively sensitive database is no small feat, either. Some archaeologists don't want to engage with the military for ethical reasons; even if their efforts might help contain the destruction, they don't want to help those who make war. Or they have practical objections to such a collaboration. One of the biggest problems archaeologists face in the field is looting and plundering; in war zones, looting often helps finance the conflict. And in a leaky world, did archaeologists want the sites they knew about on some government list? It was like flagging your antiques for the movers, so they would take extra care of the valuable stuff. In the right hands, they did take care. In the wrong hands—well, what do you know, here was an excellent list of things to loot and plunder, conveniently ranked, most valuable first.

The man from the Air Force acknowledged the sensitivity of this data to those of us around the table. "We're cautious, very conservative right now, and pretty confident that we can control it," he said. Wegener thought the success in Libya would help their efforts. "We do have good networks, but it will take time for trust to build," she said.

The idea of a shared cultural responsibility that persists through war and conflict is growing. "How can you worry about culture when there are all these people dead or homeless and suffering?" Wegener was often asked that question, she told Smithsonian.com, and when somebody asked "for the millionth time," she realized, "it's always an American who asks that. I have never been asked that by somebody on the ground when I'm working."

---

*McGuire Gibson is the name of that professor at the University of Chicago's Oriental Institute.

· 196 ·

MY SMALL GROUP spent less than a minute and a half relishing its success, then turned to the task of consolidating gains and moving on to the next challenge. Tim Melancon said, "This train's already moving. Any country in the news, we want the data." The group agreed that Mali is a likely hot spot. Wegener said, "Let's draft policy suggestions. We have a good relationship with Tim now, but what if a new person comes in and goes, 'What culture?'" She wanted the channel that had been opened up to work when future conflicts arise. "We want it to say, *Here, this is our responsibility.*"

Meanwhile, the others in the room were coordinating with their international counterparts and developing educational tools for soldiers. As one archaeologist said, "We don't want to say as [the soldiers] get on the plane, 'By the way, remember not to destroy cultural heritage!'" Some of these tools were ingenious, including sets of playing cards for Iraq, Egypt, and Afghanistan—regular fifty-two-card decks, but with images and information about archaeological practices, famous cultural sites, and notable artifacts; the reverse sides could be pieced together to form a map of the most iconic site for each country. Who dreamed this stuff up? I was about to find out.

I had stumbled into the beating heart of a professional conspiracy—to save the world's archaeological heritage in the most dangerous places on earth. I had witnessed a moment in history: archaeologists had offered their expertise to the military and, after years of patient groundwork, the offer had been accepted and acknowledged. I talked to the young woman who works with a nonprofit that makes massively detailed 3-D maps of at-risk heritage sites for the site stewards.* I collected the promise of a deck of playing cards. I also collected a fistful of business cards. The only

---

*Jaime Pursuit is the partnership and development manager of CyArk, the non-profit organization working on capturing at-risk cultural heritage sites with laser scans. See their fascinating website at www.cyark.org.

person who hesitated before handing hers over was Cori Wegener, and her card, I couldn't help noticing, featured a photo of a suit of Italian armor, faceless and impenetrable. The first American Monuments, Fine Arts, and Archives Officer since World War II had had some unpleasant experiences with the press, and still chafed at the overwrought coverage of the looting of the museum in Baghdad ("170,000 items reported stolen"—the number was more like 15,000; "the Americans opened the doors to looters"—they did no such thing; "looters whacked the heads off statues"—with one exception, those statues were headless when excavated; and so on). She used to send angry e-mails to the *New York Times* to correct their coverage; even ten years later, the newspaper of record still referred to the National Museum of Iraq, which "looters nearly emptied." (The galleries were mostly empty because staff had hidden the portable artifacts.) Nor did Wegener appreciate "reporters climbing on displays in the Assyrian gallery to get a better vantage point."

She headed down the hotel corridor, frowning behind her rectangular black glasses, worrying about the cultural heritage of Haiti and Egypt and Syria. No sooner did she leave than the creator of the cultural heritage playing cards and dozens of other creative tools for training soldiers and archaeologists, Laurie Rush, fell into step with me as we headed out the door. She was in charge of cultural protection at a military fort with a mighty archaeology program that I might like to see.

AVOIDANCE TARGETS

Mission: respect

❧

B Y THE time I met Laurie Rush, she had been working to build respect for cultural heritage among U.S. troops for almost eight years. The news report that spurred her into action came over her car radio in the summer of 2004. "I was driving to work, to Fort Drum, the morning the story of the destruction in Babylon hit," Rush said, referring to the NPR story, "U.S. Base Damages Ancient Babylonian Temple." A civilian archaeologist who worked for the Army, Rush listened with dismay: after the National Museum of Iraq fiasco a year earlier, U.S. troops had been assigned to protect Babylon, yet now they had situated their base on top of the ruins and bulldozed ancient temples into helicopter landing pads, causing "vastly more damage than we had suspected," archaeologist John Russell, the Coalition's cultural advisor in Iraq, told listeners. NPR's Renee Montagne asked Russell if the damage was reversible. In a controlled voice, Russell explained, "You can't repair damage to an archaeological site. Every time you put a shovel into an archaeological site, you're destroying some evidence from the past. . . . All the damage is permanent." He suspected the same or similar destruction was occurring elsewhere in Iraq—for instance, at the air base in Kirkuk, where an archaeological site had been plundered to fill sandbags.

Rush, the cultural resources manager for Fort Drum, in northern New York State, near the Canadian border, manages the archaeology and historic properties on its 169 square miles. She is employed by the Department of Defense, which she has described as "one of the most robust and proactive cultural resources programs in the world." She noted that "archaeologists working for all branches of the services have inventoried hundreds of thousands of acres, have discovered tens of thousands of archaeological sites, have set aside thousands of sites for preservation, and have made many significant archaeological discoveries on the North American continent and Hawaii." Protecting cultural resources is "a fundamental part of the Department of Defense's primary mission," Fort Drum's website declares, and the DoD spends more on cultural heritage protection than almost any other entity in the United States. It budgets billions for environmental management, which includes cultural preservation. This is a matter of pride to the archaeologists who work for the military and their fellow federal archaeologists at branches like the National Park Service—and a shock to almost everyone else, including me. The Department of Defense has archaeologists?

The DoD's record in the United States was of particular pride to Laurie Rush and her team, who had brought a parade of honors and commendations to Fort Drum. "When I began working for the DoD, I expected that I might be pressured to rubber-stamp project proposals without regard for archaeological integrity," Rush has written. "My experience has been in direct opposition to my expectations." In fact, she enjoyed something alien to most archaeologists—enthusiastic support. "My bosses say, 'This is so exciting,' or 'My wife is Native American,' or 'We watch the Discovery Channel at home,'" Rush said. When she asked her Fort Drum superiors to set aside part of an artillery range because it held a sacred Native American site, they agreed. She is in an extraordinary position for an archaeologist: she doesn't have to beg.

So she and her colleagues were particularly embarrassed. "It is difficult to imagine a group of professionals who could have been more dismayed than U.S. military archaeologists when the news of the damage done to Babylon hit the global media."

The soldiers didn't mean to mess up the 4,000- and 5,000-year-old ruins—that was the part that most bothered Laurie Rush. The archaeologist who reviewed the damage had noted that a "minimal level of background about the significance of mounds in Iraq" would have made the difference. A *minimal* level. The simplest lessons about history and preservation could have saved the ruins of Babylon from permanent harm. Convinced that "a better educated force would not have made those kinds of mistakes," Rush decided to take on the problem: "We have got to teach our deploying soldiers. I said to myself, I have the skills needed to fix this."

"Traditionally, in the U.S., the most important archaeological properties on military lands are put off-limits to military personnel as a preservation measure," Rush wrote. Perhaps the agency had been too protective. "If you manage cultural property at home by not letting soldiers anywhere near it, you can't expect them to spontaneously know how to occupy a cultural site overseas."

The morning that the U.S. military got beaten up by the press over Babylon, Rush pulled into the back gate of Fort Drum Army Garrison and headed for the computer in the Cultural Resources Building. She knew relatively little about Mesopotamia, so before she pulled her staff together and approached the command about providing direct cultural training to soldiers, she Googled the archaeology of Iraq. "I found a website and was reading about ziggurats; then I got to the bottom of the page and it said, 'The platforms are excellent for landing UFOs.' Noooo! It was a site sponsored by some crystal skull place!" Rush laughed, a genuine laugh that sounded like it came from a much bigger person. She laughed surprisingly often for someone who worked on a cold, bleak military post on complex and intractable problems.

Part of Rush's appeal was her physical presence: small and

sturdy, relaxed, no makeup, a wispy, blunt-cut blond pageboy, and a grin that split her face into two joyful parts. Her white shirts were crisp, chinos relaxed, shoes comfortable. "I'm a clunky-shoe person," Rush said. When she sent me some admiring profiles of herself that had appeared in Fort Drum's on-base newspaper, the *Mountaineer*, focusing on her accomplishments and awards—most recently the Rome Prize, a fellowship usually given to academics—she joked about being an egotist, but her self-deprecating attitude and frequent praise for her colleagues contradicted that. She insisted that the trust that the command at Fort Drum had placed in her was the key to everything. "I have the two best bosses in the world," she said. When Rush told one, a retired colonel, about her idea to give cultural training to deploying soldiers, "He looked at me and said, 'If I'd had that kind of information, that would have made all the difference in the Balkans.'" He told everybody else on the base, "'Anything she needs trumps anything we need for Fort Drum.'"

Outside Fort Drum, archaeologists, preservationists, and military people were coming to the same conclusion Rush had—that knowledge of archaeology was of vital importance to the military— but they tended to be isolated, not organized. The bewildering bureaucracy of the military prevented any number of archaeologists from communicating their expertise and alarm. Archaeology itself is not easy to navigate; it is a broad and complicated profession, and the archaeologists of the Old World (who study Iraq and the ancient civilizations of the East and Middle East, including classical Rome and Greece) tend to go to different conferences and read different journals from the archaeologists who work in the New World of the Americas. But Rush is a proud product of American archaeology, which locates itself firmly in departments of anthropology, the study of humans (unlike in Europe, for instance, where archaeology is a branch of history). She is trained to bridge cultural gaps.

First Rush applied for, and won, a DoD Legacy grant to develop that deck of playing cards that would teach deployed soldiers the basic archaeology of Iraq and Afghanistan. Then she began adapting archaeological sites for cultural-heritage training at Fort Drum. By the time I visited her base, she was wired to a deep and impressive range of colleagues from archaeology and the military; and everywhere I went to read more about this issue, there was the name Laurie Rush.

THE HEADQUARTERS OF the Cultural Resources department at Fort Drum is upstairs in an Army-issue-beige building, in a spacious storeroom divided by a row of yellow metal shelves and lined with gunmetal-gray file cabinets and map drawers. Rush opened a cabinet and pulled out stone projectile points and beads, the focus of her work for years. She pointed to multiple jagged pieces of stone arranged in a circle on a workbench. "This is what an Indian grinding stone looks like after being run over by a truck," she said. Things got messy sometimes with tanks rolling around. The last eight years of emergency international activism had taken Rush to Iraq, Afghanistan, Jordan, Turkey, Austria, the United Kingdom, and Italy, but home base was this storeroom, the offices for her and two other full-time archaeologists, plus the workroom downstairs where artifacts were sorted and cleaned. As head of Cultural Resources, Rush was responsible for the residue of the culture of all the people who have lived on Fort Drum's land, from Native Americans of ten thousand years ago, to twentieth-century farmers and pig-iron workers, to the current population of soldiers. Since she started working on the base full-time in 1998, her team has made discoveries that included a sacred Native American site and the remnant shoreline of a prehistoric glacial lake. When you consider that finding sites was not even their mission—the team's purpose was to find places for the military to safely build on, not go looking for archaeology—these discoveries were impressive.

"In 1998, nobody was finding anything around Fort Drum," said Rush, "though we did find old tools next to ravines—were people trapping animals there?" She had an idea about glacial lakes and shorelines, and called up the map experts on base. She asked the global information system (GIS) people if they could show her the ravines. "There was this magic moment when I was looking at the map with the hills shaded, as if the sun was setting. You could see the sites, bing, bing, bing. That's where the tributaries had been flowing into the lake." Finding the shoreline of prehistoric Glacial Lake Iroquois added a previously unknown layer to the history of the area. "Fort Drum—building boats for ten thousand years!" Rush said.

The team also made discoveries in its own storage cabinets. Rush said a curator had been going through a collection of objects found at a nineteenth-century farmstead when he pulled out a French gun flint. "This doesn't belong in a farmstead!" he told Rush. "And sure enough," she elaborated, "we started finding trade beads and Indian assemblage and seventeenth-century cedar posts and all this material that made us realize we were looking at a very different site." The cultural resource management company that had done much of the early archaeology at the garrison had labeled all the objects from this particular site *19th Century Farmstead*. "In fact," said Rush, "a major component of it turned out to be a seventeenth-century fur-trading and Jesuit site, which for many people is much more interesting. And actually very important—it turns out to be the only one on the New York side of the border."[*]

Rush was reflexively generous about the CRM company's error. "So much depends on the personal interests of the principal investigators. The one on this team was interested in when cement barn floors first appeared in this part of the country." Cement barn floors! She laughed, as if to say, *I know, archaeologists are weird*, and then she told me about a mistake she and her group had made. She

---

[*]Rush's team also found an eight-thousand-year-old hearth beneath the seventeenth-century trading post.

said that discovering evidence of boat-building along the remnant shoreline had attracted a prominent archaeologist interested in ancient maritime routes. "We opened up our debitage bag to him—all the bits of stone that we had no idea about but had saved—and he started finding channel flakes in it. Those are really important! This archaeologist could have been so mean. He could have looked at me and said, 'You stupid, stupid woman, you're not qualified to be working here. Anyone who can't identify a channel flake . . . !'"

We were both laughing, though I had to admit I had no idea what a channel flake was. Rush gave me an indulgent look and explained; it was a better story if you understood the punch line. Fluted paleo-Indian points have a channel or groove in the middle, and to form that groove, someone had to chip out a piece of stone. "*That* piece is the channel flake," she said. "The point is, this man found really important things in my debitage bag, but instead of making us miserable and demoralized, he was like, 'This is so exciting!' Then he patiently said, 'Would you like me to show you the characteristics?' So it became a fabulous learning experience. We have a motto here, that our most exciting days are the days we discover we were wrong. That means we discovered something new, and we're learning."

LAURIE RUSH HAD a preppy upbringing in Connecticut but decided to head to the Midwest for college, because she had heard the people there were nice. Seriously, that was her priority. She met her husband, Jack, at Indiana University in Bloomington, and after he got his medical degree from the University of Chicago and she earned her master's and doctorate at Northwestern, the couple moved to the Thousand Islands region of Lake Ontario, the North Country, where he could work off a public-health scholarship by practicing in an underserved area. They began their family, which soon totaled five children, and Laurie started to find archaeological work from local engineering firms and the Antique Boat Museum. The Doctors Rush thought *Northern Exposure,* that early-nineties television series about a new doctor taking a post in Alaska, had been created for their amusement; they referred to it as "The Jack and Laurie Show" and "we swore they were bugging our house to get the dialogue." The wind howled across Lake Ontario and through the nearby Adirondack Mountains every winter; snow started falling in October. When I visited Rush at Fort Drum, it was mid-May, but a chilly rain blew sideways during our tour of the base; I could have used a pair of warm gloves. "Fort Richardson in Alaska might be a little colder than us, but we get more snow," Rush said.

The extreme weather was one reason Fort Drum became the eventual home of the Tenth Mountain Division, the U.S. Army's first ski-trained soldiers, who fought in World War II and wrested key posts in the mountains of Italy from the Nazis. They "were the guys who started the ski industry in this country," Rush said. The climate challenges both humans and hardware. After technological disasters caused by torrential thunderstorms, the division's field computers were reconfigured as "ruggedized" iPads that transmit electronic notes directly to the lab. It isn't just precipitation that was a problem; in summer, everything gets sticky with bug spray. "It gets buggy here?" I asked. Rush's rumbling laugh was my answer.

The physical discomforts of fieldwork had discouraged Rush early on from a career in archaeology. Unlike the other professionals I met, she had imagined an alternate career for herself; her doctorate, in fact, is in medical anthropology. But there were no jobs in the Thousand Islands in public health, while CRM firms in this area were begging for trained practitioners in archaeology. She adjusted her expectations and, ever practical, returned to the field.

RUSH, TWO MEMBERS of her archaeology team, and I all put on bright-orange reflector vests and headed out in the rain to see the home of the Tenth Mountain Division. The base was a network of streets with names like Operation Iraqi Freedom and Enduring Freedom, set against a beige-and-brown landscape striped with evergreen and punctuated by functional prefab offices. We drove past giant open stalls fitted with water hoses and liquid soap—car washes for tanks.

Our first stop was the interactive map room in the Range Division, where a security team kept a sharp eye on the troops training in the field. Live ordnance was a hazard; we were wearing orange hunters' vests so we wouldn't get shot, but all those lit-up firing ranges on the map made me skittish. It didn't help to hear that one of Rush's colleagues, who supervises much of the fieldwork on the base, has the bomb squad on speed dial. A display case outside the map room showed some of the weaponry found on Fort Drum—bombs, grenades and rockets from the past century, sleek, barbed, and menacing, the modern version of a museum case full of points, spears, and arrowheads.

There were over six hundred historic sites and more than two hundred prehistoric sites at the fort, but Rush wanted to show me several replicas of Afghan villages, built for training purposes and made of rubber and recycled construction material. A low wall enclosed an area of "avoidance targets"—a mock mosque and a pretend Muslim cemetery—so that soldiers and aerial gunners could train for combat while trying to minimize damage to sacred sites. Another site featured low, flat-roofed shelters, several occupied by bearded dummies in turbans, and a painted car made of sculpted spray polyurethane foam. The cost of each site, Rush said, was less than $2,500, the maximum amount one could then charge on a government credit card. She was especially pleased with the mosaic tower, a copy of one from Uruk, in Iraq, that was made of sonotubes (cheap but durable paper tubes, usually used to pour concrete in), scavenged from the base's construction supply.

Fort Drum's fake sites looked almost cartoonish, but they represented the first efforts by the military to give soldiers explicit practice at being both effective warriors and sensitive occupiers. "We've been short on practical solutions. We're like, 'Guys, be more careful.' But we never tell them how," Rush said. Fort Drum's sites are now being duplicated on other bases, and Rush and her team are in demand to guide other military archaeologists in the construction of replica archaeological features.

Archaeology is full of creative improvisation, but that usually means pulling trucks out of ditches or figuring out how to excavate in hard-to-reach places, not sculpting replica sites. But the top priority of everyone at Fort Drum was to support the troops, so Rush, who has a reputation as a pragmatist willing to work with the command, is resourceful almost by definition, a mission-oriented archaeologist. She recalled an early presentation on cultural sensitivity she made to Iraq-bound soldiers, and the soldier who said, " 'What do we do when they shoot at us from cemeteries? Is it all right to shoot back?' I said, 'Hell, yes!' and another soldier said, 'You're my kind of archaeologist.' "*

We drove past the historic village of Leraysville, with its old mansion and servants' quarters, now used for visiting officers and military celebrations, and the rural outpost of Sterlingville, both acquired by eminent domain around World War II. The residents were resettled, and in the 1990s the empty villages were placed on the National Register of Historic Places. Cultural Resources guided the repairs to the LeRay Mansion (even advising volunteers how to decorate it authentically during the holidays) and took over management of the ruins and crumbling foundations of Sterlingville's old homes for preservation purposes. Rush and her team gave a tour

---

*The Afghanistan heritage playing cards are each stamped with the motto "ROE First!" (ROE stands for "rules of engagement," which state, in short, that a soldier has the right to defend him- or herself.)

to the former residents of Sterlingville and their descendants, and were surprised to hear complaints that the land was off-limits to soldiers. What, these people wondered, had been the point of sacrificing their homes if the soldiers couldn't train here?

The feedback gave the Cultural Resources crew the idea to adapt the real archaeological site at Sterlingville to help prepare troops who were soon to deploy. They got the top layers of vegetation cleared, then began stabilizing the site so it could be used without damage—"hardening the site," Rush called it. They reinforced crumbling walls with sandbags and covered open foundations with tough but permeable geotextiles or recycled tank treads, then spread clean sand and dirt on the coverings. The result was a site strengthened at its vulnerable points, but still an obvious and authentic ruin where soldiers could practice combat scenarios that avoided damage to its archaeological features. With the blessing of Sterlingville's former residents and the gratitude of the commanding officers, the first archaeological site in the United States was opened to train soldiers headed overseas, two years after the Babylonian temple was damaged in Iraq.

And Rush continues to reach young soldiers and to arm them with respect: one of her former Army commanders, now in cadet command, has incorporated her cultural heritage lessons into the curriculum, where they will become a part of every cadet's ROTC training.

BECAUSE RUSH DROVE us the long way around the base, we had to reenter at one of the gates. She passed her team's Army IDs and my driver's license to the soldier in the booth. "One alien?" he said, looking at me. Certainly I had started the day as an alien, trying to find my way through this big base and all those roads with Freedom in their name, and following directions like "turn right at the bomb" (there was a big painted bomb at the corner on Rush's team's road). But hadn't I made progress since then? Hadn't Rush invited me to come back in the buggy summertime and toil with the shovelbums? "Yes," I admitted to the guard. "One alien."

We parked in a sandy area at the edge of pine-and-birch woods and walked through a strand of pine trees to a clearing. The air was saturated, and mist hung over the site, making it feel hushed and separate from the rest of the base—like a place where people gathered to chant and sing, not fire weapons. One of Rush's team wandered off to track native flora, such as the British soldier lichen, which look like little red hats. Another inspected the ground like a diligent archaeologist, and found a tiny porcelain doll's head with a seam across its skull.

Laurie Rush stood looking over the sandy site. She had sent a survey team here years ago, knowing it was a sensitive area; it bore recent evidence of tanks rolling through, but was also scattered with stone tool debris thousands of years old. Rush remembered getting the call from one of the surveyors: " 'I think I'm standing in a stone circle.' " An arrangement of standing stones could mean a sacred gathering place.

The process of archaeological identification can take a long time; this site took Rush's team years to scope out. "Over four hundred hearths on the site, but—no pottery! That was a big clue that something special happened here. This was not a place where the work of daily life happened." Eventually, Cultural Resources radiocarbon-dated most of the hearths in the area back to A.D. 375, and consulted one of the pioneers of the field of archaeoastronomy [the cultural history of astronomy]. The field had more than five hundred stones bigger than ten inches, and some were arranged in pairs—"that's an important part of the site. Some of them line up with the Dog Star [Sirius] at the midpoint of the Iroquois lunar calendar," Rush said.

Once the archaeologists figured out that the stones were aligned with the stars, they invited local Mohawk families to a gathering. The children danced that night, then they all camped out and assembled before dawn the next morning. Rush recalled her own silent prayer that day: Please, God, let the sun rise here. And it did: gloriously, the sun shone at dawn "for a whole ten minutes," she said, "before a cloud bank moved in." The archaeoastronomer, Anthony Aveni, told Rush that other boulders probably lined up on the equinox, one of the two days each year when the sun is directly above the equator. Was Aveni right? "Yes," Rush confirmed. "Me and a porcupine were there for that sunrise."

The site was made accessible to the Native Americans anytime but is off-limits to Army soldiers and employees, though the Cultural Resources crew and their guests are an exception. "Once the Army decides to protect it, our work is done," Rush said. "This frustrates the crew. Archaeologists like to dig, not leave things *in situ*. To them, they're just getting started." But for the Iroquois nations, including the Mohawks, "that suited them." Rush loved to talk about the Native American visits to the base, the time one of the elders took a stick and drew a constellation in the sand, then poked holes for stars to represent the Pleiades and "smoothed all the marks—very theatrical," or the poetic moment when the spiritual leader of the New York tribes, the Iroquoian Tadodaho, thanked " 'the stars whose names we have forgotten.' "

Rush viewed her connection with all of the Iroquois, who call themselves Haudenosaunee, as one of the outstanding benefits of her job. "We've learned so much about them since working for the Army." Whether she was making presentations with her playing cards, or lobbying to include an archaeologist in the planning of international war exercises, she promoted the rewards of consulting other cultures about archaeology, depicting the Army's relationship with the Iroquois as a model. Rush referred to Native Americans not as stakeholders or descendant communities, but as the Army's "host nation"; when the Haudenosaunee chiefs, clan mothers, and Tadodaho visited the base, they were received with ceremony, as heads of state.

Heads of state? It hasn't always been like this. After a costly lawsuit between the Makua Military Reservation in Oahu and native Hawaiians, the Department of Defense decided to try a new tack late in the nineties. The DoD consulted tribal leaders throughout the country, asking them how they expected to be treated. The results were made policy in October 1998, formalizing the new government-to-government model—essentially a resolution by the Department of Defense to consult Native Americans in all matters that related to them and a pledge to treat them respectfully.

Rush has been honored by the Secretary of the Army and the Secretary of Defense multiple times and by her fellow professional archaeologists, for her innovative leadership, but when she was cited for her work with the Iroquois, her husband shrugged. "I don't get it," he said. "All you did was treat them with respect. And they gave you an award for that?"

"Yes," she told him. "That's the point!"

THE IRAQ AND Afghan Heritage playing cards are a triumph of geekery, handsome black decks of cards that work just fine for solitaire or poker or war, but are rich with archaeological images. The decks display an internal logic that a poet would love: each suit stands for a different aspect of culture—diamonds for artifacts, spades for digs and sites, hearts for "winning hearts and minds," and clubs for heritage preservation. Each card contains a different message, from the most basic ("Stop digging if you find ancient artifacts or archaeological features") to the revelatory ("Karez, the ancient water system tunnels in Afghanistan, look like ant hills on aerial imagery"). The decks can also be laid out as puzzles, with the backs of each card forming part of a larger picture of an archaeological icon. As artifacts themselves, the cards tell a great deal about the conscientiousness, creativity, and playfulness of the people who devised them.

Laurie Rush found her first partner in the creation of these playing cards at her high school reunion. There she renewed her teenage friendship with Roger Ulrich, now an archaeologist teaching classics at Dartmouth and an Old World expert who could link her to specialists in classical archaeology. These specialists advised Ulrich and Rush on the content on the cards; Ulrich's students fact-checked the information, did the photo research, and secured the rights to reprint the images of sites and artifacts; and the Colorado State University Center for Environmental Management of Military Lands was enlisted to design and produce the cards. Soon there were three decks, one for Iraqi and Afghan heritage, one a dedicated Afghan deck, and one for American and Egyptian troops, who participated in war maneuvers every two years.

The only complaints Rush heard from the troops about the cards and the training on replica sites was, Where were these years ago? Stories about the cards appeared in *Archaeology* magazine and in *USA Today*—positive stories about the military and cultural heritage. Rush was heartened. The cards reached the soldiers in desert tents who could deal themselves useful and interesting facts about the heritage of the area, while studying images of landmarks captioned pointedly: "This site has survived 17 [or 23 or 35] centuries. Will it and others survive you?" But the cards were equally valuable as business cards that directed those working on these issues in the compartmentalized world of archaeology and the bureaucratic maze of the military to an open and direct channel of action. Information about the Cultural Resources staff of Fort Drum and the Colorado center, where one could find a network of professionals who were dedicated to preserving heritage and minimizing military harm, was printed on every deck and accompanied every press story. "It's funny how many military people found out about the project through the mass media," Rush said. The cards had been beacons.

For all the approval she's earned from military leadership and the troops, Rush has been criticized by some archaeologists for deigning to work with them at all. At the 2008 World Archaeological Congress, in Dublin, she faced so much resistance that she needed police protection while presiding over a panel about the benefits of collaborating with the military: a post in an online chat room had proposed storming her session, so the Irish Garda accompanied Rush and her fellow speakers throughout the conference. "One of the Gardaí said, 'Ma'am, we need to review the evacuation plan with you,'" Rush recalled. "I must tell you, if you're ever worried about your speakers getting there on time, this will solve that!" Then she added, perhaps unnecessarily, "This work is not for the fainthearted."

Responding to her critics, Rush wrote an essay titled "Mars Turns to Minerva: Thoughts on Archaeology, the Military, and Collegial Discourse," a defense of the U.S. military's efforts to protect cultural heritage and a plea for reasoned and dignified dialogue—essentially, a call for everyone to please be nice and remember that there are lives at stake. Rush began working full-time at Fort Drum the year after the sudden death of her oldest child, at seventeen, and there is something extremely personal about her indefatigable efforts to help soldiers appreciate every scrap and crumb of human culture. She saw young men and women going off to war, and she wanted to help them earn and offer respect. The old complaint—why would we worry about potsherds and graves and ruins when we should be worrying about people?—was moot to her. Potsherds and graves and ruins were the stuff of people.

Rush welcomed the debate. "Even the most seasoned and analytical anthropologists can find themselves becoming rapidly acculturated when exposed to a military environment," she acknowledged, "and our colleagues can play a very important role in helping us to continually question the nature of our participation and the . . . effects that our work may have." But she couldn't condone withholding knowledge because you refused to work with those who waged war. "We had Iraqis die at checkpoints," she said, "because our soldiers were extending their hands with the palms up to indicate 'Stop.' To Iraqis, extending the hand palm up means 'Welcome.' Now, as an anthropologist, if you have knowledge that could save people, how can you not share that?"

Rush didn't want to silence archaeologists who disagreed; she didn't want to silence any constituency. She felt there should be room for everybody at the cultural table. TV reality shows featuring treasure hunters who used metal detectors, for instance, were roundly decried by archaeologists, but Rush saw the treasure hunters as potential allies in preservation. "The legislation is not going our way at all, and the archaeologists are all angry. That's our image now, angry archaeologists. I want to say, 'Wait, you have a constituency who loves these resources [the artifacts]. Can't we figure out how to channel that enthusiasm?' We are missing a tremendous opportunity here.

"We still have that potential, but I think I have colleagues who forget that to be paid to do this is such an incredible privilege. We have jobs that other people dream about. I find myself at cocktail parties with doctors gathered around me, all saying, 'Oh, I always wanted to be an archaeologist.' I do a lot of pinching myself."

It was almost invisible, what she had done to shift the conversation: she waded into a contentious and thorny professional problem, and came out the other side hopeful and eager to make friends, even with treasure hunters.

THE NIGHT I visited Fort Drum, I had dinner at a pub in Sackets Harbor with Laurie and her husband, Jack, a general practitioner with a droll sense of humor, along with their daughter Cait and her new husband. We watched the sun set over the harbor that had been the scene of several battles in the War of 1812. Our table was arrayed with different kinds of craft beer. The late rays flooded through the picture window and refracted through our drinks, turning each a different jewel-tone—amber, ruby, gold. Laurie told me about when she used to be afraid to speak in public or in front of generals. She took up ice dancing and entered competitions to get over her performance anxiety. Once you've literally fallen on your face in front of a crowd, she said, you could talk to anyone.

Cait teased her mother about another experience she'd had with a journalist. A student had asked for an interview, so Laurie invited her to the fort. Cait quoted the resulting story: " 'You would never in a million years notice this woman. She is plain and short.' " Laurie led the laughter.

Early in my research, an elder of the profession suggested that I follow at least one archaeologist who worked for the government. I said I was interviewing an archaeologist for the Army, Laurie Rush. The man lit up. "I *like* her!" he said, then added, hastily, "not that that should matter."

But in this case, being likable did matter. Her friendly and engaging manner helped bridge cultures, not to mention compartmentalized professions. And consider: niceness, as wielded by Rush, turned out to be quite the formidable weapon.

HERITAGE

HERITAGE

BUCKETS OF ARCHAEOLOGISTS

If archaeologists tried to save the world

❦

OVERHEARD AT 5:30 a.m. in the clean and charming railway station of Poroy, Peru, a shiny Disneyfied terminal dropped into the slummy, narrow-roaded, dog-clotted outskirts of Cusco: "I heard your paper." "Yes, I heard yours!" (Many languages, many accents—simple English or Spanish would have to suffice at this hour.) The gathering of the UNESCO International Committee on Archaeological Heritage Management has concluded, four days of archaeologists from six continents talking about how to manage World Heritage sites, forty years after the ambitious program began—how are we doing? Now it's time for their treat: the field trip to the king of archaeology sites, Machu Picchu. Few of the participants have four days to hike in on the Inca Trail, so they opted instead for the Vistadome train and its three-and-a-half-hour ride to Aguas Calientes at the base of Machu Picchu—neither as luxurious as the first-class Hiram Bingham rail nor as funky as the backpackers' train. This is my dream, to ride a train stuffed with archaeologists and talk archaeology and cultural identity and repatriated artifacts and other burning topics while the scenery shifts dramatically and a real-life fantasy kingdom comes into view.

So much archaeological knowledge and experience is gathered in this pleasant terminal, embodied by the cheerful Elizabeth; the grandfatherly Willem; John, the Brit; Veysel, the handsome young doctoral student with two silver earrings who, while the rest of us hiked or taxied to the ruins above Cusco last night, rode a horse hired for the occasion; Monique, tiny and pretty with a severe haircut who made an impassioned presentation about the Palestinian heritage sites that no one can visit; Fritz, the German; Neale and the other sardonic Australians; Sato and his colleague Yo. Yo Negishi particularly enjoys the idea of a train full of archaeologists. It is the start of an amusing article, he thinks. Or an Agatha Christie mystery? There are apparently no murderers in our midst. In fact, we could not be a milder bunch. Professor Dr. Willem J. H. Willems, for instance, the copresident of the International Committee on Archaeological Heritage Management (ICAHM),* is sporting enough, even at this ungodly hour, to spar with Negishi as he tries to come up with a good collective noun for this group. A wheelbarrow? A dump? A field of archaeologists? Here, on the sanitized floor of the train station, we put it to a vote: *a bucket of archaeologists* sounds just right. But before the bucket of archaeologists can be transported, it is spilled and scattered: the seats on the Vistadome to Machu Picchu have been assigned already, based on when each of us booked our tickets. The archaeologists are sprinkled through the multiple cars of the train, mixed in with tourists, and indistinguishable. Only one is seated in my car: Ashton Sinamai, who works at a World Heritage site in Zimbabwe that has been all but abandoned by the local population, but I am separated from him by a family of chatty Canadians. Sinamai closes his eyes; I open my book.

While the train's stewards fuss over us like flight attendants, serving miniature food with unnecessary flourish, and as "El Cóndor Pasa" and other trembling pan pipe music plays over the train's speakers, the scenery shifts from green plots and llama farms

*ICAHM advises the International Council on Monuments and Sites (ICOMOS) and the World Heritage Committee about archaeology and heritage.

framed by picturesque mountains to jagged desert-like canyons to jungle terrain with giant, vivid flora. The huge windows on the side and roof of the train are spotless, the better to see the rock formations and succulent plants as we descend via switchbacks from very high ground into the Sacred Valley of the Incas.

In *Andes*, my companion book for this journey, Michael Jacobs writes about geographer Alexander von Humboldt and botanist Aimé Bonpland's expedition to South America at the turn of the nineteenth century: their "sensory intoxication," excited by "absolutely everything, almost incapable of taking in so many new phenomena: the climate, the natural abundance, the unusualness of the plants . . . the overwhelming sensuality of a world in which even the crabs were sky-blue and yellow." It's an astute and amusing read for a journey like this, and Jacobs's accounts of traffic accidents involving plunging buses are fresh in my mind as the bus we transfer to in Aguas Calientes barrels up the mountain toward our destination.

We are within reach of what is arguably the most iconic archaeological find in a world that includes Pompeii, Petra, Angkor Wat, Stonehenge, and the great pyramids of Egypt, but anticipation is mixed with trepidation. Our driver meets another bus rocketing downhill and stomps the brakes; then slowly, painfully, and without any promise of success, our bus eases toward the unfenced edge, where a spectacular vista opens perilously close to our outer wheels. Then the buses creep past each other, close enough to suggest the Inca stonework that somehow features massive stone blocks wedged together so tightly that a credit card cannot fit between them. What would happen to world heritage if a bus full of archaeologists on the road to Machu Picchu tumbled over the edge and into the Urubamba River? For half an hour, such a fate is easy to imagine.

Perhaps it is fear that turns Elizabeth Bartley talkative. All the way up the mountain, she chats about the mounds of Ohio, the archaeology near her home in Cincinnati that remains largely unstudied. For years, the University of Cincinnati didn't even have a specialist in Ohio archaeology. Why don't more people care about mounds? she wonders. I feel guilty hearing this. *Because they're dirt!* is the phrase I swallow all the way up the mountain. Then I remember Poverty Point and silently vow to make a pilgrimage to some really big, really obvious mounds soon. It's not just my bias, though: stone always trumps dirt in archaeological destinations. We are, after all, a busload of people, a parade of buses, ascending to a site carved out of stone.

Several archaeologists spoke at the conference about the problem of "invisible archaeology," significant sites that are so humble in appearance, or buried, or otherwise hidden from the view of tourists, that they have trouble winning support. It's an interesting problem. Fritz the German—Friedrich Lüth, the president of the European Association of Archaeologists—mentioned the European continental shelf, which was above ground 20,000 years ago and now lies drowned along the current coastline and throughout most of the North and Baltic seas, a vast Paleolithic site. Scientists are working to try to map and preserve this tremendous resource, but because it will never be visible to tourists, it will probably never earn World Heritage protection. The millions of boots that trample through Machu Picchu and Petra take a toll, but they also support archaeology and help make the case for investing in preservation.

The travelers ascend the trail from the turnstile entrance, then gather on one of the terraces overlooking Machu Picchu: archaeologists from five continents standing on the sixth. We have reached a spectacular pinnacle of civilization. You don't have to know a thing to have your breath taken away. No amount of grooming—weeding, fitting stones back into place, keeping the golf-course-green grass tamed on terraces that once would have spilled over with potatoes and beans—can spoil the wildly improbable and spectacular jewel of a city, carved out of a mountain and brushed by clouds. But make no mistake, this site has been tidied. Look at old pictures of Machu Picchu when it was discovered by the American explorer Hiram Bingham (in the quaint way that representatives of empire nations could "discover" a site that local families lived on) to see what an effort has been made to strip out its overgrowth and tame its unruly and jungly tendencies.

We look down on the lawns of the ceremonial plazas of Machu Picchu, nestled by a pretty maze of stone walls, with banked terraces and cliff faces forming a natural bowl; a game of badminton or croquet could be played on the plazas where a few alpaca roam. A European archaeologist turns to John Schofield, who used to work for the agency that oversees the historic buildings and monuments of England, and says wryly: "Looks like English Heritage is managing this." They laugh, and those nearby laugh, too. Schofield points out one crucial difference—an English Heritage site would be crawling with tourists with self-guided tours clamped to their heads. And look at this gorgeous site, he says admiringly, and no personal audio devices!

Even with the help of trains and buses, we are breathless. How did the Incas live here, much less haul up the stones to create this? We get as close as we dare to the edge of the terrace, but there are few railings, and thousands of opportunities to misstep and tumble off the mountain. "Do you think the Incas raised children here?" someone says speculatively. "How did they keep them from falling off?"

The place is swarming with people, primarily people with gray hair and canes, and even one in a wheelchair, being lifted like a litter from terrace to terrace. Machu Picchu is a bucket-list destination, and, apparently, many people take the full span of their lives to work down their list. By the time we emerge on a ledge above the site and look down, we are 8,000 feet in the air and my heart is fluttering. Before descending to the plaza, we see two men carry a stretcher to a terrace above us and then hustle off with a stricken, strapped-on tourist. *Buena suerte, turista.* Like a band of monkeys who watch a tiger snatch one of their kind and carry him away, we blink and return to the alluring vista.

There are so many of us that we split into two groups, each with a guide. I fall in with the Brits, the Japanese, the African, and the American. As is the custom, our guide is native—in this case, a Peruvian descendant of the Incas. I am a descendant of those geniuses who built the Fishkill Supply Depot and used it to manage and win the War for Independence; I am also a descendant of the geniuses who boiled mammoth and buffalo bones for bone grease. But our guide, Miguel, is the descendant of the geniuses who built Machu Picchu, and he stands here, magisterial, his eyes locked on ours as he details in a musical voice the wondrous accomplishments of the Inca from half a millennium ago. His ancestors did not just haul tons of stone a ridiculous vertical distance (without wheels, no less), carve them with great skill and artistry, and engineer the remote site with an ingenuity we can still learn from—they also apparently laid out the whole thing so at certain times of year, the light of the sun or moon would beam on particular sacred spots. For a stargazer who squints at the night sky through the ambient light pollution of New York City, this is almost impossible to imagine, but our guide tells us something new about astronomy at every stop—this tiny window in this stone wall lights up only on the winter solstice; that structure was an observatory—until the displays of mathematical and celestial expertise of those old Peruvians begins to feel like the work of superhumans. And they were artists, as well. On one of the center terraces I see an elegant, jagged rock sculpture placed squarely in front of an elegant, jagged mountain, a harmonic echo of the sort that can be seen all over the site. Day and night, summer and winter, the human construction chimes with nature.

The archaeologists move single file along one terraced level and circle down to the main court level, descending into the bowl of Machu Picchu, all professional eyes appraising the architecture. Miguel gestures toward the stone buildings we pass, various residences and storerooms, but as he leads us past the entrances, Sinamai and John Schofield and Yo Negishi and Elizabeth Bartley peel off and duck beneath the lintels to explore, marveling at the window frames and door frames and niches, and snapping photos. Our guide scrupulously avoids enclosures, but archaeologists are happy to wiggle into tiny spaces. I follow one into a room the size of a closet. "Do you think Miguel is claustrophobic?" he says.

You can tell the archaeologists, of course, by their photos. The tourists' photos feature people in front of mountains, terraces, stone structures, sundials. The archaeologists wait until the people move away to take theirs: they want the terrace, the stone wall, the lintel, the human-made thing, all sans humans.

I think the archaeologists are like the alpacas that roam the site, scrambling in the heat for hours without food or water. No snacks or drinks inside the gates of Machu Picchu, and the *baños* are back at the entrance and require a single *sol*. These arkies are tough. And ultimately they agree: this is one sweet archaeology site, even if there are too many tourists streaming through. One archaeologist leans over to look at the lower slope, overgrown with vines and trees— the groomed and mapped and guided part of Machu Picchu is only the beginning. Up and down the sides of this mountain, more sites are waiting to be excavated. The guide tells us that teams are working now to uncover other parts of the hidden city. Machu Picchu will grow. There are limits now on the number of people allowed to enter the site and hike the Inca Trail. The United Nations, in the form of its committees and advisory groups like ICAHM, will lean on Peru to limit even further the number of people tromping over the site. But as we learned at the conference, Peru, counting the tourists pouring in, is contemplating new entrance gates and information centers, expanded rail service, perhaps a nearby airport in its future.

Meanwhile, the dashing Veysel Apaydin, a generation or two younger than most of the other archaeologists on this jaunt, has gone off to climb the insane peak of Huayna Picchu, risking life and limb to clamber up to the Incan priests' summit. Hours later, he catches up with us, sweating testosterone, biceps bulging—and then he's gone again. While we ride the bus down the mountain, hugging the inside track this time, Veysel makes the ninety-minute descent down the ancient staircase/donkey trail that Hiram Bingham used a century ago. "We're all old people to him," one of my companions notes.

On the tour, our guide, Miguel, mentioned with pride the great Peruvian archaeologist Ruth Shady Solís, who discovered the oldest city in the Americas, Caral, located near the Peruvian coast a few hours north of Lima. How wonderful to hear Shady's countryman brag about her on this peak, and I think about her as I descend the mountain. Ruth Shady—not Machu Picchu—was what drew me to Peru. Don't get me wrong. I'm thrilled to see Machu Picchu, but Shady was the reason I came here.

I LIKE ARCHAEOLOGISTS who throw their whole beings into the work and fight for scraps of rock and bone and their own vision and interpretation of the past. I like originals, and Shady is clearly one of those. As a young archaeologist, she combed aerial photographs of Peru and found some odd-looking features rising out of the Supe Valley. Guided by the photographs, she ventured out into the Peruvian desert a few hours north of Lima. According to a riveting article in *Archaeology*, "Shady endured an almost unimaginable regime of poverty and lawlessness as she tried to start work," including being shot at by masked robbers. She dug during the day and went to school at night. She began teaching at Universidad Nacional Mayor de San Marcos in Lima and used students and soldiers from a nearby base to help her excavate the big hills, exposing the pyramids underneath. She was a force: somehow, over the course of fifteen years, she managed to get most of the road from the coast to Caral paved; somehow, she protected Caral from flagrant looting; and, eventually, her efforts led to

Caral's recognition and designation as a World Heritage site. And in another good move, she renamed the site Caral from the original Chupacigarro Grande (East).

Shady's only misstep seemed to be inviting a husband-and-wife team of American archaeologists, Jonathan Haas and Winifred Creamer, to help her complete the expensive work of carbon-dating that would allow her to calculate the age of Caral. An article in *Discover* titled "Showdown at the O.K. Caral" recounted Haas's pitch to Shady about the advantages of a partnership: "as a stateside co-author, he could secure grants for her project—hard to come by in impoverished Peru—from U.S. sources." The Americans took the samples from Caral and sent them to the lab, which established the surprisingly ancient date of 2,627 B.C.; then they published the results in *Science* under all three bylines. This was sensational news. It meant Caral was as old as the Egyptian pyramids! Haas and Creamer were hailed as discoverers and quoted widely, particularly in the English-language press. Though the couple later tried to correct the misconception that they were anything but latecomers to this research, Shady was furious; she refused to work or speak with them again.

Haas and Creamer weren't going away, however; they had seen mounds all over the river valleys near Caral and were eager to dig in. In spite of the damage to their reputation and prominent archaeologists denouncing their appropriation, they won additional funding, hired Shady's graduate assistant and other students from her university, pulled together a big team of American students, and began their own dig just north of Caral.

For two years I'd been following the indomitable Ruth Shady, though she had no interest in corresponding with me, and I had seized on this cultural heritage conference as, among other things, a chance to see her keynote. I had settled into my front-row seat the first morning with such anticipation. At least I would get to see her imposing, fierce self, Peruvian earrings and necklaces gleaming, describe the place she had discovered in rapid Spanish, about one in ten words of which I might grasp. The conference organizer, Helaine Silverman, welcomed us to Cusco in both English and Spanish and began with the announcements, which led with the news: Alas, due to the urgent press of work, Ruth Shady Solís had, regrettably, canceled.

I had a ticket. I came here for her. She was one of those archaeologists whose challenges had been epic, even operatic, whose accomplishments had rewritten human history—and she would not come out of her hole. I bit my cheek and swallowed the blood. I've lost count of the archaeologists I've chased who got away. They are an elusive bunch, in motion or in the thrall of another time. Even the ones who alight on a terraced ledge long enough to have a conversation would, before I knew it, shimmer like the good witch Glinda before evaporating into thin air.

TOO BAD RUTH Shady wasn't here at the ultimate archaeological conference, with two hundred of her international peers. She missed the PowerPoints from every corner of the globe. She missed the disappointment that rippled through the audience that had come to hear her—disappointment that conveyed our admiration.

I considered the woman who announced her absence, Helaine Silverman, our fluent host. In English, she was all elbows and bustle, the brisk professor of archaeology at the University of Illinois at Urbana-Champaign and force behind the conference celebrating and reevaluating forty years of UNESCO's World Heritage list. In Spanish, Silverman turned fluid and charming; her whole body came to life, hands moving gracefully, face animated. By day she wore glasses and sensible shoes and ran archaeologists on and off the raised stage, one every fifteen minutes, so we'd have time to hear everyone: scores of presentations from sites low and high, humble and spectacular, neglected and thriving. At night, Silverman switched into contacts and makeup, and in a woven shawl, swept a few of us to her favorite place to have drinks at a stunning former monastery on the steep hill overlooking Cusco, decked out with old tapestries and Baroque paintings. It was a place where you order one expensive pisco sour, then nurse it for hours on leather cushions, basking in the luxury of this historic and beautifully restored piece of Peru. When we got hungry, we followed Silverman as she threaded her way through the narrow streets and a snakelike passage to the perfect hole-in-the-wall for a feast of quinoa soup for a few *soles*: a lesson in how to dine well on an archaeologist's budget. I watched her talking to the waiter, hands like hummingbirds, ordering our casks and tureens.

Those hands had dug deep into Peru, particularly the culture of the Nasca, a mysterious people who lived in the southern desert of Peru between 1,200 and 2,000 years ago. (Even the spelling of their name is mysterious; scholars are split on whether they are Nazca or Nasca; I follow Silverman, who calls the culture Nasca and the place and the lines Nazca.)* The Nasca left behind vivid textiles, pottery covered with creatures like the Fan-headed Mythical Killer Whale, and preserved human heads, their lips pinned together with cactus spines, with holes punched in the forehead and base of the skull to string a cord for carrying. The Nasca also left behind those gigantic lines etched in the desert ground, visible by airplane. The Nazca Lines, called geoglyphs by the archaeologists, had been made by removing the red rubble on the top layer of ground and etching shapes in the gray layer underneath. Millions of people knew them as the landing strips for ancient astronauts from *Chariots of the Gods* and other books by Erich von Däniken, the Swiss hotelier whose

* Not to be confused, in the Googling, with the stock car racers of NASCAR or the swingers of NASCA International, a sex club.

sensational books ruled the bestseller lists in the 1960s and '70s.*
Von Däniken is still manufacturing reasons, in books with names
like *Gold of the Gods* and *History Is Wrong*, for why ancient natives
could not possibly have been smart enough to create their own civilizations. "It is difficult to believe that it originated from a jungle
people," he wrote of the Mayans' ability to calculate the length of
a year on Venus. Silverman was a young student when von Däniken got his start; she has since written extensively about the Nasca,
and rather than simply ignore those popular books, she has spoken
up for archaeologists and tackled "the more egregious of the pseu-
doscientific theories about the Nazca Lines" and those people who
have done so much harm to archaeology and the Peruvians by their
"willful appropriation and misrepresentation of the past." She did
battle on behalf of the real history of Peru and in one of her books
plucked out von Däniken's heart; she feels archaeologists have a responsibility to call nonsense as they see it. To ignore it is costly.

When Silverman finally took the stage at the conference to deliver her own talk, she didn't mention the dramatic Nasca or any
wacky pseudoarchaeology. She spoke about the neighborhood we
were in, the historic center of Cusco and its Plaza de Armas, the
World Heritage site that must accommodate both tourists and regular Cusqueños. How can it preserve its authenticity in the midst
of a vibrant, changing city? In the past, Silverman tells us, she registered her dismay in the usual way of archaeologists when Inca walls
were damaged during hotel construction, and when the beloved
local Café Ayllu, the last "truly Cusqueño space, frequented for decades by intellectuals, the local middle class, and visiting anthro-

---

* I've read von Däniken's *Chariots of the Gods,* and I've read Silverman and Donald A. Proulx's *The Nasca,* and the Nasca people were far wilder and more interesting than any ancient astronauts. And after reading von Däniken's take on the
Mayan calendar—and other advances from so-called "primitive" people— it
seems his motive was essentially racist.

pologists," was displaced by its landlord for a KFC.* Silverman had been an outspoken voice for authenticity and preservation.

Now, she said, she would like to revisit the idea of authenticity and explore the culture of the contemporary space. Cusqueños have taken the three fast-food franchises in the tourist center, KFC, McDonald's, and the Peruvian chain Bembos, and made them their own. All three are decorated with Cusqueño art, and in a square that belongs to locals only on Sunday mornings or on holidays, they have become places where tourists and Cusqueños regularly interact the rest of the time. Finding contemporary authentic culture in the bright wrappings of fast-food restaurants was not just creative and inclusive; it represents a real shift in the scope and outlook of archaeologists. An archaeologist's work wasn't over when she lost a battle to freeze a corner of history in time. As long as there were people remaking that corner, Silverman seemed to be saying, there would be chapters upon chapters for archaeologists to write.

The World Heritage movement began to preserve monuments and historic buildings after World War II and it has expanded in multiple ways since; that's the job of this particular kind of conference, sponsored by an international scientific committee of UNESCO and its advisory group, to stretch and test and fine-tune our definition of heritage, and answer the question, What parts of human history are worth preserving? The last four decades have ushered in some mind-boggling adjustments to that question. Natural heritage, historic city centers, historic parks and gardens, underwater cultural heritage, and even intangible culture like dance, music, oral traditions, and festivals have all been added to the idea of heritage. Heather Gill-Frerking took the stage at the conference to make the

---

*The story of the displacing of the Café Ayllu by the landowner, the local archbishop, is a heartbreaking one, detailed at http://www.cuzcoeats.com/2011/07/cafe-ayllu/; and at http://www.cafeayllu.com/Cafe_Ayllu_1/cafe_ayllu.html.

case for mummies to be officially considered for the list. Though burial places like Pompeii and ancient Thebes, with its necropolis, have been designated World Heritage sites, human remains are not specifically covered in its mission. Tollund Man, who resides now in the Silkeborg Museum in Denmark, and Ötzi the Iceman, a naturally preserved mummy over five thousand years old, discovered in ice in the Alps, are not eligible for World Heritage designation—but, Gill-Frerking wondered, weren't they important parts of our archaeological patrimony?

As more than one archaeologist pointed out to me, the field advances one obituary at a time. Archaeologists took ages to embrace historical archaeology as a legitimate branch of the profession. And once they accepted the idea that sites with seventeenth-, eighteenth-, and nineteenth-century artifacts could be understood in fresh ways by field methodology, what was to stop them from turning to twentieth- and even twenty-first-century sites? Could archaeologists bring their observational and scientific skills to bear on the room you just inhabited? The field that once counted classical or prehistoric bones, stones, and pottery as its turf now excavates (and observes and ruminates about) everything from 2.5-million-year-old ancestral human tools to the context of the chicken nugget you just threw away.

BETWEEN TECHNICAL PRESENTATIONS about some of the dazzling tools of archaeology and testimonies on the success and failure of various sites to engage local communities, thwart looters, and survive human and environmental threats, there were talks like Silverman's with a humble and surprising human focus. These are the ones that end up fixed in my memory.

John Schofield, now a professor at York University, in the U.K., gave a presentation with a particularly populist and modern take on archaeology. An unprepossessing guy with a mobile, everyman's face, Schofield specializes in what he calls "the archaeology of the contemporary past"—what I think of as the archaeology of five minutes ago. He once worked with a team that "excavated" a worn-out Ford Explorer that had been used for archaeological excavations. They documented the van like a piece of material culture. They scrutinized it, measured it, swept up the dirt and fragments of seventeenth-century pottery found in the van's corners, sampled the rust on the frame, recorded the dents on the roof where it had been used as a diving board, and then dismantled the body and the engine. For two months, they studied the van as a thing that had been made and altered and littered by human beings. Partly an exercise, even a kind of stunt, this was also a fascinating application of controlled scientific investigation: observe, measure, record, take apart. One conclusion the team reached struck me as illuminating: the interior of the van was in excellent shape; it had been well-maintained by its archaeologists, regularly serviced and repaired. But its body and exterior were so battered by the rough demands of fieldwork that it looked like a wreck. Everywhere in and on the van were traces of the archaeologists and evidence from their various digs.* Even things we use every day and think we know can, when rigorously investigated, tell us something new.

Schofield talked to the auditorium full of archaeologists about this shift, from thinking about cultural heritage as icons and buildings to thinking about it as another way to document the lives of ordinary people. He mentioned in particular the Maltese capital of Valletta, the city chosen as a World Heritage site because of its den-

---

*Another finding intrigued me: after the team took the engine apart, they dusted it for fingerprints and found none. Archival research turned up the fact that the van had been one of the first turned out in a fully robotized factory. Schofield's talk, and the field of contemporary archaeology, remind me of the pioneering archivist Howard Gotlieb, who instead of waiting till his subjects were old and had gone through their files, would sign them up while they were relatively young and have them sweep their desks each week and send him the scraps and papers.

sity of historic monuments, a beautiful city in the southern Mediterranean, largely unchanged, at least in its architecture, since the late 1700s. Malta had been a port stop for various nations' navies for years, and the visiting sailors would head to the bars and cabarets of Strait Street in Valletta. The bars have been shuttered since 1970, the street all but abandoned, and the powers in Malta, including the Catholic Church, have no interest in preserving that part of the city or even acknowledging it. But some of those who once worked on Strait Street have been found living in its ruins, including a former dancer, a man named Joe. Schofield wondered: Isn't Joe's Valletta an important part of the history and heritage of the city?

I thought about what John Schofield sees when he looks around this conference, the multicolored faces squinting up at the elevated stage in the dark, funky municipal building, the headphones that transmit rough simultaneous translations in Spanish or English, our litter of flyers and notes and business cards and the wrappers from the coca candy for those suffering from the *soroche* (altitude sickness). What does Schofield see when he stands on one of the terraces of Machu Picchu? The fifteenth-century Inca ruins and the remains of shepherds' huts a century or more old, the traces of boot marks and shovel bites from various digs, the clearing and repairs and planting marks made by the landscapers, and the material residue from the tourists who walk over it now. He sees what people left a couple centuries ago, or last season, or even earlier that day: coins and buttons and tickets and sunglasses and candy wrappers, bandannas, empty suntan lotion containers, smuggled-in water bottles, protein-bar wrappers, little holes where people's canes punched into the path or where the waffle design on their sneakers or jelly sandals or hobnail boots made marks. He sees the additional wear on the path near the entrance where the flow of the crowd in high season bottlenecks; he sees the wear on the moss of the boulder where the backpackers rest before climbing Huayna Picchu. It is possible to read a piece of their stories in what they left behind. And it is worthwhile to gather evidence that doesn't turn up anywhere else in the historic record, or the visitor logs, or turnstile counts, or the time cards of the landscapers, bus drivers, and guides, that takes into account the various subversive or alternative ways that people might use the site.

"We look for and recognize those often subtle traces," Schofield said. "Archaeologists see the world in a very particular way. Archaeologists of the contemporary past are no different: we look for traces of past human activity, but recently passed—the day before, perhaps." He smiled. "What we see could be useful."

WHEN I WASN'T sitting in Cusco's auditorium, I wandered across town to the other venue, the Casa Concha Museum. There, next to displays of the artifacts from Machu Picchu that Hiram Bingham had hauled back to Yale University (and Yale had just returned to Peru), I saw more presentations of archaeology in action. I could watch slide shows about the health of the stunning Rock Islands in Palau and the New Caledonia Coral Reef or the excavations in the wilds of Peru and the desert of Chile endlessly. The very poor archaeologists touched me, those who had little support for their work—"We dig wherever there is a hole," said one archaeologist from Buenos Aires—but I was also fascinated by those with money to invest in their cultural heritage, like the Germans who sent their archaeologists flying over the Black Forest with lidar equipment, to take piercing photos of the underbrush—and look, here's an old castle we found!

One evening, after a long day of presentations, I sat above Cusco in a restaurant where the tables doubled as aquariums in white old-fashioned bathtubs: you ate on a glass top as fish swam beneath your plate around algae and arrangements of shells. Around the rim of the bathtub, a United Nations of archaeologists ordered pisco sours and, naturally, beer. Odd, stuffed angels were suspended from the ceiling, the chairs and benches cushioned with fake tiger-skin pillows, the light pink and murky, as if we were underwater, drowning in the eclectic. We ate alpaca steaks on top of the aquariums. Well, the vegetarians didn't eat alpaca, nor did Douglas Comer. The American copresident of ICAHM had started his trip with a hike up to the ruins of Saqsayhuamán, above Cusco, and one of the stray alpacas that roam the site fell in love with him; he couldn't eat alpaca since he'd been nuzzled.

I sat between Comer, an expert in space archaeology, and Yo Negishi, an expert in the ancient Jomon hunter-gatherers who lived 14,000 years ago in Japan. Comer ran a CRM firm in Baltimore, where he specialized in collecting and analyzing satellite and aerial data. He worked with NASA and encouraged archaeologists to make use of its library of recently declassified satellite photographs to study sites through time. Yo Negishi handled some of the oldest pottery in the world. He told me that ninety-nine percent of the excavations in his country were emergencies, conducted to clear land for development. The image of archaeologists might be dashing and romantic in the rest of the world, but in Japan, Negishi and his colleagues suffered scorn for their profession. He recalled working on one emergency dig, knee-deep in a muddy hole while the man whose construction was interrupted when the equipment turned up skeletal remains stood on the edge, mocking him. " 'You call this a job?' " Negishi imitated him, laughing.

JUST BEFORE LEAVING Peru, I paid homage to the spirit of Ruth Shady Solís and made a pilgrimage to the oldest city in the Americas. I rode with a guide named Bratzo, an affable and chatty half-Peruvian/half-Balkan man who plucked me out of Lima and drove me up the coast. We passed through some of the massive slums of

Lima, where people lived atop cemeteries, he told me. We passed numerous houses bristling like porcupines with wires standing up from their roofs. "Our houses are never done," he told me. "My own, which I built, has wires, because someday my son might want to build a floor above me to live. And look! Here are already the connections for him!" He played addictive *chicha* music on the car's CD player, Amazonian instruments and rhythms with a psychedelic influence and a dash of Carlos Santana, the perfect soundtrack for a jaunt up the Pan-American Highway, through steep foggy hills and coastal desert.

We turned east after several hours at a burnt cane field edged by palm trees. We saw naked men bathing in an irrigation ditch, one stretched out napping, workers on break, and horse-drawn carts piled high with produce. We drove and drove on a half-rutted road as mountains rose around us. We followed fields of marigold and corn and asparagus on either side through the fertile Supe Valley. We passed open trucks with men hanging off the back, and adobe houses, and, finally, a blue billboard that read: "Conozca: La Ciudad Sagrada de Caral, 23 km." We waited for a herd of black and brown-and-white goats driven by a skirted woman in a flowered hat to pass; the goats traveled with a dog, a burro, and a spotted pony. In the middle of this farmland, another huge billboard announcing *La Zona Arqueológica* had a squatters' lean-to propped against its base, guarded by two dogs.

And suddenly the landscape was desert, all beige and sere and dried riverbed; the green mountains and green fields had become a distant backdrop. The approach to Caral was as monochromatic as the moon, and the sun that had been shining on us all the way inland was hidden. *Overcast* didn't capture the atmosphere; this wasn't exactly fog—it was as if everything had become shrouded, humid, chilly. Six buff-colored pyramids loomed over a bleak plateau; bleached-out expanses of plazas lay between them, defined by low walls of stone. The site had been fitted for tourists and students with informative signs, simple open thatched huts with low-tech displays, big parking spaces for buses, clean restrooms. Waiting for Dino, who would guide us through Caral, we read about the *shicra*, the loose-woven reed containers that held the rocks that formed the foundations of the pyramids. The site stretched out for 165 acres. On a distant pyramid, we saw people who looked to be the size of goats. Dino joined us and identified them as archaeologists who worked here for twenty-two days and then took an eight-day break. "This is like a prison for archaeologists," he said with a smile. Until a late bus full of schoolchildren arrived, Bratzo and Dino and I and the busy, faraway archaeologists were the only signs of life at Caral.

I can't imagine what it was like for Ruth Shady Solís here before she realized what she had found, when the walls were buried and the pyramids looked like dunes. She excavated the humble and exotic remains, the *shicra* bags, the drug inhalers carved from bone, the piles of sardine and anchovy bones twenty miles from the ocean, the cache of flutes made from the bones of cranes. It took fifteen years to appreciate that these finds were not just traces of an ancient population but evidence of an organized society with an extensive trading network. And such a sophisticated physical infrastructure—altars, for instance, with underground flues for ventilation, the kind of thing you might find in European ruins, but not until thousands of years later. And just over the lip of the plateau, irrigated farms had grown an abundance of beans and pumpkin and cotton in four different natural colors year round. Some of those beans and cotton crops had made their way to the coastal site of Aspero, where they were exchanged for sardines and anchovies, caught in cotton nets. That's where Shady worked now, with Michael Moseley, the American archaeologist who had defended her against Haas and Creamer's "academic imperialism"; in a recent speech, Moseley charged they had "jumped claim, quite literally." Shady, Haas, and Creamer were all engaged in "spectacular and revolutionary" archaeology. He blamed their feud on the character flaw that plagues so many archaeologists: "They have huge egos."*

I was standing by the largest pyramid as Dino talked on about the thousands of his ancestors who must have lived here—perhaps we were walking on the remains of their houses, he suggested. Bratzo asked intelligent questions; he had been hooked on archaeology since he hiked along the coast with a friend and came upon a mummy in one of the caves.

Ruth Shady Solís had been obsessed with the precolonial story of her people. That obsession led her to discover what is, so far, the oldest city in the Americas; with it she has restored a piece of the ancestral past to her people. Recognizing Caral's importance was evidence of her skill as an archaeologist. But here's the thing about archaeologists: Caral or no Caral, she probably would have done what she did anyway. Whether or not what she found was the oldest or first, she would have given up vacations, slept in her car, awakened each morning and kept working, with nobody encouraging her and no guarantee she'd find anything. I suspect she would have pursued her stubborn vision no matter what she unearthed.

I thought of all the archaeologists I had met, what their drive and stubborn insistence on their own visions had meant. I thought of Adrien Hannus, the long-haired Sioux Falls archaeologist who sat eating burnt bacon in a diner at the beginning of my story, describing how the Native Americans of the plains used to extract bone grease from animal bones. A Vietnam veteran, Hannus had ended his military service in bad shape, with a case of amoebic dysentery that had left him sixty-five pounds lighter, and a powerful aversion to the "grotesqueness and violence and gore" he'd witnessed. After discharge, he abandoned the study of law and turned to anthropology, the study of human beings.

*Moseley's lecture, "Four Thousand Years Ago in Coastal Peru," can be heard at https://peabody.Harvard.edu/node/581.

What was archaeology to him? It was the opposite of killing things. It was trying to will life back into stuff that had been forgotten and buried for thousands or millions of years. It was not about shards and pieces of bone or treasure; it was about kneeling down in the elements, paying very close attention, and trying to locate a spark of the human life that had once touched that spot there.

THERE WAS NO one in sight as Bratzo and I left Caral. We rolled slowly away over the rocky riverbed in this remote moonscape, and then . . . what's this? A man in a yellow jacket and cap on a moto-taxi—a three-wheeled motorbike—with a yellow cooler strapped in front of him, coming from the other direction. Bratzo rolled down his window and they had a little chat in the middle of the dry riverbed. He handed over a few *soles*, and the man handed us back some ice cream bars, and we pressed on through thousands of years to return to the present.

Acknowledgments

MY THANKS TO the archaeologists and experts who opened their doors to me and whose stories make up this book. Grant Gilmore, Laurie Rush, Bill Sandy, and John Shea led me to others as well, and Sandy took me along on numerous digs. I am also indebted to Robert Ashworth, Jim Burr Sr., Joey Cabaccini, Zoe Contes, Terri Jentz, Leedom Lefferts, Ricah Marquez, Duane Quates, Cristina Scalet, Meg Schulz, Willa Skinner, Mike Sprowles, Ruud Stelten, Penny Steyer, and Joe Wallace; to Leila Amineddoleh and Thomas R. Kline at the Lawyers' Committee for Cultural Heritage Preservation; and to my digging partners, especially Jillian Banks, Alex Denning, Kelly Riemersma, and Talia Varonos-Pavlopoulos and the whole NYU crew.

Thanks to those who talked to me about their work and who made incalculable contributions to this book, including Andy Bobyarchick, Bill Caraher, Jennifer Everhart, Joel Grossman, Rachel Hallotte, Kris Hirst, Sandra Hollimon, Fumiko Ikawa-Smith, Dave Johnson, Jessica Johnson, Judy Kelley-Moberg, Rungsima Kullapat, Edward J. Lenik, Brian Lione, Taylor Middleton, Andrew Reinhard, Friedrich T. Schipper, Christopher J. Stackowicz, Margaret Staudter, and Louise Pothier and Sophie Limoge of Pointe-à-Callière, Montreal's stunning museum of archaeology.

I took advantage of many programs that are available to anyone interested in archaeology, particularly through the AIA and its local societies, the New York State Archaeological Association and its local chapters, Brown University's Joukowsky Institute for Archaeology and the Ancient World, and NYU's Center for Ancient Studies, and Coursera, and am grateful for all. The Society for American Archaeology (SAA), the Paleoanthropology Society, and Stony Brook University were particularly welcoming.

I could not have done the research for this book without the help of Purchase College, its Writers Center, and its library. Thanks especially to Louise Yelin and Suzanne Kessler, and to Darcy Gervasio, and Marie Sciangula. Margaret Fox, Carolyn Reznick, and Meryl Sprinzen led me to sources, and Sherry DeBoer led me to several. Jim Nicholson gave me great advice when I began this project. Thanks to E. Jean Carroll, Pete Dexter, and Nick Trautwein for crucial support, and to Bob Brutting, Betsy Carter, Lee Eisenberg, Eric Himmel, Christine Lehner, Jay Lovinger, Bruce McCall, Becky Okrent, Dan Okrent, Caroline Miller, David Smith, Roy Solomon, and Yvonne vanCort. Carol Caldwell went above and beyond to help me at an important point, as did Chris Dodge.

My friends and readers are an extraordinary crew. Catherine Anderson, Marcelle Clements, Mary Ellen Hannibal, Abby Rosmarin, Kristen Munnelly, and Barbara Rowley gave me useful and much-appreciated comments. Martha Alcott read and fact-checked on deadline. Kate Buford, Ben Cheever, Gay Daly, and Mark Golodetz listened to and/or read several versions of these chapters, and Susan Squire read it no fewer than three times. Esmeralda Santiago and Larkin Warren offered steady feedback and endless patience and support. My friend Ruth Liebmann traveled with me to Peru, and I stole all her great observations. Mary Murphy and Bob Minzesheimer have been there for me throughout, as have Jackson Fleder, Carolyn Fleder, and Nick Fleder, and my extended and forgiving family.

I want to thank my publishers, Jonathan Burnham and Michael Morrison, for their faith and support, and Jane Beirn, Ed Cohen,

Acknowledgments

Barry Harbaugh, Annie Mazes, Sydney Pierce, and Virginia Stanley for their hard work and steady hands on this book. How many writers these days can count on the same team across a decade? I have had the benefit of David Hirshey's humor and savvy through every stage of three books. Milan Bozic has designed three wonderful covers. Chris Calhoun has guided me wisely throughout. And Rob Fleder, who shares my life, has given me three fantastic titles, priceless editorial advice, and courage.

That is very many excellent people—and others unmentioned besides—but none could talk me out of some of my decisions or save me from all errors. I take full responsibility for those.

Select Bibliography

DOWN AND DIRTY

"Archaeology's Dirty Little Secrets," online course, Sue Alcock, Brown University, 2014: www.coursera.org/course/secrets.

Birmingham, Robert A., *Spirits of Earth: The Effigy Mound Landscape of Madison and the Four Lakes* (Madison: University of Wisconsin Press, 2010).

Gill-Frerking, Heather, and W. Rosendahl, "Use of Computed Tomography and Three-Dimensional Virtual Reconstruction for the Examination of a 16th Century Mummified Dog from a North German Peat Bog," *International Journal of Osteoarchaeology*, vol. 23, issue 6, November/December 2013.

Glob, P. V., *The Bog People: Iron Age Man Preserved* (Ithaca: Cornell University Press, 1969).

Karr, Landon, with L. Adrien Hannus and Alan K. Outram, "Bone Grease and Bone Marrow Exploitation on the Plains of South Dakota: A New Perspective on Bone Fracture Evidence from the Mitchell Prehistoric Indian Village," A Bush Foundation Research Project, November 3, 2005.

"Kingship and Sacrifice: Iron Age Bog Bodies and Boundaries," Heritage Guide no. 35, Archaeology Ireland.

Lange, Karen, "Tales from the Bog," *National Geographic*, September 2007.

Renner, C., "Hard Evidence," *NDSU Magazine*, Fall 2007 (profile of Heather Gill-Robinson, now Gill-Frerking).

Robinson, Ron, with contributions by L. Adrien Hannus, *The Village on the Bluff: Prehistoric Farmers/Hunters of the James River Valley* (Sioux Falls: Archeology Laboratory, Augustana College, 2011).

Sanders, Karin, *Bodies in the Bog and the Archaeological Imagination* (Chicago: University of Chicago Press, 2009).

"Top 10 Discoveries of 2013," *Archaeology*, January–February 2014.

Vergano, Dan, "Bog Bodies Baffle Scientists," *USA Today*, January 16, 2011.

FIELD SCHOOL

Deetz, James, *In Small Things Forgotten: An Archaeology of Early American Life*, rev. (New York: Anchor, 1996).

Gilmore, Richard Grant, "All the Documents Are Destroyed! Documenting Slavery for St. Eustatius," in Jay B. Haviser and Kevin C. MacDonald, eds., *African Re-genesis, Confronting Social Issues in the African Diaspora* (London: Routledge, 2006).

Gilmore, R. Grant, "Shawn Lester Burials: White Hook or *Witten Hoek* Area Excavation," St. Eustatius Center for Archaeological Research, 2011.

Gilmore, R. Grant, III, M. L. P. Hoogland, and Corinne L. Hofman, "An Archaeological Assessment of Cul-de-Sac (The Farm)," Phase 2, report to NuStar, June–August 2011.

Gilmore, R. Grant, III, and Madeline J. Roth, "Fort Oranje, St. Eustatius, An Historical Archaeological and Architectural Assessment," *Fort: The International Journal of Fortification and Military Architecture*, vol. 41, 2013.

Hofman, Corinne L., Menno L. P. Hoogland, and Annelou L. van Gijn, eds., *Crossing the Borders: New Methods and Techniques in the Study of Archaeological Materials from the Caribbean* (Tuscaloosa: University of Alabama Press, 2008).

Morrison, Bethany, guest ed., "Special Forum: Innovations in Archaeological Field Schools," in *SAA Archaeological Record*, vol. 12, no. 1, January 2012.

Parker, Matthew, *The Sugar Barons: Family, Corruption, Empire, and War in the West Indies* (New York: St. Martin's Press, 2011).

Siegel, Peter E., and Elizabeth Righter, eds., *Protecting Heritage in the Caribbean* (Tuscaloosa: University of Alabama Press, 2011).

THE SURVIVALIST'S GUIDE TO ARCHAEOLOGY

American Museum of Natural History, Podcast: Land of Painted Caves with Jean M. Auel and Ian Tattersall, April 29, 2011.

Auel, Jean, *The Clan of the Cave Bear* (New York: Crown, 1980; Brilliance Audio, 1986).

———, *The Land of Painted Caves* (New York: Crown, 2011; Brilliance Audio, 2010).

———, *The Mammoth Hunters* (New York: Crown, 1985; Brilliance Audio, 1986).

———, *The Plains of Passage* (New York: Crown, 1990; Brilliance Audio, 1991).

———, *The Shelters of Stone* (New York: Crown, 2002; Brilliance Audio, 2002).

———, *The Valley of Horses* (New York: Crown, 1982; Brilliance Audio, 1986).

Bataille, Georges, *Lascaux; Or, the Birth of Art: Prehistoric Painting* (Lausanne: Skira, 1955).

Cochran, Tracy, "The View from Mount Auel," *Publishers Weekly*, April 22, 2002.

Edgar, Blake, "Chronicler of Ice Age Life," *Archaeology*, November/December 2002.

Finlayson, Clive, *The Humans Who Went Extinct: Why Neanderthals Died Out and We Survived* (New York: Oxford University Press, 2010).

Hornblower, Margot, "Queen of the Ice Age Romance," *Time*, October 22, 1990.

Klein, Richard G., *The Human Career: Human Biological and Cultural Origins*, third ed. (Chicago: University of Chicago Press, 2009).

McBrearty, Sally, and Alison S. Brooks, "The Revolution That Wasn't: A New Interpretation of the Origin of Modern Human Behavior," *Journal of Human Evolution*, vol. 39, issue 5, November 2000.

Shea, John, "Bleeding or Breeding: Neandertals vs. Early Modern Humans in the Middle Paleolithic Levant," in Susan Pollock and Reinhard Bernbeck, eds., *Archaeologies of the Middle East: Critical Perspectives* (Malden, MA: Blackwell, 2005).

———, "The Human Revolution Rethought," *Evolutionary Anthropology*, 15:42–43 (2006).

———, "Child's Play: Reflections on the Invisibility of Children in the Paleolithic Record," *Evolutionary Anthropology*, 15:212–16 (2006).

———, "Homo sapiens Is as Homo sapiens Was," *Current Anthropology*, 52:1, February 2011.

———, "Neanderthal News: Extinct Species Exhibit Variability," book review, *Evolutionary Anthropology*, vol. 20, no. 5, September/October, 2011.

————, "Refuting a Myth About Human Origins," *American Scientist*, 99:2, March–April 2011.

————, "Stone Tool Analysis and Human Origins Research: Some Advice from Uncle Screwtape," *Evolutionary Anthropology*, April 12, 2011.

————, *Stone Tools in the Paleolithic and Neolithic Near East: A Guide* (Cambridge, U.K.: Cambridge University Press, 2013).

Shea, John J., and Ofer Bar-Yosef, "Who Were the Skhul/Qafzeh People? An Archaeological Perspective on Eurasia's Oldest Modern Humans," *Journal of the Israel Prehistoric Society*, 35:451–68.

Stringer, Chris, *Lone Survivors: How We Came to Be the Only Humans on Earth* (New York: St. Martin's/Griffin, 2012).

Trinkaus, Eric, and Jiří Svoboda, eds., *Early Modern Human Evolution in Central Europe: The People of Dolní Věstonice* (New York: Oxford University Press, 2006).

Zielinski, Sarah, "Neanderthals . . . They're Just Like Us?" National Geographic News, October 12, 2012, http://news.nationalgeographic.com/news/2012/10/121012-neanderthals-science-paabo-dna-sex-breeding-humans/.

EXTREME BEVERAGES

McGovern, Patrick E., *Uncorking the Past: The Quest for Wine, Beer, and Other Alcoholic Beverages* (Berkeley: University of California Press, 2009).

Tucker, Abigail, "Dig, Drink and Be Merry," *Smithsonian*, July–August 2011 (appears digitally as "The Beer Archaeologist").

PIG DRAGONS

Adovasio, J. M., Olga Soffer, and Jake Page, *The Invisible Sex* (New York: HarperCollins, 2009).

Nelson, Sarah M., *The Archaeology of Korea* (Cambridge, U.K.: Cambridge University Press, 1993).

————, "The Development of Complexity in Prehistoric Northern China," *Sino-Platonic Paper*, no. 63, December 1994.

————, "How a Feminist Stance Improves Archaeology," http://www2.nau.edu/~gender-p/Papers/Nelson.pdf.

————, "In the Trenches: A Sister Archaeologist Joins a 'Band of Brothers,'" in manuscript.

————, *Jade Dragon* (Walnut Creek, CA: Left Coast Press, 2009).

————, "RKLOG: Archaeologists as Fiction Writers," in John H. Jameson Jr., John E. Ehrenhard, and Christine A. Finn, eds., *Ancient Muses: Archaeology and the Arts* (Tuscaloosa: University of Alabama Press, 2003).

————, *Shamanism and the Origin of States: Spirit, Power, and Gender in East Asia* (Walnut Creek, CA: Left Coast Press, 2008).

————, *Spirit Bird Journey* (Walnut Creek, CA: Left Coast Press, 1999).

————, *Tiger Queen*, in manuscript.

Nelson, Sarah Milledge, and Myriam Rosen-Ayalon, eds., *In Pursuit of Gender: Worldwide Archaeological Approaches* (Walnut Creek, CA: AltaMira Press, 2002).

Stark, Miriam T., ed., *Archaeology of Asia* (Malden, MA: Blackwell, 2005).

MY LIFE IS IN RUINS

"University Guide 2014: League Table for Archaeology," *Guardian*, June 4, 2014.

ROAD TRIP THROUGH TIME

"Archaeological Investigations in Deadwood's Chinatown, 2002," *Black Hills Historian* (newsletter of the Friends of Case Library, Black Hills State University), Fall 2002.

Brokaw, Chet, "Gambling Brought Deadwood, S.D., Back to Life," *USA Today*, November 11, 2009.

"Deadwood Dedicates Tribute to Its Chinese Heritage," *Rapid City Journal*, July 23, 2013.

Floyd, Dustin D., "Doomed: The Rise and Fall of Deadwood's Chinatown," *Deadwood Magazine*, February 1, 2006.

Griffith, Tom, "Deadwood Tapping into Its Chinese Heritage," rapidcityjournal.com, June 11, 2013.

Harvey, Andy, "Wing Tsue Demolition Affects Research," Keloland.com, February 10, 2006.

Katchadourian, Raffi, "Where East Met (Wild) West," *Smithsonian*, March 2005.

Loken, Maria, "Pair of Historic Buildings Razed," *Rapid City Journal*, December 28, 2005.

————, "Razing Spurs Deadwood to Take Action," *Rapid City Journal*, January 19, 2006.

Wong, Edith C., "Ancestral Legacy," *Deadwood Magazine*, February 1 and March 1, 2006.

————, "Chinatown's Conundrum," *Deadwood Magazine*, March 1, 2007.

Zhu, Liping, and Rose Estep Fosha, *Ethnic Oasis: The Chinese in the Black Hills* (Pierre: South Dakota State Historical Society Press, 2004).

UNDERWATER MYSTERIES

Abbass, D. K., "A Marine Archaeologist Looks at Treasure Salvage," *Journal of Maritime Law and Commerce*, vol. 30, no. 2, April 1999.

Chera, Constantin, "The Future of Underwater Archaeology," *UNESCO Scientific Colloquium on Factors Impacting the Underwater Cultural Heritage*, Royal Library of Belgium, December 13–14, 2011.

Gould, Richard A., *Shipwreck Anthropology: The School for American Research* (Albuquerque: University of New Mexico Press, 1983).

McLeish, Todd, "Seeking Sunken Ships," *Quad Angles*, February 2007.

Mooney, Tom, "Treasures So Near, Yet So Far," *Providence Journal*, October 13, 2008.

EXPLORERS CLUBS

Bintliff, John, "Why Indiana Jones Is Smarter Than the Post-Processualists," *Norwegian Archaeological Review*, vol. 26, no. 2, 1993.

Canby, Vincent, "Raiders of the Lost Ark" (ecstatic movie review), *New York Times*, June 12, 1981.

Connelly, Joan Breton, *Portrait of a Priestess: Women and Ritual in Ancient Greece* (Princeton, NJ : Princeton University Press, 2007).

Fagan, Brian, "An Archaeologist Whips Indy," *Wall Street Journal*, May 24, 2008.

Indiana Jones and the Ultimate Quest (movie), directed by Nikki Boella and Kevin Burns, Prometheus Entertainment, 2008.

Munsell Soil Color Charts, Munsell Color Company, rev. ed., 2000.

Polk, Milbry, and Mary Tiegreen, *Women of Discovery: A Celebration of Intrepid Women Who Explored the World* (New York: Clarkson Potter, 2001).

Wiese, Richard, *Born to Explore: How to Be a Backyard Adventurer* (New York: Harper, 2009).

Wilford, John Noble, "New Analysis of the Parthenon's Frieze Finds It Depicts a Horrifying Legend," *New York Times*, July 4, 1995.

FIELD SCHOOL REDUX

Connelly, Joan Breton, *The Parthenon Enigma: A New Understanding of the West's Most Iconic Building and the People Who Made It* (New York: Alfred A. Knopf, 2014).

————, "Twilight of the Ptolemies: Egyptian Presence on Late Hellenistic Yeronisos," in V. Kassianidou, R. Merilees, and D. Michaelides, eds., *Egypt and Cyprus in Antiquity* (Nicosia: Cyprus American Archaeological Research Institute and the University of Cyprus, 2009).

————, "Yeronisos: Twenty Years on Cleopatra's Isle," *Explorers Journal*, Winter 2010–11.

Stone, Webster, "Cleopatra's Secret," *Departures*, July/August 2008.

THE BODIES

Bumiller, Elisabeth, "Air Force Mortuary Sent Troop Remains to Landfill," *New York Times*, November 9, 2011.

Carola, Chris, "Saving NY's Valley Forge: Revolutionary War Patriots' Graves Besieged by Development," *Gaea Times*, July 3, 2009.

Chastellux, Francois Jean, Marquis de, *Travels in North America* (Chapel Hill: University of North Carolina Press, 1963).

Goring, Rich, "The Fishkill Supply Depot and Encampment During the Years 1776–1778," New York Office of Parks & Recreation, Division of Historic Preservation, December 1975.

Hasbrouck, Frank, ed., *The History of Dutchess County, New York* (Poughkeepsie, NY: S. A. Matthieu, 1909).

Maynard, W. Barksdale, "The Fight to Save Fishkill," *American Spirit*, May–June 2014.

Randall, Michael, "Fading into History: Fishkill Depot Defenseless Against Mall," *Times Herald-Record*, September 16, 2006.

Rhinevault, Carney, and Tatiana Rhinevault, *Hidden History of the Lower Hudson Valley: Stories from the Albany Post Road* (Charleston, SC: History Press, 2012).

Smith, Philip Henry, *General History of Duchess [sic] County from 1609 to 1876, Inclusive* (Pawling, NY: Self-published, 1877).

Sullivan, Robert, *My American Revolution: A Modern Expedition Through History's Forgotten Battlegrounds* (New York: Farrar, Straus and Giroux, 2012).

Ward, Christopher, *The War of the Revolution* (New York: Skyhorse Publishing, 2011).

Washington, George (John C. Fitzpatrick, editor), *The Writings of George Washington from the Original Manuscript Sources 1745–1799*; prepared under the direction of the United States George Washington Bicentennial Commission and published by authority of Congress (Westport, CT: Greenwood Press, 1970).

EVIDENCE OF HARM

Barry, Dan, "At Morgue, Ceaselessly Sifting 9/11 Traces," *New York Times*, July 14, 2002.

Bryson, Bill, *A Short History of Nearly Everything* (New York: Broadway Books, 2003).

Dunlap, David, "Ground Zero Forensic Team Is Posted to Seek Remains," *New York Times*, October 21, 2006.

Hockenberry, John, "Sherlock Holmes: Connecting Fiction and Forensics," *Takeaway*, NPR, December 17, 2013.

McPhee, John, *The Pine Barrens* (New York: Farrar, Straus and Giroux, 1981).

Robbins, Elaine, "Archaeological Crime Fighters," *American Archaeology*, Summer 2006.

Tattersall, Ian, *Masters of the Planet: The Search for Our Human Origins* (New York: Palgrave Macmillan, 2012).

ARCHAEOLOGY IN A DANGEROUS WORLD

Binkovitz, Leah, "Q&A: How to Save the Arts in Times of War: From Iraq to Libya, Corine Wegener Works to Preserve Priceless Objects of Human History," Smithsonian.com, January 24, 2013.

Bogdanos, Matthew, with William Patrick, *Thieves of Baghdad* (New York: Bloomsbury, 2005).

Joffe, Alexander, H., "Museum Madness in Baghdad," *Middle East Quarterly*, Spring 2004.

Kane, Susan, "Lessons Learned from Libya," *SAA Archaeological Record*, vol. 13, no. 3, May 2013.

Myers, Steven Lee, "Iraq Museum Reopens Six Years After Looting," *New York Times*, February 23, 2009.

Parker, Diantha, "Treasure Hunters in Uniform: 'Monuments Men' Remembered," *New York Times*, February 20, 2013.

Power, Matthew, "Letter from the Hindu Kush: The Lost Buddhas of Bamiyan: Picking Up the Pieces in Afghanistan," *Harper's*, March 2005.

Rush, Laurie, ed., *Archaeology, Cultural Property, and the Military* (Woodbridge, U.K.: Boydell Press, 2011); see esp. Laurie Rush, "United States Department of Defense Cultural Property Protection Program for Global Operations."

————, "CEAUSSIC: Mars Turns to Minerva," blog of the American Anthropological Association's Ad Hoc Commission on Anthropology's Engagement with the Security and Intelligence Communities, July 21, 2009: http://blog .aaanet.org/2009/07/21/ceaussic-mars-turns-to-minerva/.

Wegener, Corine, guest post, The Punching Bag blog by Larry Rothfield, November 29, 2009: http://larryrothfield.blogspot.com/2009/11/guest-post -from-maj-corine-wegener-on.html.

AVOIDANCE TARGETS

Cutshaw, Jason B., "Post Archaeologist Will Train Soldiers to Preserve Historic Sites," June 22, 2006: http://www.drum.army.mil/mountaineer/Article.as px?ID=1287.

Eugene, Toni, "Army Project Teaches Cultural Awareness to Deployed Troops," *Army*, March 2008.

"Fort Drum Archaeologist Offers Lessons Learned While Studying in Rome," December 9, 2010: http://www.drum.army.mil/mountaineer/Article.aspx ?ID=4979.

Ghiringhelli, Paul Steven, "Fort Drum Archaeologist Spreads Influence During Studies in Rome," February 24, 2011: http://www.drum.army.mil/moun taineer/Article.aspx?ID=5115.

————, "Fort Drum Archaeologist's Influence Grows After Year at Prestigious Academy in Rome," October 6, 2011: http://www.army.mil/arti cle/66827/.

Greenleese, Nancy, "Archaeologist Saves Cultural Treasures with Cards,"

Deutsche Welle, August 27, 2012: http://www.dw.de/archeologist-saves -cultural-treasures-with-cards/a-16195430-1.

McHargue, Georgess, *In the North Country: The Archeology and History of Twelve Thousand Years at Fort Drum* (Hollis: Puritan Press, 1998).

Montagne, Renee, "U.S. Base Damages Ancient Babylonian Temple," *Morning Edition*, NPR, June 24, 2004.

Schlesinger, Victoria, "Desert Solitaire," *Archaeology*, vol. 60, no. 4, July– August 2007.

Wagner, Heather, Laurie W. Rush, and Ian Warden, *Protecting the Past to Secure the Future: Best Management Practices for Hardening Archeological Sites on DoD Lands*, Legacy Resource Management Program, March 2007.

BUCKETS OF ARCHAEOLOGISTS

Adams, Mark, *Turn Right at Machu Picchu: Rediscovering the Lost City One Step at a Time* (New York: Plume, 2012 reprint ed.).

Atwood, Roger, "A Monumental Feud," *Archaeology*, 58:4, July–August 2005.

Bailey, G., et al., "Sic Transit Gloria Mundi," *British Archaeology*, 92: January– February 2007.

Council of Europe Framework Convention on the Value of Cultural Heritage for Society (Faro agreement, 2005): http://conventions.coe.int/Treaty/EN/ Treaties/Html/199.htm.

Creamer, Winifred, Jonathan Haas, and Ruth Shady Solís, "Dating Caral, a Pre-ceramic Site in the Supe Valley on the Central Coast of Peru," *Science*, April 27, 2001.

Drake, Barbara, "Totally Offensive: McDonald's Opens at Cusco Plaza de Armas," An American in Lima (blog), September 24, 2008.

Harrison, Rodney, and John Schofield, *After Modernity: Archaeological Approaches to the Contemporary Past* (Oxford, U.K.: Oxford University Press, 2010).

Jacobs, Michael, *Andes* (London: Granta, 2010).

Mann, Charles C., *1491: New Revelations of the Americas Before Columbus* (New York: Vintage, 2006).

Miller, Kenneth, "Showdown at the O.K. Caral," *Discover*, September 9, 2005.

Moseley, Michael Edward, "Four Thousand Years Ago in Coastal Peru," Gordon R. Willey Lecture, Peabody Museum of Archaeology and Ethnology at Harvard University, April 8, 2010.

———, *The Incas and Their Ancestors: The Archaeology of Peru* (New York: Thames & Hudson, 2001 revised ed.).

———, *The Maritime Foundations of Andean Civilization* (Menlo Park, CA: Cummings Publication Company, 1974).

Munro, Kimberly, "Ancient Peru: The First Cities," *Popular Archaeology*, vol. 5, December 2011.

Parcak, Sarah, "Eat Your Heart Out, Indiana Jones," *Future Tense*, October 3, 2013.

Ruggles, D. Fairchild, ed., *On Location: Heritage Cities and Sites* (New York: Springer, 2012).

Shady, Ruth, "Reply of Dr. Shady to PANC (Proyecto Arqueológico Norte Chico) (English version)," Caral Civilization Peru blog, January 17, 2005: http://caralperu.typepad.com/caral_civilization_peru/2005/01/reply_of_dr_sha_1.html.

Shady, Ruth, and Christopher Kleihege, *Caral: The First Civilization in the Americas: La Primera Civilizacion de America* (Chicago: CK Photo, 2010).

Shady Solís, Ruth, "Caral: Ruth Shady Solís," en Perú (blog), November 17, 2007: http://enperublog.com/2007/11/17/caral-ruth-shady-solis/.

———, *Caral, The Oldest Civilization in the Americas: 15 Years Unveiling Its History* (Proyecto Especial Arqueológico Caral-Supe, Instituto Nacional de Cultura, 2009).

Silverman, Helaine, and William H. Isbell, eds., *Handbook of South American Archaeology* (New York: Springer, 2008).

Silverman, Helaine, and Donald A. Proulx, *The Nasca* (Malden and Oxford: Blackwell, 2002).

ALSO OF INTEREST

Brinkley, Douglas, *The Wilderness Warrior: Theodore Roosevelt and the Crusade for America* (New York: HarperPerennial, 2010).

Carmichael, David L., Robert H. Lafferty III, and Brian Leigh Molyneaux, *Excavation (Archaeologist's Toolkit)* (Walnut Creek, CA: AltaMira Press, 2003).

Carver, Martin, *Making Archaeology Happen: Design versus Dogma* (Walnut Creek, CA: Left Coast Press, 2011).

Ceram, C. W., *Gods, Graves and Scholars* (New York: Vintage Books, 1986 second rev. ed.).

Childs, Craig, *Finders Keepers: A Tale of Archaeological Plunder and Obsession* (New York: Little, Brown, 2010).

Select Bibliography

Christie, Agatha, *Murder in Mesopotamia: A Hercule Poirot Mystery* (New York: William Morrow Paperbacks, 2011 reissue ed.).

Cuno, James, *Who Owns Antiquity? Museums and the Battle over Our Ancient Heritage* (Princeton, NJ: Princeton University Press, 2008).

Curtis, Gregory, *The Cave Painters: Probing the Mysteries of the World's First Artists* (New York: Anchor, 2007).

deBoer, Trent, *Shovel Bums: Comix of Archaeological Field Life* (Walnut Creek, CA: AltaMira Press, 2004).

Eiseley, Loren, *The Night Country* (Lincoln: University of Nebraska Press, 1997).

Fagan, Brian M., *Ancient North America: The Archaeology of a Continent* (London: Thames & Hudson, 2005, 4th ed.).

———, *In the Beginning: An Introduction to Archaeology* (Boston: Little, Brown, 1972).

Felch, Jason, and Ralph Frammolino, *Chasing Aphrodite: The Hunt for Looted Antiquities at the World's Richest Museum* (Boston: Houghton Mifflin, 2011).

Feldman, Mark, *Archaeology for Everyone* (New York: Quadrangle/New York Times Books, 1977).

Flatman, Joe, *Becoming an Archaeologist: A Guide to Professional Pathways* (Cambridge, U.K.: Cambridge University Press, 2011).

Geier, Clarence R., Jr., ed., *Look to the Earth: Historical Archaeology and the American Civil War* (Knoxville: University of Tennessee Press, 1996).

Grann, David, *The Lost City of Z: A Tale of Deadly Obsession in the Amazon* (New York: Doubleday, 2008).

Hallote, Rachel S., *Death, Burial, and Afterlife in the Biblical World: How the Israelites and Their Neighbors Treated the Dead* (Chicago: Ivan R. Dee, 2001).

Herridge, Victoria, "TrowelBlazers: In Search of the Female Indiana Jones," CNN.com, June 20, 2013 (and TrowelBlazers blog).

Jansen, Gemma C. M., Ann Olga Koloski-Ostrow, and Eric M. Moormann, eds., *Roman Toilets: Their Archaeology and Cultural History* (Leuven: Peeters, 2011 supplement ed.).

Kansa, Eric C., Sarah Whitcher Kansa, and Ethan Watrall, eds., *Archaeology 2.0: New Tools for Communication and Collaboration* (Los Angeles: UCLA Cotsen Institute of Archaeology Press, 2011).

Leakey, Mary D., *Disclosing the Past: An Autobiography* (New York: McGraw-Hill, 1986).

Lenik, Edward J., *Rocks, Riddles and Mysteries: Folk Art, Inscriptions and Other Stories in Stone* (Franklin: American History Press, 2011).

Mallowan, Agatha Christie, *Come, Tell Me How You Live: An Archaeological Memoir* (New York: William Morrow, 1946).

Mann, Charles C. *1493: Uncovering the New World Columbus Created* (New York: Vintage, 2012).

MacManamon, Francis P., and Alf Hatton, eds., *Cultural Resource Management in Contemporary Society: Perspectives on Managing and Presenting the Past* (New York: Routledge, 2000).

Sebastian, Lynne, and William D. Lipe, *Archaeology and Cultural Resource Management* (Santa Fe: School for Advanced Research Press, 2009).

Thomas, David Hurst, *Skull Wars: Kennewick Man, Archaeology, and the Battle for Native American Identity* (New York: Basic Books, 2001).

Wilson, Lanford, *Lanford Wilson's The Mound Builders* (New York: Broadway Theatre Archive, 1976).

Wynn, Thomas, and Frederick L. Coolidge, *How to Think Like a Neandertal* (New York: Oxford University Press, 2012).

Zeder, Melinda A., *The American Archaeologist: A Profile* (Walnut Creek, CA: AltaMira Press, 1997).

———, "The American Archaeologist: Results of the 1994 SAA Census," *SAA Bulletin*, March 1997.

Index

About the author

About the book

Read on

Insights,
Interviews
& More . . .

Meet Marilyn Johnson

© Rob Fleder

MARILYN JOHNSON is the author of *The Dead Beat: Lost Souls, Lucky Stiffs, and the Perverse Pleasures of Obituaries* and *This Book Is Overdue!: How Librarians and Cybrarians Can Save Us All*. She has worked as a magazine editor and writer, notably at *Esquire* and *Life*, and lives in New York's Hudson Valley with her husband, Rob Fleder. Visit her website at marilynjohnson.net.

Q&A with
Marilyn Johnson

Conducted by Alex Belth

Your first book was about people who write obituaries, and your second was about librarians. This is your third book. What led you to archaeologists?

I thought it would be fun to go on a dig.

And is it?

It is! It totally is. I do feel a kinship with each of these professions. I wrote obituary tributes for several years for magazines and wanted to know how real obit writers who worked on daily deadlines managed to breathe so much life into their writing. And I worked as a page for my public library as a teenager. I might have gone on to library-science school, except when the board wouldn't raise my pay a nickel— from ninety-five cents an hour to a dollar— I quit out of pride. That ended my library career. I still hang out with librarians, though; they're my people.

And you still read obits all the time.

Are you kidding? I get most of my ideas from the obits. I read an obituary of Lewis Binford, for instance, who helped spark a revolution in archaeology in the United States and who was married six times, often to fellow archaeologists. Archaeology obits, I noticed, were full of curious facts about tantalizing history and places I didn't recognize. I wondered who else was making a mark in the field in these turbulent times. I figured they had to be obsessed. ▶

3

Q&A with Marilyn Johnson *(continued)*

Did you ever want to be an archaeologist when you were a kid?

Sure. When I was young, I loved to dig and collect fossils. I was mad about archaeology. Who wasn't? But I jumped off the science track early and took only one class in anthropology in college. I guess you'd call archaeology my fantasy profession, and though I have no gift for the work, I do share archaeologists' curiosity and stubbornness, and their enchantment with the past. Archaeologists, librarians, and obit writers—they all work passionately and for little personal reward to save bits of our cultural history. They all connect us to the people and objects and stories of our past.

The first time I ever heard about archaeology was in the fifth grade when we learned about Richard Leakey. Is he the big cultural touchstone?

Definitely. The Leakeys—Richard; his parents, Louis and Mary; his wife, Maeve; and daughter Louise—are an archaeological dynasty. Richard, Maeve, and Louise are all affiliated with Stony Brook University, and John Shea, the Ice Age expert in the book, teaches down the hall and has been on-site with them in Africa.

And while we're talking pop culture, what do archaeologists think about Indiana Jones?

The archaeologists I met talked about Indiana Jones with real affection. He has given that profession a swagger that, let's face it, few other professions have. More than thirty years after *Raiders of the Lost Ark*, Indiana Jones is still luring people into the field, and Harrison Ford himself has been a sport—he served on the Archeological Institute of America's board for years. But the character is a cartoon, a plunderer, a throwback to an acquisition-oriented era as opposed to our current era, which emphasizes cultural-heritage management and respect for native cultures. No archaeologist with any standing is going to talk seriously about some of the stuff in the movies, the crystal skulls and aliens and haunted artifacts. They know it's nonsense—but they appreciate the publicity.

So what makes an archaeologist in real life?

Resourcefulness. Curiosity. Physical sturdiness, mental toughness, and endurance. Patience. The capacity—not to mention, the desire!—to kneel all day in the sun inside a big hole, which might be a grave or a privy, while clouds of mosquitoes feast on you. Archaeologists have an uncanny ability to ignore the discomforts and channel the time period and the people they're studying. They have one foot in, say, the contemporary Caribbean sun with underbrush spreading in front of their eyes and bulldozers hovering, and one foot in the eighteenth-century plantation that used to stand there.

And yet it's such a physically demanding job.

It's terribly hard on the body, and some of the archaeologists reminded me of pirates: scarred, limping, sun-damaged, sweating under their rakish bandannas—and they do have a kind of pirate's swagger. But how is it they never lose that hunger to turn over the next shovel of dirt? That amazes me. It's the quest for the unknown. Once you have had the privilege of unearthing something that humans haven't seen or touched for centuries, I think you get a kind of archaeological fever. I certainly got infected.

I was impressed by how many young and old people are in the profession. You'd think it'd require a young person's stamina, but that's not the case.

The archaeologist Sarah Nelson is in her eighties, and she would go dig in China this minute if she could get grant money. She is a great role model and is absolutely representative of the archaeologists I met in her indomitable drive. Nothing will stop her from figuring out novel and creative ways to apply her knowledge and get her hands on some unfiltered history.

You write about women as well as men. Even though the field was traditionally male dominated and women had to fight stereotyping, it's clear that some of the brightest and most prominent archaeologists are women. Did you consciously try to include a mix of men and women, or did your nose just lead you to the most interesting and/or cooperative subjects?

Of course I tried to get a mix of archaeologists in all ways: male and female; ancient, classic, post-Colombian, and contemporary; academic, independent, and contract archaeologists. I included archaeologists in their twenties, several in their thirties and forties, a bunch in their fifties and sixties, one almost seventy, and one in her eighties. But my nose ruled. I was looking for characters, originals, people who could articulate what they were doing in colorful ways.

Also, about women, Nelson told you, "My archaeological writings presume that what women did in the past is recoverable and interesting." And you add: "And interesting. That she felt the need ▶

to add that phrase was telling. To some extent, archaeologists find what they're looking for, and if you never look for evidence of powerful women, even if the hills and valleys are full of queens and warriors, they'll be invisible." This brings up one of the book's central themes. That archaeology is subjective. That it's not comprehensive. History is written by the winners. But it seems to be as if archaeology is, in some sense, about honoring the losers' story, too, right?

This is one of the most subtle and touching aspects of the profession. Archaeology is about paying attention to things that have been or could be undetectable or invisible to others. As Joan Connelly said, "Good archaeology fills in the blanks of history. It tells the losers' stories. It teases out the history that falls between the cracks." That, to me, is beautiful.

Do you think, by nature, archaeologists are drawn to the losers' stories?

I'm not sure if archaeologists are naturally drawn to "losers"—or can we call them overlooked people?

Yeah, that's better because it doesn't imply any kind of judgment. It's about being neglected, overlooked.

That's right. I'm drawn to such people, too. That's probably obvious from the subjects of my previous books. Certainly the most interesting stories to me are the ones that have not yet been told. How did children live two thousand years ago? Where are the women of ancient Greece? How did ordinary soldiers manage in colonial times? In the absence of written records, archaeology is one of the few ways to understand how these people lived, and even when there are written records, archaeology can add new evidence, or even contradict accepted history. Bill Sandy was surveying for a mall development in Fishkill, New York, when he uncovered what might be the largest graveyard of Revolutionary War soldiers that we know about. It's part of the Fishkill Supply Depot, the largest and least-known supply center from that war. This is a tremendous find, not just because we think he discovered all these veterans of our first war in a vacant lot. How did Washington and his generals keep those men and munitions hidden? How did they tend their dead and wounded in such secrecy?

What role does technology play in all of this?

The field is exploding, only partly because of technology—wars, climate change, and economic development are all tearing into the earth and giving us access to some of that buried history. But technology certainly helps. The use of satellite remote sensing by pioneers like Sarah Parcak and Douglas Comer has shown us sites we never knew were there, and it has tracked the erosion and degradation of others. There are increasingly sophisticated geophysical, chemical, and biological tests available—not to mention the crazy cases where archaeologists have been able to extract and analyze DNA material from ancient bones. But none of this is as magical as it sounds: the hard work of excavation and analysis still requires human verification and interpretation; "ground proof," they call it. I agree with most of the archaeologists in *Lives in Ruins*: There's no substitute for a trained field worker with a sharp eye and a simple trowel.

I found the section of the book on forensic archaeology fascinating.

The forensic archaeologist I dug with, Kimberlee Sue Moran, is attractive, young—she's in her thirties—and perfectly at ease unearthing a murder victim crawling with maggots. She likes to emphasize that forensic archaeology is simply archaeology that can stand up in court: anything excavated or recovered has to be handled with gloves, remain uncontaminated, logged, identified, and accounted for at all times. You don't bag something and leave it by the trench while you go back to the truck for your lunch. If you can stomach lunch—forensic archaeology can be disgusting.

You were certainly challenged by your level of seaworthiness a few times during the reporting of this book, weren't you?

The gross stuff was incredibly gross. I learned some things I can never unlearn about organic decomposition and human bone. And now that you mention it, I also got seasick, had altitude sickness, and had to be rescued a few times. But the killer bees that gave chase one day didn't get me!

Earlier on you mentioned how secretive archaeologists are. Was it hard to get close to them?

Archaeologists are much harder to reach and get close to than the subjects of my other books. I mean, think about it: obit writers' names are in the newspaper almost every day, and librarians are roaming around the library wearing big CAN I HELP YOU? buttons. Where are archaeologists? They're scattered all over the world, anywhere humans have left their mark. They dislike cell phones, and they are, for various practical reasons, somewhat secretive. The archaeologists I did connect with were not interested in drive-by interviews. I didn't want that, either. I didn't want a few quotes from ▶

an underwater archaeologist; I wanted to see the sunken fleets and drowned artifacts through the archaeologist's eyes. It took years of groundwork to get next to some of them. In the book I admit, "I've lost count of the archaeologists I've chased who got away. They are an elusive bunch, in motion or in the thrall of another time. Even the ones who alight on a terraced ledge long enough to have a conversation would, before I knew it, shimmer like the good witch Glinda before evaporating into thin air."

What about Ruth Shady? Was she like your Bobby Fischer, your white whale?

Ha! Ruth Shady isn't *my* anything; she is her own completely original force in archaeology. She is a Peruvian archaeologist who uncovered the oldest city in this hemisphere and fought a very public feud with a couple of Americans. I don't blame her for not talking to me; she had no reason to trust Americans. I flew to Peru to hear her give a keynote speech at an international conference. I was hunkered down in my seat in the Municipalidad del Cuzco and thrilled—my heart was beating so fast!—and then . . . no Shady. She didn't show up! Of course I was frustrated, but writers deal with disappointment all the time, and so do archaeologists. And I think it ended up being a funny way to tell her story. That's who she is, after all, an archaeologist who was so engrossed in her current dig, she couldn't stop to speak to her colleagues.

On the other hand, I interviewed Grant Gilmore with the hope that I could take his field school in the Caribbean in six months, and he said, "Don't wait. Come now." So I leapt. And I was so entertained by John Shea that I impulsively asked to take a class with him (though it meant a 160-mile commute twice a week)—and he said sure, here's a list of textbooks, see you next week.

Yeah, one thing that John Shea said struck me: "Narratives close off the complexity of reality." Then you go on to observe that we study archaeology "to gather authentic fragments of our human past, but the further back we go, the more we see what an incomplete picture we have of human history." There is so much mystery involved. How do archaeologists wrap an empirical mind around capturing history?

We're conditioned by narrative to expect some resolution, whether it's answers to our questions or solutions to a mystery. We expect a neat wrap-up to the story, but in fact there are many things we don't understand and might never understand. Why were some people of the Iron Age tortured and their bodies thrown in bogs? How did the Inca get giant blocks of stone up mountains five hundred years ago without the use of wheels? Why did earlier people go to all the trouble to build mounds? Laurie Rush, the military archaeologist, admitted, "Our most exciting days are the days we discover we were wrong." The past is a wilderness that we've just begun to explore.

Are archaeologists in a rush or are they Zen-like in taking all the time they need?

It depends on the archaeologist and the circumstances, but I think they would all take their sweet time if they could. They're all trying to balance doing things in a timely fashion (and, if they're contract archaeologists, on the clock and on deadline) with doing things carefully, so as much information as possible is preserved, and other archaeologists coming behind them can reexamine the site in a few years or decades or eons. Then there's Kathy Abbass, who has been preparing more than twenty years for the excavation of a fleet of historic ships sunk in Newport Harbor hundreds of years ago. She has to be able to preserve what she hauls up, and she'll have only one chance to get it right. History *will* judge these people, so they want to get it right.

What do you think future archaeologists will make of our time?

We don't know what will survive in a thousand years. Will Yankee Stadium and its monuments lie in ruins? Will only the bobblehead dolls and plastic Dippin' Dots bowls linger in the rubble? I think it's entirely possible that future archaeologists will puzzle, for instance, over the prevalence of the number 2 in these regions. Maybe they'll think we attributed magical properties to the number 2! Derek Jeter's identity and legacy will have to be reconstructed from fragments of commemorative cups; perhaps they'll note the fact that, curiously, he was always depicted with one large webbed hand. 〜

Alex Belth is the creator of the blog *Bronx Banter* and curator of literary journalism for The Stacks at *Deadspin*. This Q&A originally appeared in the *Daily Beast*. It is here reprinted with permission.

Discussion Questions for *Lives in Ruins*

1. The demolition of the last building in Deadwood's Chinatown and the bulldozing of ruins in Babylon by US soldiers making a base camp are two examples from this book of archaeological sites destroyed, intentionally or inadvertently. Can you think of other sites that have been spoiled for archaeology? What are the penalties for archaeological destruction? How can archaeologists and others encourage historic preservation?

2. Why do you think the author included fictional characters like Indiana Jones and Jean Auel's Stone Age hero Ayla in a book about real archaeologists?

3. Archaeologists divide themselves according to:
   - the time period they're interested in (Paleolithic or Neolithic; classical, historical, or contemporary)
   - the type of archaeology they study (forensic, underwater, public, military, or contract archaeology)
   - the kind of people they specialize in (Greco-Roman, Woodlands Indian, Mayan)
   - the places where they dig (the Mediterranean, Central America; Old World, New World)
   - their theoretical orientation (feminist, processualist)
   - their training (American, European)
   - and whether they work primarily at a desk or in the field.

   What do you think most archaeologists have in common? Which specialty most appeals to you?

4. What is the point of archaeological excavation? What are archaeologists looking for? What do you think should happen to the artifacts that they unearth?

5. The archaeologist in the "Field School" chapter found evidence that, in the eighteenth century, enslaved people on the island of St. Eustatius lived under different and relatively less odious constraints than enslaved people on other Caribbean islands. Can you think of other examples of archaeologists finding evidence that modifies the historic record?

6. Why do some archaeologists make stone tools, re-create beverages based on the chemical residue found in ancient jars, and try to boil animal bones in pits instead of pots? How might such activities—sometimes called experimental archaeology— be used to make the past come alive for students? Can you think of other historic practices that might be interesting to re-create?

7. Why is the underwater archaeologist in the book taking so long to excavate a fleet of sunken ships?

8. Discuss how the following problems are leaving their mark on the field of archaeology:
   • natural disasters, global warming, and rising oceans
   • looting
   • war and armed conflict
   • and funding challenges.
   How does modern technology help archaeologists? In what ways can it be problematic? ▶

Discussion Questions for *Lives in Ruins*
(continued)

9. The archaeologist in *Lives in Ruins* who excavated a Ford Explorer and the one who surveyed fast-food restaurants in the Plaza de Armas in Cuzco, Peru, were practicing contemporary archaeology. What can we learn by conducting archaeology in current landscapes? Can you think of any places in your community that might benefit from the methodology and insight of a contemporary archaeologist?

10. What kind of archaeology has been done near your town?

11. How might future archaeologists read—or misread—the residue of your life and the activities of your household? ∽

Have You Read?
More by
Marilyn Johnson

THE DEAD BEAT: LOST SOULS, LUCKY STIFFS, AND THE PERVERSE PLEASURES OF OBITUARIES

Marilyn Johnson, a one-time obituary writer, explores the cult and culture of obituaries, finding new life and fresh connections to history in the unusual lives we don't quite appreciate until they're gone.

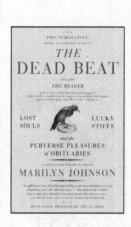

"A smart, tart, and often hilarious tiptoe through the tombstones." —*Parade*

"In *The Dead Beat*, Marilyn Johnson— an obituarist herself—acts as our Virgil through the back pages, introducing the knowledgeable, eccentric, and talented writers responsible for sending off the just and the unjust, the famous and the not-so famous." —*The Observer* (London)

"This delightful quirk of a book is not dark or morose; it's an uplifting, joyous, life-affirming read for people who ordinarily steer clear of uplifting, joyous, life-affirming reads. Of all the personalities captured in *The Dead Beat*, few are more endearing than Johnson, a former obituary writer. Her enthusiasm is infectious. Writers interested in honing the craft should inhale this book. Who else might profit or delight from reading about obituaries? Just about anyone who's not yet in one, I'd wager." —Mary Roach, *Los Angeles Times*

13

Have You Read? *(continued)*

"A fascinating book about the art, history, and subculture of obituary writing. Johnson's analysis of the form and its top practitioners is absorbing, [and] her account of the culture of obituary lovers is downright amazing."

—Jane and Michael Stern,
New York Times Book Review

THIS BOOK IS OVERDUE!: HOW LIBRARIANS AND CYBRARIANS CAN SAVE US ALL

What is it like to be a librarian in a world with too much information? Constant change, exploding technology, shrinking budgets, growing numbers of the baffled . . . could there be a better spot to watch the digital age unfold than behind the librarians' desk?

"Energetic, winningly acerbic, and downright fun, *This Book Is Overdue!* will leave you convinced that librarians really can save the world." —*BookPage*

"As Johnson amply shows in her romp through the brave new world of the profession, [the] new librarians cum information scientists are building on the work of their pioneering predecessors as they branch out in sometimes surprising directions." —*Boston Globe*

"Johnson's exquisite book taps into the radical changes that libraries are going through. She blows apart the librarian stereotypes. . . . In Johnson's eyes, they are committed 'intellectual social workers,' educating whoever comes through their doors in the face of brutal budget cuts."
—*Newark Star-Ledger*